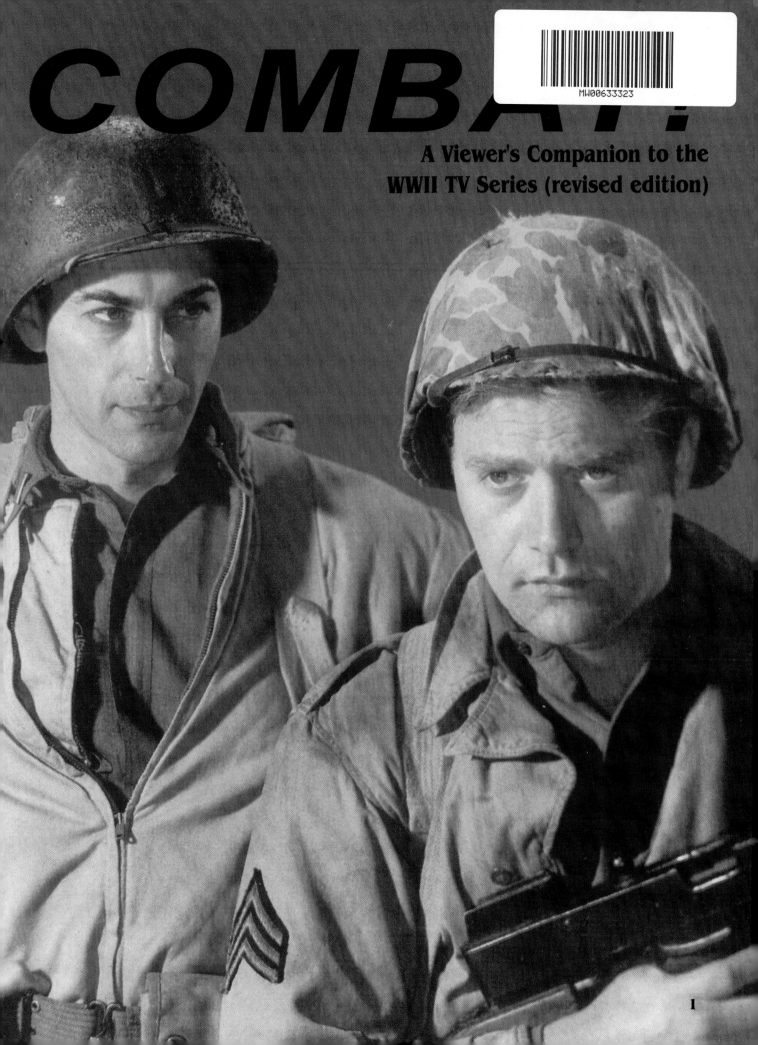

COMBAT!

A Viewer's Companion to the WWII TV Series (revised edition)

Acknowledgements

I thank the following people, who helped create *Combat!,* for their generosity in discussing their work with me: Robert Altman, James Best, Robert Blees, Conlan Carter, Georg Fenady, Jack Hogan, Pierre Jalbert, Rick Jason, Tom Lowell, Earl Parker, and Dick Peabody. My thanks also to Masahiro Asaka, James Beaver, Andrew Bellenkes, Marty Black, William Brinson, Rob Chellis, Nancy Durgin, Carolyn Elliott, Golden State Autographs, Lee C. Glaeser, Bill Groves, Margie Healey of Korbel, Debora Hosey, Toshiyuki Kikuzuki, Anita Kreger, Rob Lingelbach, Rick Lubben, Mark Marmer, Susan Moar, Ignacio McGuire, Graham Niven, Jean Noack, Dion Osika, Janice Payne, Jill Pochek, Ken Paruti, Don Roberts, John B. Roberts Jr., Steve Rubin, Dave Sanders, Linda Schweitzer, Charles Schauer, Deb Simicich, Melle Starsen, Joanne Strobl of Hop Kiln Winery, Karen Thorson, Ed Walton, Mikako Watabe. The help and support of these, and so many other fans of the show, made this book possible.

It has been a thrill putting this book together. I've had the opportunity to meet and talk with so many other fans who were touched by this show. Most exciting for me was meeting the actors and discovering what genuinely nice people they are. These fine gentlemen are very giving and kind to their fans. I'm continually bemused by their surprise that something they created forty years ago has made such a stir and is so fondly remembered. Words alone cannot express my gratitude and appreciation for what these actors gave to me as a writer and to all of us as fans.

And thank you so much to my parents for their love and support. I have long since forgiven them for banning me, as a child, from watching the last seasons of *Combat!*

Copyright © 1997, 2002, 2008
by Jo Davidsmeyer

Cover Art by Paton Design

Printed in the USA.

Original Edition, 1997
Revised Edition first printing 2002
2nd Printing 2008

Combat! was produced by the American Broadcasting Company and is owned by Paramount Pictures.

Publisher:
Strange New Worlds
5591 Shady Brook Trail
Sarasota, Florida 34243
www.StrangeNewWorlds.com

Right: Louis Mercier (wearing beret) guested as a French resistance fighter in the episode "Missing in Action." Also pictured are Pierre Jalbert, Barton Heyman, Rick Jason.

Above: Vic Morrow takes the beach in a publicity photograph for the pilot episode.

3

The Author

In a writing career spanning twenty-five years, Jo Davidsmeyer has been editor for several non-fiction publications (everything from real estate to internal medicine) and was creator and managing editor of *Strange New Worlds,* a magazine for science fiction collectors and enthusiasts.

Her articles about television and media collectibles have appeared in *The Military Trader, Television Chronicles, Gateways, The New Monthly, Just Write!, Fantastic Collectibles Magazine,* and many others.

She is a published and award-winning playwright, as well as an accomplished musical director. Her play "Angel," a drama about the trial and execution of a Nazi war criminal, was a winner of the Open Book/Fireside Theatre National Playwriting competition. It was produced in New York City and has enjoyed regional performances.

Jo Davidsmeyer

She organized Comboat! '96, a Caribbean cruise that was the first reunion of the cast since the series had ended. Two years later, she again reunited cast and fans for Recon '98 in the Simi Valley, California, which included a tour of Franklin Canyon, where so many *Combat!* episodes were filmed. She is webmaster for the *Combat!* Fan Page, where fans have gathered for information and discussion since 1996. Visit Jo and fellow *Combat!* fans at www.CombatFan.com

Jo Davidsmeyer with the men of Combat!

Contents

Foreword
by Rick Jason

Combat! has been in constant reruns all over the country, and indeed, in many other parts of the world since we ceased production thirty years ago. I now get fan mail from the grown children who watched the show with their parents when it first played on ABC. And now they watch it on cable and the satellite with *their* children. It seems to have become a rite of passage that engenders in me a weird feeling—sort of akin to becoming immortal before I've died.

A devoted fan of *Combat!* contacted me not long ago with some amusing information. A station in Anaheim, California, had been "stripping" the show; that is, playing a segment nightly Monday through Friday. They suddenly took it off the air, and several days later the fan I speak of called the station to complain. "The operator, as if ready to jump out of her skin said, 'Oh, no, not *again!* That makes over a hundred and fifty calls we've had during the last two days. Would you please tell your friends that we'll be running *two* episodes every Saturday afternoon?'"

When I first started out to be an actor, all of this was beyond imagining. My training was in New York City, and then all I wanted was to be a good stage actor. Memories of that medium only remain in the minds of those who have seen the performance live, and in the actor's scrapbook. I have a lousy sense of personal history, so I've never kept a scrapbook. My lovely wife made one up of all the clippings that for years I tossed into paper shopping bags in a dark closet (why, I have no idea), but I think it's been mislaid. I hope so, anyway. How nice it's going to be for visitors, when I'm in my dotage, that I won't have tons of those pasted-up folders to trot out and bore them with.

Combat! was probably the best thing that ever happened in my career, and this book on the series dusts off long-forgotten incidents. Many memories well up—so many it's difficult to choose, but here are some that stands out. (I may be plagiarizing from myself, since some are in a memoir I'm writing—and I must tell you that the memories are out of context. I'm writing them as they come to mind.)

Vic Morrow as Sgt. Saunders on the field radio.

Vic and I were having lunch in the MGM commissary one day toward the end of the fourth year. He was reading a trade paper (the Hollywood Reporter) and chuckling to himself. "What's funny?" I asked. He handed me the paper and pointed to an article on the first page. "So what," I said after scanning it. "Kirk Douglas is about to start his thirty-fifth picture after twenty years in films. Good for him." He smiled at me as if at the village idiot. "Do you realize," he said, "that by the end of next year we will have completed the equivalent of *seventy-six* motion pictures? And all of them on the same subject? In *five* years?"

There was the time Charles Bronson guested on the show. I used to smoke cigars on the set, but since I never got a chance to finish one, I settled for cheapies that I didn't mind stamping out if they were a third or halfway smoked when I was called into a shot—Grenadiers at three for a dollar. Matter of fact, they're what George Burns smoked because he said they're a cheap cigar, but unlike expensive ones, they stay lit.

Anyway, Charlie and I were sitting off to the side on Stage Twenty-four, which was our "outdoor set," used for special constructions, snow scenes, etc. I was smoking a Grenadier, and there was some leak light behind me. Charlie isn't what one might term a great conversationalist, so we just sat. And waited.

Presently he said, *"That* is not a good cigar."

"Oh, I don't know," I said, taking it out of my mouth and looking it over.

"It is *not* a good cigar," he insisted.

"I like 'em."

"Well, it's not a good cigar!"

"Uh . . . what's wrong with it, Charlie?"

"The smoke."

"The *smoke?* What's wrong with the smoke?"

"It's *brown*. If it was a *good* cigar, the smoke would be blue."

I looked carefully at my stogie. "Uh huh," I said. "Well, thanks." I got up and stepped into my dressing room, where I smoked the Grenadier until we were called into the set.

Then there was the famous "Hard Boiled Egg Ploy." About the second or third year into the show I began to put on weight from all of our caterer's good food, so I started brown bagging three days a week. Just two hard boiled eggs, a couple of tomatoes and some celery. At lunchtime I'd just disappear into my trailer and quietly consume my meal. One day toward the end of the break there was a knock on the door and Dick Peabody stepped in.

I invited him to a seat at the table, opposite me; the venetian blind at the window was drawn and partially slanted shut to keep out the hot sunlight. I was just finishing my first egg.

Rick Jason from the 1996 "Comboat!" Cruise

"What's going on?" I asked innocently.

"Oh, not much," he said. "Good lunch today. As always."

"Uh huh."

He dropped something on the floor that he'd taken out of his pocket, and as he started to reach for it I noted it was close to me. "I'll get it," I said as I leaned over and picked it up.

I then finished the first egg and cracked the second one on the table top. A raw egg ran all over the table. I couldn't believe what I was seeing. "That is the damnedest thing," I said. "I put them both in the water at the same time, and this one didn't cook!"

Dick told me later, while the whole company was having a great good laugh, that my reaction almost broke him up and he had to exit my trailer as soon as he could. Our caterer, Millie (who had supplied the raw egg for the switch), was laughing so hard she was crying. I gave Millie a big hug.

Dick, who later became a columnist for his local newspaper in Northern California where he retired, even wrote it up in one of his columns.

I consider the two-parter, "Hills Are for Heroes," not only the best thing we did in five years, but quite possibly one of the best feature film war movies (or more to the point ANTI-war movies) ever made. Vic directed and had a major

hand in writing. At the completion we had a wrap party where I reminded Vic that he'd gone over budget by almost twice the time and twice the money allotted. "Screw it!" he said. I agreed with him. I think he may have felt that this project, in some way, was possibly to be his legacy. But we had no title.

Selig Seligman, our executive producer, Gene Levitt, our very capable and hard working producer, and I were standing in a small triangle on Stage Twenty-four (at MGM) having a quiet drink and trying to come up with a title. Frank Kowalski, our revered, insolent, and very funny script supervisor (He told me my first Polish joke one day just as the cameras were about to roll and I laughed so hard the director had to call "Cut!" and wait until I got control of myself.) was well into his cups as he half strolled and stumbled over to our little group.

"What's goin' on, fellas?" he managed to get out.

"We're looking for a title," Selig said, almost dismissing him.

Frank was too drunk to be put off. Besides, he was an unproduced writer on the side. "Wha's th'matter with you saps?" he said. "There's on'y one title for this sho'. 'Hills Are for Heroes'"—and he lurched away.

Selig looked at Gene, Gene looked at me, and we all looked at each other.

During the Christmas-New Year's time of 1969-1970, I fulfilled a promise I'd made to myself by accepting the USO request to make a personal tour of Viet Nam. I signed up for a seventeen-day tour and eventually extended it to the maximum twenty-one days. *Combat!* was playing daily on armed forces television, in Tokyo at the armed forces hospital, and all over Nam in any camp where they could get an antenna up.

I was welcomed as a personal friend by every soldier I met. The show, if they could catch it off duty, was almost a religion with them. There was even a squib in *The Reader's Digest* about the soldier recuperating from wounds at the hospital in Tokyo and watching our show one afternoon in the rec room. A Red Cross lady approached him and asked, figuring he'd seen enough action to last a lifetime, "Why are you watching *Combat!?*"

"Oh," he answered laconically, "I want to see what I did wrong."

I was so touched by the continuous welcome I received as I flew from base to base, from the Delta in the far South to the DMZ (demilitarized zone, a couple hundred yards of no man's land) at the northernmost post. Just jawing with the guys, visiting the hospitals, having chow with the enlisted men every night at a different base (army food hadn't improved much since I'd been in the service in WW II) made my trip and broke the boredom for some of them. Whatever the politics were at the time, and since then, is not and was not important to that venture. These were my fellow Americans, and I'm happy that I was able to make some little contribution to their time there.

I'd made several movies in Japan after *Combat!* wound up, then from the mid- to late seventies I did a series of commercials for the Toyota Celica that played only in Japan, where *Combat!,* playing in reruns today, is still rated one of the top shows. I was going to Tokyo on a shoot for a new model Celica, and they didn't want it seen out of the country until its release date. I'd be working there just one day, but the president of Toyota made sure my visits to Japan were always auspicious. I was invited to spend a few weeks in my favorite town of Kyoto, all expenses paid.

I called Simon Tse, a Chinese film producer who had been born and grew up in Japan, to tell him I'd be in Tokyo in about two weeks and perhaps we could have dinner together. I'd worked in a movie, with George Kennedy, that Simon made on location in New York several years before.

"Wonderful, Rick, and I have a surprise for you."

"Oh?"

"Vic is making a movie for me. Shooting in Kyoto."

"Wonderful. I'm going down there to stay at my favorite Japanese inn for a week or so."

"Good. Call me when you get to your hotel in Tokyo, and in the meantime, I'll tell Vic to expect you."

"Wait, Simon. Don't tell him; let it be a surprise. I'm the last person he'll expect to walk on the set." He was laughing gleefully as we hung up.

The day after I got settled at Yoshikawa Inn in Kyoto, Simon had laid on a car and driver to take me out to the location where they were shooting. We'd had a great dinner in Tokyo several nights before and ended, as usual, fighting for the check.

The car drove out of town several miles to the studio back lot. As it stopped about a hundred yards from the set, I stepped out and began to walk toward where the camera and crew were setting up. Someone got Vic out of one of the buildings, facing away from me, on the pretext that they needed a few still photos. I could see from his back that he didn't understand why it was so important to get some shots right this minute. I stopped a few feet behind him and slightly off to his right. The photographer kept shooting stills. Then Vic felt a presence behind him and turned slowly around. I was standing casually, hands in my trouser pockets, smiling. He looked at me and turned away, walked toward the photographer a few steps and stopped. He suddenly spun around, and stared. It was one of the greatest doubletakes I've ever seen. Everyone was in on the joke except him, and the entire company burst out laughing and applauding.

"What. . . . Are you crazy? . . . What? . . . ." He walked up to me for a closer look and stopped about a foot away. "What the hell are you doing here?"

"I heard you were making a picture in Japan, and I figured I'd just drop over and help you with the shopping."

My fear that this book might end up as a cut-and-dried recitation fit only for a dark corner in some librarian's sanctum, or as just a reference work, is assuaged by the writing talent of the author, Jo Davidsmeyer, with whose work I am well acquainted.

Not only is she highly capable as a writer, but her love of our series from its inception, her continuing devotion of time and energy to *Combat!'s* website on the internet, her interconnection and friendship with the cast members, makes this a very personal journey. Being the vivacious and funny lady she is, I'm sure you'll enjoy traveling with her. Your friends may try to borrow this book. My advice is, don't lend it to them. I have a feeling you're going to want to read it again. And, quite possibly, after a time, you will want the entertainment of reading it, even again.

Rick Jason
Moorpark, California, 1997

Anna Lee and Rick Jason in "The Enemy."

Introduction

by Jo Davidsmeyer, Author

The "Hills are for Heroes" episode was promoted with this Worldvision publicity photo captioned "Combat: Generic Action."

"We had a ball," says Tom Lowell, who played Billy Nelson for the first two seasons of *Combat!* "There are several things I've done in my career that I'm very proud of. But my remembrances of having worked in the business are focused toward one area only, and that's the two years that I spent on *Combat!* It was the best. Yes, I worked at Disney, at all sorts of other things, but this was the most fun time with these guys. I could not wait to get to work every day."

Tom Lowell's sentiment is shared by many fans of the show. Those, like myself, who were children when *Combat!* first aired in the sixties, couldn't wait for Tuesday night when we would sit before our television sets, hanging on every action of the men of King Company. Between Tuesdays, we recreated the battles in our backyards, terrorizing the neighborhood pets. The show appealed to a variety of ages, from young children to veterans of both world wars. Teens watched the show with parents who served in the war, using the series as a bridge between generations. Drill Sergeants watched *Combat!* with their men, using it for object lessons or to critique the military operations.

Something about this particular TV series resonated with its audience. Baby-boomers who re-discover *Combat!* as adults find that the show holds up well over the decades. They are surprised that it has a depth and meaning they had not perceived as children. Forty years after the cameras stop, *Combat!* is still fresh and vital. The characters of Hanley, Saunders, and the rest of the squad continue to entertain and engage new audiences.

For the youngest fans of *Combat!*, World War II and Normandy sound as distant as Shiloh and Antietam did to the World War II generation. Still, *Combat!* attracts new fans around the world, as it enjoys renewed life in syndication. It has a message still relevant to a world that has since entered into another millennium.

Many viewers are drawn to *Combat!* by the special chemistry among the characters. *Combat!* rises above the typical action show because the stories are about people, not just explosions and hardware. The strong acting and superior scripts of the "human drama of men at war" are remarkably compelling.

I first saw *Combat!* when I was six years old. That started a love affair that's lasted a lifetime. In 1993, I began seeking others who remembered *Combat!* Then, I was thrilled just to discuss the show with others who remembered its haunting drama. I had little notion that my search would lead me to meet the actors, get to know them and their art well, and to be personally blessed by the loving friendship of both Dick Peabody and Rick Jason, who have since gone to their reward.

This is a revised version of the original book printed in 1997. The 2002 edition includes updates of cast and crew information. I've also added short reviews of all the episodes and an index.

This book expresses the admiration and affection I have for this show and the people who created it. I hope that readers will find this book useful as an armchair companion for viewing the episodes. I have no desire to be coldly objective about *Combat!*

First and foremost, I am a fan, happy to scout ahead and "take the point."

—*Jo Davidsmeyer*

The World War II drama *Combat!* premiered October 2, 1962 against unexpected competition. On the east coast, the male audience that the show was intended to attract was more interested in the World Series, which had gone into extra innings. Despite the distraction, the overall ratings were excellent and the premiere garnered good reviews. The ABC series *Combat!*, much like the squad it depicted, would often encounter unexpected problems and come out victorious against overwhelming odds.

1962 was an odd time to premiere a realistic war series. In the previous year, Congress began hearings about TV violence and its effect on America. Network executives were pressured to tone down the violence on the small screen. In this environment, ABC premiered two war shows: *Combat!* and "The Gallant Men."

Though a tribute to the average G.I. who fought (and died) on the front lines of Europe, *Combat!* did not glorify war or violence. But it did show the kind of glory that men and women can rise to when tested under fire. *Combat!*, at its best, shows soldiers struggling to find and keep their moral center in the midst of a world torn apart by war. In *Combat!*, war is a furnace that either destroys a man, or tempers him like hardened steel.

The filming of this series tempered and destroyed a few behind-the-scenes personnel during its five-year run. The June 15, 1963 *TV Guide* observed that the show's success "would sometimes seem to be based on the clash of opposites. The filmmaking team responsible for the show has held such diverse opinions of how the war should be treated that the battle has often appeared to be taking place not so much in Normandy as in the front office."

Either despite these offstage battles, or because of them, *Combat!* is a show of remarkable quality that withstands the test of time. This gritty drama redefined the TV action/adventure genre and became a proving ground for the next generation of feature film directors and stars. Few shows of the sixties, or of today, match *Combat!* for production values and script quality.

The story of the making of this series is one of constant change and conflict. *Combat!* had no single creator with an overriding vision to form the character of the show. Unlike David Dortort with "Bonanza" or Gene Roddenberry with "Star Trek," *Combat!* had no steady

"Vic Morrow, as Sgt. Chip Saunders, and Rick Jason, as Lt. Gil Hanley, star in the dramatic episodes of G.I.s in Europe during World War II on Combat! *on ABC-TV Tuesdays at 7:30-8:30 p.m. EDT," so read this press information photo from an early promotion.*

CHAPTER 1

Getting There

hand at the helm. Instead, a remarkable parade of talented, strong-willed artists marched through the five years of *Combat!* All left their mark and defined the show on their own, sometimes conflicting, terms.

Broadcast history

Combat! premiered in 1962 and was broadcast for five seasons. TV's longest-running World War II drama, *Combat!* aired 152 hour-long episodes. The first four seasons were produced in black and white, with the final season (25 episodes) in color.

It was often among the top ten network shows. *Combat!* had world-wide distribution, popular in Spanish-speaking countries and the Far East.

The show followed King Company's second platoon as they battled their way across Normandy. The series offered an unvarnished view of men in conflict — both with the enemy and with themselves. While striving for authenticity, *Combat!* focused on intimate character studies, showing the war in microcosm. The show's realism was enhanced by merging actual war footage into the episodes.

Robert Pirosh: From Bastogne to the MGM backlot

Combat! was developed by World War II veteran Robert Pirosh, who wrote and produced the pilot episode. Before serving in World War II, Pirosh co-wrote many popular comedy films, including *A Day at the Races,* starring the Marx Brothers, and Danny Kaye's *Up In Arms.*

During the war, Pirosh rose to the rank of Master Sergeant serving with the 320th Regiment, 35th Division. He saw action during both the Ardennes and Rhineland campaigns and was awarded the Bronze Star. During the Battle of the Bulge, Pirosh led a patrol into Bastogne to lend support to the beleaguered defenders. Profoundly affected by these experiences, Pirosh spent much of his later career paying tribute to the frontline infantry soldier.

Pirosh won an Academy Award for his original story and screenplay to *Battleground* (1949), starring Van Johnson. *Battleground* chronicled the siege of Bastogne, telling the story from the point of view of the ordinary G.I. It became the biggest box office hit of 1949. Two years later, Pirosh was again nominated by the Academy for best story and screen play for *Go for Broke,* which he also directed. *Go For Broke* is the true story of the American-born Japanese who served heroically as U.S. infantrymen in the 442nd Regimental Combat Team in World War II.

Pierre Jalbert (standing), Vic Morrow and Dick Peabody.

Robert Pirosh on the set of the pilot episode in 1962.

Pirosh again paid tribute to the infantry in the feature film *Hell Is for Heroes,* which he wrote, produced, and directed. But conflicts arose between Pirosh and his star, Steve McQueen. Pirosh walked away from the film before it was finished. Later that year, he approached Selmur Productions with the idea for a series about frontline infantry soldiers.

Pilot: A Day in June

ABC, interested in making its own shows, found promise in Pirosh's proposal for a new series, "Men in Combat," and ordered a pilot. Pirosh centered his story around a small squad of men. Pirosh excelled at writing about the ordinary soldier and his compatriots. Before the show went into regular production, this core concept of a small squad of enlisted men would change.

The pilot episode introduces the audience to a squad of men about to embark upon the invasion of Normandy. The squad consists of: Private Braddock, the platoon comic and resident hustler; Paul "Caddy" Cadron, a Cajun soldier; Beecham, a G.I. terrified of what awaits him on the beach; and Doc, a young,

The troops hit the Normandy beach in the pilot episode: Steve Rogers, Vic Morrow, Shecky Greene, Frankie Ray and Rick Jason.

sensitive medic. Leading these soldiers are two skirt-chasing sergeants: Saunders, the fearless veteran; and Hanley, the untried soldier, an attractive charmer who outranks Saunders, both on duty and with the ladies.

Tension runs high among these soldiers as they are confined to their camp in Britain, awaiting the invasion order. Fist fights break out among the uncertain G.I.s, until the order arrives to move out. Though Braddock is thrilled at the news, since he won the platoon's $800 D–Day pool, his happiness is short-lived. They're to hit Omaha beach in the first wave of troops.

In alternately dramatic and comic moments, the squad pays a high price to take Omaha beach, goes on an inland patrol, and joins with a motley group of French resistance fighters. Braddock loses his winnings and his lunch, Caddy deals with the loss of his best friend, and Doc and Hanley both face their fears and survive their baptism of fire. For good measure, the squad liberates captured paratroopers and take out a German tank with improvised weapons. And, of course, they meet and dazzle

a female resistance fighter. The episode ends with the squad marching jubilantly into the heart of France, saying "Paris, here we come!"

Rick Jason

Fresh from his star turn as suave insurance investigator Robin Scott in the syndicated series "The Case of the Dangerous Robin," Rick Jason was cast as Sergeant Gil Hanley. This was not Rick Jason's first time in uniform. Rick volunteered for military service in 1943 and became a cadet in the Army Air Corps. After washing out of flight school because of problems with the required math, he says he bravely fought the battle of Nashville, working in public relations. Later, he was transferred to his home state of New York, where he worked in a convalescent hospital with combat fatigue patients and amputees in a special rehabilitative program. Rick finished his military career by teaching horseback riding at an Army Air

Fifth season publicity photo of Rick Jason as Lt. Hanley.

Corps hospital.

Richard Jason was born in New York City on May 21, 1923 into a wealthy family. In a 1962 *TV Guide* article, he laughingly described himself as second generation *nouveau riche* and a born romantic. A hell-raiser as a child, he was expelled from eight prep schools before finally graduating.

Expecting him to follow in his footsteps, Rick's father bought him a seat on the Curb stock exchange (now the AMEX). But while in the Army Air Corp, Rick sold the seat. After the war, he attended the American Academy of Dramatic Arts on the G.I. Bill. While learning his craft, he lived in a cheap, furnished room and paid the bills with odd jobs as a riding instructor, soda jerk, auditor, and hotel clerk.

Actor-director Hume Cronyn discovered him in the audience of a play and cast him in the Broadway show "Now I Lay Me Down to Sleep." The part earned Rick a Theater World Award and offers for contracts with four movie studios.

After success in the 1952 film "Sombrero," one movie fan magazine proclaimed him as a star of the future. He had featured and leading roles in films with Columbia, RKO, and 20th Century Fox and was signed to a multiple-picture contract with Fox. His first project, an adaptation of John Steinbeck's "The Wayward Bus," earned him critical acclaim and a string of roles in films and on television. It also brought him to the attention of Orson Welles, who cast him in the only project Welles directed for television: "The Fountain of Youth."

Rick received over 30 offers for leads in television series and eventually accepted the "Dangerous Robin" series in 1960. The show ran 38 episodes and is notable as the first TV series that featured karate. Though Rick was adept at karate, the martial arts were not widely established at the time, so no knowledgeable karate stuntman could be found for Rick to challenge in the weekly battles. Jason's instructor was pressed into service for on-screen action.

Rick Jason originally turned down *Combat!* But his agent convinced him to take a chance on the series, pointing out that no war movie (up to that time) had ever lost money at the box office.

After *Combat!* ended in 1967, Rick returned to theater. He also made films in Japan and Israel. In 1970, he took the lead in the pilot, "Prudence and the Chief." In this take-off on "The King and I," Rick played the Chief of the Cheyenne nation opposite Sally Ann Howes, the teacher of the Chief's children. The network didn't pick up the series. In 1973, he became a regular on "The Young and the Restless." Rick's TV career remained strong; he guested on dozens of prime-time shows through the seventies and eighties. He also was in demand for voice-overs and commercial work.

In retirement, Rick lived with his wife Cindy in Moorpark, California. He was an avid collector of wines and created The Wine Locker, a 4,000 square-foot facility to store fine wines under optimal conditions. He continued to indulge his many and varied interests: woodworking, carpentry, cooking, photography, and breeding tropical fish. Most of all, he enjoyed outdoor adventures, especially hunting and fishing.

In his book *Scrapbooks of My Mind: A Hollywood Autobiography,* Rick provided an intimate look at Hollywood's star machine, sharing his unique perspective and memories of MGM, 20th Century Fox, and the other big studios in their heyday.

Rick died in October, 2000, taking his own life. He is survived by his wife Cindy. As *Combat!* resurged in popularity, Rick was generous and warm with fans, always answering mail personally with more than was asked for, and sometimes even responding to a fan letter with a personal phone call. He attended the first three cast reunions and delighted regaling all with his stories.

HANLEY'S WOUNDS

Beatings:
• Cold-cocked with rifle butt on right side of jaw [Rescue]

Bullet Wounds:
• Left upper arm, Luger [Entombed]
• Left shoulder [A Sudden Terror]
• Left shoulder [Finest Hour], the bullet is cut out
• Left shoulder, on the back [A Distant Drum], bullet passes through
• Left shoulder, rifleshot [Rescue]
• Left wrist/hand, rifleshot [Pillbox]
• Left thigh, outside, pistol shot [The Convict]
• Right arm, just below shoulder [Anniversary]
• [Beneath the Ashes]

Explosions:
• Knocked unconscious in church during air raid [Any Second Now]
• Shrapnel passes through upper left arm [The Volunteer]
• Bumps head falling down hill [The Volunteer]
• Possible concussion, or just shell-shock [Rescue]
• Concussion [Escape to Nowhere]
• Possible left leg broken [Any Second Now]

Miscellaneous:
• Sprained wrist [A Walk with an Eagle]

Passes out:
• [Rescue] twice: at opening and after beating in Act 3
• [Escape to Nowhere] Begins episode unconscious
• [A Distant Drum] Begins episode unconscious
• [The Volunteer] Three times (in woods, on cart, in bed-room)
• [Escape to Nowhere] Passes out when trapped under beam (being trapped under beams was a common occurrence in the series)

Vic Morrow, autographed photo, as Saunders.

Vic Morrow

Vic Morrow was cast to play the second sergeant in the pilot. In an entertainment career that spanned 27 years, Morrow is perhaps most fondly remembered for the role of Sgt. Saunders in *Combat!*

Vic Morrow was born in the Bronx, New York, on February 14, 1929. Along with a bother and sister, he was raised in a typical, middle class family. At 17, Vic quit high school and joined the Navy. After completing his service, he earned his high school diploma at night school, then enrolled under the G.I. Bill as a pre-law student at Florida Southern College. But the acting bug struck and he forsook law for the stage. Vic studied acting at Mexico City College in 1950, performing in bilingual pro-

ductions. When he finished college, Vic worked with various theater groups, ultimately joining the New York Actors' Workshop under Paul Mann. Vic studied diligently for two years, driving cabs in his off-hours to pay for classes.

Morrow's big break came in 1955 in MGM's *The Blackboard Jungle*. Critics praised his portrayal of the tough street-kid Artie West, who menaces Glenn Ford, but the role typecast him. Following this success, he had featured roles in the films *King Creole*, *Tribute to a Bad Man*, *Men in War*, *God's Little Acre*, *Cimarron*, and *Portrait of a Mobster*, in which he portrayed the notorious Dutch Schultz. His desire for realism led him to spend days absorbing criminal lore from Barney Ruditsky, the former New York policeman who helped capture Schultz.

In 1962, Vic's new manager, Harry Bloom, pushed Vic's sex appeal and leading man qualities to gain him a screen test for *Combat!*

Vic escaped his villain image during his five seasons on *Combat!* Vic used his clout on *Combat!* to assume the director's chair, eventually directing six episodes for the series, including the acclaimed two-part, anti-war saga "Hills Are for Heroes." His other directorial credits include the New York off-Broadway stagings of "Deathwatch" and "The Maids" and the Desilu Professional Theatre Workshop presentation in

Lt. Hanley (Rick Jason) armed with his M1 carbine.

SAUNDERS' WOUNDS

Bullet Wounds:
- Right thigh (inner thigh?) [Rear Echelon Commandos]
- Left abdomen [Reunion]
- Left foot, in the heel [Duel]
- Left leg, outside, just above knee [The Walking Wounded]
- Left leg, outside, just above knee [Main Event]
- Left leg, outside, just above knee [Masquerade]
- Left leg, outside, just above knee [Barrage]
- Left leg, inside, just above knee [Conflict]
- Left leg, just above knee [The Celebrity]
- Left shoulder, flesh wound [Encounter]
- Left shoulder [More Than a Soldier]
- Left heel [The Duel]
- Right temple, rifle shot [The Leader]
- Right abdomen, machine gun [The Gantlet]
- Right leg, just above the knee [Ollie Joe]
- Right thigh, just above the knee [The Letter]
- Right thigh, upper [The Letter]
- Right thigh, high, outside [The Hostages]
- [The Little Carrousel]

Beatings:
- Blow to the left temple from rifle butt [The Gantlet]
- Cut: crop welt over left eye [The Long Way Home 1]
- Crop welt on left cheek [The Long Way Home 1]
- Possible injury to left ribs from beating [Long Way Home]
- Blow to left temple with club [The Long Way Home 2]
- Broken lip and cut on left cheek [Mountain Man]
- Blow to head [The Convict]
- Slapped around [Barrage]

Burns:
- Hand and shin [Chapel at Able-Five]
- Both hands [Survival]

Explosions:
- Knocked unconscious by bomb [The Walking Wounded]
- Concussion from mine causes blindness [Chapel at Able-Five]
- Knocked out by barrage [Far from the Brave]
- Knocked out from grenade and fall down hill [The Partisan]
- Neck wound, left side, from grenade [The Partisan]
- Leg wound [Hills are for Heroes]

Miscellaneous:
- Right hand, cut by flying debris [One More for the Road]
- Bruises and contusions causing unconsciousness from motorcycle wreck [The Gantlet]
- Rope burns on both palms [The Gun]
- Left eye gouged by Steiner [The Long Way Home 2]
- Pinched nerves in both legs from being trapped under beam [The Hard Way Back]
- Caught on barbed wire, cuts to both hands and left cheek[The Medal]
- Debris blasted in cheek, eyes from rifle shot [The Sniper]

Passes out:
- [The Gantlet] Three times: blow to head, gunshot, wreck
- [Rear-Echelon Commandos] Passes out on Crown's shoulder, fatigued by bullet wound
- [The Walking Wounded] Twice: from bullet and from bomb
- [Conflict] Passes out between acts 3 and 4
- [The Partisan] Twice
- [The Long Way Home 1] Passes out at end from beating
- [The Long Way Home 2] Overpowered in struggle
- [Masquerade] Passes out from earlier wounding
- [Chapel at Able-Five] Twice: from land-mine and from grenade
- [The Convict] Blow to head
- [Survival] Passes out four times from pain
- [Far from the Brave] From concussion of barrage blast
- [Barrage] From exhaustion and loss of blood after dragging himself into cave.

Hollywood of "The Firstborn," starring Lorne Green. He later directed the film version of "Deathwatch," working with long-time friend Leonard Nimoy.

An ABC press biography of Morrow said his professional goals were to attain the same recognition as a writer and director that he enjoyed as an actor. That ambition eluded him. In 1965, Vic was divorced from his wife of six years, actress Barbara Turner, and became estranged from his children Carrie Ann and Jennifer (actress Jennifer Jason Leigh). This, plus the cancellation of *Combat!* in 1967, sent him into a personal and professional decline.

Morrow's image as the "heavy" overtook him in his post-*Combat!* career. At first, he was in demand as a guest on hit TV series. A starring role in another series was proposed, but he wanted quality films, wanted to develop his own projects, and, most of all, he wanted to continue to direct.

He appeared in supporting roles in mini-series and made-for-TV films, most notably *The Glass House* and the "Police Story" pilot. Despite critical acclaim for his role in *The Bad News Bears,* his roles got smaller. He was plagued with misfortunes: a broken second marriage, the death of his beloved mother, a reputation as a heavy drinker, the failure of his film *A Man Called Sledge,* and the death of long-time companion Joanne Lee. When offered the chance to appear in a Spielberg film, Vic eagerly accepted. He saw it as a way to revive his film career.

Vic Morrow died in the early morning of July 23, 1982 while filming *Twilight Zone: The Movie.* As he waded across a river carrying two children, a helicopter crashed beside them, killing all three.

In remembering Morrow, Tom Lowell says, "Vic was very kind to me. Here I was, this young kid, and I was really awestruck by him. His reputation, not only as an actor, preceded him, but also a person who knows acting. I learned a great deal by watching him. I always tried to listen very carefully when he was working in a scene. I would always ask these stupid ques-

The cast of Combat!, *(back row, left to right) Dick Peabody, Jack Hogan. (Front row) Rick Jason, Vic Morrow and Pierre Jalbert.*

COMBAT!

tions, which I'm sure is why Peabody would always razz me, and I asked Vic, 'What does it feel like to be a movie star?' And he said 'I'm not a star, I'm a comet. Because it will burn brighter, but go out faster.'"

Shecky Greene in "The Prisoner."

Shecky Greene

Top nightclub comedian Shecky Greene made his TV acting debut as the bumbling, wise-cracking Private Braddock in *Combat!* To make the pilot, he had to get time off from his hotel commitments in Las Vegas, where he worked twenty weeks a year as one of the strip's most prominent lounge entertainers. Greene was ready to make the leap into dramatic acting and was sought after by television and film producers.

Sheldon Fred (Shecky) Greene began his show business career in 1944, after three years of Navy service aboard the aircraft carrier *Bon Homme Richard,* based in the Pacific.

"I planned to become a gym teacher," Shecky says in his press bio. "I took a summer job at a resort near Milwaukee called Oakton Manor. They paid me $20 a week and gave me a fancy title, 'Social Director.' We couldn't afford to bring in acts, so I'd get up and tell a few jokes, do pratfalls and whatever came to mind." He spent a year working toward his degree, while con-

tinuing to do club dates.

In the late forties, Greene was booked for two weeks at the Prevue Lounge in New Orleans. He stayed three years. Greene eventually wound up owning a share of the Prevue and planned to settle permanently in New Orleans. But when the club burned down, he returned to Chicago and college. "I was in the dorm one night when Martha Raye called from Miami and asked me to play her club down there. I quit school again when they held me over for six weeks. This time I made up my mind, I would stick with show business. I was only 25 years old and making $500 a week."

In 1953, when the Golden Hotel in Reno offered him over $1,000 a week, Shecky made a beeline for the Wild West. The owners tore up his four-week contract on opening night and made him a deal for $20,000 a year. Over the years, Shecky played many Las Vegas casinos and lounges, including the Starlight Lounge, the Tropicana, and the Last Frontier, becoming one of the biggest names in lounge entertainment in Nevada.

Robert Blees says of Shecky Greene, "He's a much better actor than people think. He's a sensational comic. He's a very witty guy — well read and intelligent. He wanted to establish himself on film, but wasn't being offered the right roles. He got offers to play third-rate Henny Youngmans, but he thought he was better than that. I thought so, too."

Shecky Greene is considered by many to be the consummate nightclub performer. Shecky admits that all this success has come to him with no pursuit on his part. Rather than help his career along, he's probably been his own worst enemy. Tales are legion of his drinking, carousing, gambling, turning over crap tables and busting up entire casinos; many of the stories are even true. However, Shecky has a different attitude about himself and his career today.

Several years ago, he stopped drinking. Then he had surgery for his throat and lost his voice for over a year. He was told he would never perform again. But through faith, his own courage, and the support of friends, he completely recovered. Later, he underwent cancer surgery and was cured.

Shecky has won numerous awards for nightclub performances, including the Las Vegas Entertainment Award for Best Lounge Entertainer, the Jimmy Durante Award for Best Comedian, and Male Comedy Star from the Las Vegas Academy of Variety and Cabaret Artists. He did eventually work in films, including *Splash,* Mel Brooks' *History of the World—Part 1,* and *Tony Rome.* He has appeared on many game shows and was a substitute host on Johnny Carson's "Tonight Show."

Shecky has appeared on television series ranging from "Laverne and Shirley" to "Northern Exposure" to "Roseanne." He spends several hours a day helping fellow talents to improve their acts and continues to perform his stand-up act.

BRADDOCK'S WOUNDS
Explosions: • Concussion from falling out of a land-mined jeep [The Prisoner]   **Passes Out:**   • [The Prisoner]   **Misc:**   • Wounded right hand from unknown injury [The Chateau]

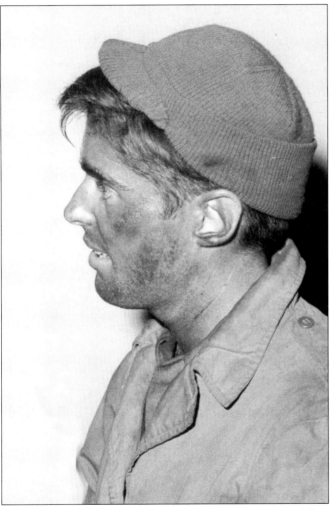

Steve Rogers as Doc Walton.

Steven (Rick) Rogers

The role of *Combat!'s* young medic went to the youthful Rick Rogers. This slim-featured young man seemed perfect to portray medic "Doc" Walton, a gentle, sensitive youngster who is profoundly affected by his battlefield experiences. Viewers of the pilot would scarcely guess from his appearance that not too long before, he weighed a lumbering 230 pounds. He had become drastically overweight as a kid and stayed that way throughout his childhood and youth.

He credits his acting aspirations for lopping off the weight and the comedy facade that he adopted as a defensive device. Rogers' real first name is Rick, but by the time the series aired, he had changed it to Steve, so as not to be confused with *Combat!* co-star Rick Jason.

An only child, he was born in Chicago on April 18, 1937. His father, Ted Rogers, a salesman, had been the first announcer for KSL and had also announced for KDYL in Salt Lake City. Later, Steve moved to Southern California with his parents. He attended elementary school in Northridge, a suburb of Los Angeles. He got his first taste of on-stage performing there when, while delivering the commencement speech at his sixth grade graduation, he forgot his lines and ad libbed his way through it.

He attended Notre Dame High School in Van Nuys, California, then finished his high school education at the Menlo School, Menlo Park, California.

During 1958 and part of 1959 he studied at Nevada Southern, then left there to join the acting school of Estelle Harman in Hollywood. He studied with her for three years, including the six months he spent on active duty with the Army, during which she conducted an informal correspondence course for him. Subsequently, Steve appeared in the 1962 Columbia feature picture, *13 West Street* and several TV productions, including "The Lawman," "Cheyenne," and "Straightaway."

His 1962 studio biography states his main hobby is reading, and he pursues it vigorously, being partial to law texts, biographies of famous lawyers and jurists and novels dealing with lawyers. Steve Rogers had hoped that *Combat!* would launch him into larger roles. But after leaving *Combat!* in its first season, the stardom that he sought never materialized. He eventually gave up acting and pursued a profitable t-shirt venture.

Pierre Jalbert

For the French-speaking Cajun G.I. from Louisiana, Paul "Caddy" Cadro, the producers brought film editor Pierre Jalbert out of the cutting room and into the spotlight.

Pierre was born the son of a newspaperman in Quebec City, Canada on January 9, and christened Joseph Jacques Pierre-Paul Jalbert. There, he attended Ouellet College and Laval University. While at university he was in the army reserve a year. "Then the air force created the University Air Training Corps," says Pierre Jalbert, "so I transferred to that. I was there from '41 to the end of the war. I became a sergeant. I was the drilling sergeant for my squad." Pierre was studying to be a pilot when the war ended.

Pierre Jalbert as PFC Paul "Caje" LeMay.

CAJE'S WOUNDS

Bullet Wounds:
- Left shin just below knee cap [Bridge at Chalons]
- Left shoulder [The Partisan]
- Left upper arm [The Brothers]
- Right knee, outside [Anniversary]
- Upper left thigh (outside) machinegun bullet [The First Day]
- Right lower leg, outside, just below knee [The Old Men]
- Right shoulder, machine gun [Battle of the Roses]
- Right arm [Birthday Cake]
- Right thigh, outside [A Little Jazz]

Knife Wounds:
- Bayonet wound in lower left arm [Jonah]
- In gut [The Leader]

Beating:
- Injury on left cheek, possibly crop welt [Long Way Home 2]
- Punched [The Mockingbird]

Miscellaneous:
- Limping, left foot appears injured at start [Silver Service]
- Twisted left ankle in fall [Jonah]
- Twisted right ankle [Conflict]
- Scratched (bit?) on hand by woman [Weep No More]
- Compound fracture, lower left leg [The Hostages]

Passes out:
- [Long Way Home—Part 2]
- [The Mockingbird] After being slugged by spy

Pierre Jalbert was the top seated ski racer in Canada and, after the war, was hoping for a berth on the Canadian Olympic team when disaster struck. He contracted rheumatic fever and his doctor informed him that he would never ski again. By the following fall, he made an astonishing recovery from an illness that customarily leaves its victims semi-invalids. His doctor gave him the go-ahead to resume skiing. At the National Championships, he emerged as Canadian National Champ and became the Olympic team captain. Unfortunately, he broke his leg in a training mishap two days before the Olympics and didn't compete.

After the Olympics, he remained in Europe, sightseeing and later living in Paris where he studied art and art appreciation at the Sorbonne. A year later, he returned to Canada and resumed his job as editor and associate producer with the Canadian National Film Board, a federal production agency, and later with an independent film production company in Montreal. His desire was always to come to Hollywood, but he felt was not yet ready. While captain of the Canadian ski team, he competed in ski races at Sun Valley and Aspen and climaxed his Stateside trips with a visit to Hollywood. Later that year, he returned to Paris, where he worked as assistant producer for a French film company and as partner in a Parisian import-export firm.

He spent much of his spare time with film star Norma Shearer and her husband, Marti Arrougé, old skiing acquaintances also living in Paris. They suggested he turn professional and accompany them for the ski season to Sun Valley, Idaho.

Pierre agreed and became an instructor at Sun Valley.

His acting ambition still in mind, in the spring he went to Hollywood, where he has lived since. At Universal, he was hired as an assistant editor. A lull in production resulted in his being laid off. After another hiatus, he landed an editor's assignment at MGM.

An agent friend submitted his name for the pilot of Combat!, which gave him his long-sought-after opportunity to act. The part lasted five seasons. Pierre recalls, "I'd been around actors most of my life, been at MGM for ten years and knew the mechanics. I knew most of the technicians who were going to work on Combat! But I had never worked as an actor professionally. But I knew actors. I'd met Vic when he had done The Blackboard Jungle. I was the dialogue editor on it." Pierre was fascinated by the opportunity to be in front of the camera. "When we were doing the pilot, I went to Pirosh and asked why I was in his story. I wanted to find a handle to my behavior. He said, 'Pierre, I will tell you why. When I was in France, in my squad, I had two Louisiana Coonans.' Coonan is the slang word for Cajun. He said that they were the best soldiers that he had in his squad and they were the best killers and they never spoke

Right: Louis Mercier (wearing beret) guested in the episode "Missing in Action." Also pictured are Pierre Jalbert, Barton Heyman, Rick Jason.

To make the acting more realistic, the actors took boot camp training at Ft. Ord. (Note the names over the pockets of the actors.)

too much. They did their duty and they did their work and that was it." That was all Pierre needed to know, he had found the basis for his character. "Like Vic said, there's only a few laws that you must know. You apply them and it'll work. Because acting, basically, is sheer unadulterated common sense. Where am I? What am I? Who am I?"

After *Combat!*, Pierre allotted himself three years to make his acting career blossom, before considering returning to the editing room. He did several pilots. One was a spin-off of "The FBI" called "Interpol" for Warner Brothers. "It was a great part," recalls Jalbert. "I would have been our man in Paris. But the show just didn't fly." He did two more pilots, both westerns, but neither was picked up. He guested several times on "Mission Impossible" and did a few independent movies with Edward J. Lakso, who wrote many *Combat!* episodes.

Eventually, he returned to his old craft and went back into the cutting room. He worked at Paramount through 1990 as editor and dialogue editor on feature films and mini-series, including *Grease, Star Trek: The Motion Picture, The Godfather, Washington Behind Closed Doors,* and *Shogun.*

He married Joy Lee, former actress and ballerina, in January of 1961, and the couple have remained happily married. Pierre now spends his spare time refinishing furniture, remodeling houses, and writing. When time and weather allow, he keeps up his skiing.

He has actively participated in all the *Combat!* cast reunions and continues to be a fan favorite.

Selig J. Seligman

Selig J. Seligman was executive producer for *Combat!*, the first ABC series to be owned by the network. Seligman, a former ABC-TV vice president and cousin to ABC-TV president Leonard Goldenson, was the founder of Selmur productions (named for he and his wife, Muriel).

In 1958, he produced the ABC courtroom drama "Accused." It presented reenactments of real law cases, mostly criminal. Like his later series, *Combat!*, the show stressed authenticity. The judge was played by a UCLA law professor and the attorneys were real-life lawyers. According to *The Complete Directory to Prime Time Network and Cable TV Shows,* Seligman kept a staff of lawyers and law students busy researching actual court cases in his search for realism for the series.

Seligman brought to "Accused" a strong knowledge of the law. He graduated number one in his class at Harvard law school and was a former State Department attorney. Seligman

was a war veteran who served as an attorney at the Nuremberg war crimes trials.

Filming the Pilot

Veteran film director Boris Sagal directed the pilot episode. His extensive list of credits spans three decades. He has directed TV series, TV films, mini-series, and theatrical releases. A short list includes: "The Man From U.N.C.L.E.," "Night Gallery," *The Thousand Plane Raid, Hauser's Memory, The Omega Man,* "Rich Man, Poor Man," and "The Awakening Land."

The pilot took six days to shoot, including one day of location shooting on Tranca's Beach, which stood in for Omaha Beach. The stars of the show, Rick Jason and Vic Morrow, met on the second day of filming. Rick Jason recalls the excitement he had from the very first, working with Vic. "We rehearse the scene and this guy gives! I mean, he is playing the scene. He almost leads me. We start soaring on each other's characters. We're getting energy from each other. And I realize there's a chemistry . . . Don't ask me what it is. Movie makers have been trying to figure it out since the beginning of film. It was the first indication I had that this show might just go."

Pierre Jalbert, too, recalls that Vic's generous acting style and dedication to his craft was evident from the beginning. "One day we were having lunch during the pilot and Vic said to me, without being facetious, 'You really aren't an actor, are you, Pierre?' I said, 'We're all actors.' But, to be truthful, I understood his question. I wasn't a professional actor, I was and am a professional editor. I'm a technician." Vic told Pierre that if the series survived, he wanted to direct some episodes. "He said, 'Why don't we exchange knowledge?' Wasn't that nice? From then on, when I had something important to do, like a scene that needed some acting knowledge, he would take me apart and he taught me the ropes of the job. And he was a very, very good teacher."

While the pilot began filming, the Hollywood Reporter printed an ABC publicity release about the show that described it as having three stars: Jason, Morrow, and comedian Shecky Greene. "I seldom read the trade papers, so I didn't see it," remembers Rick Jason. "Dick Irving Hyland, my agent, called and said everything was taken care of. I asked what had been taken care of, and he explained about the item. And that he had telephoned ABC and reminded them of my contract. That there was only one other star in the show and everything was shared equally between us, including (if the pilot sold) alternate

COMBAT!

Omaha Beach had a "stand in"— Tranca's Beach — for the pilot, "A Day in June."

first billing on each segment. I think my only comment was, 'Okay, but when am I going to meet Shecky Greene? I'm a fan of his!'"

Though the cast formed a quick rapport, many had reservations about the project. "We were fighting a script so loaded with cliches," says Rick Jason, "and burdened with stale dialogue and predictable characters, that it threatened to sink the project. I think Vic thought so, too, although we didn't discuss it until almost a year later."

Filming on "A Day in June" finished on December 23, 1961. The wrap party was held on a sound stage at MGM. By 1:00 am, over 300 people were still celebrating the successful conclusion of the pilot, when in strutted executive producer Selig J. Seligman. He thanked everyone for an outstanding effort and then, according to Rick Jason, proudly announced on the microphone, "Tonight, at 10:55 pm, you finished your last shot. At exactly 11:00 pm, my wife, Muriel, gave birth to a son. We're calling him Adam. Thank you, all."

Pilot Cast

Rick Jason as Sgt. Gil Hanley
Vic Morrow as "Chip" Saunders
Shecky Greene as Braddock
Rick Rogers as Doc
Pierre Jalbert as Caddy
Max Dommar as Theo
Lisa Montell as Marcelle
Frankie Ray as Gardello
Harry Dean Stanton as Beecham
Brad Weston as Crowley

Pilot Technical Credits

Produced by: Robert Pirosh
Music by: Leonard Rosenman
Director of Photography: Phil Lathrop
Assistant to the Producer: Ralph E. Winters
Production Executive: Richard Caffey
Art Direction: George W. David and Merrill Pye
Film Editor: Ralph E. Winters
Assistant Director: Joseph McEveety
Set Decoration: Otto Sieger
Recording Supervisor: Franklin Milton

Above: *To announce its 1962 season, ABC gathered series stars at the Hollywood Bowl for this publicity photo.*

Right: *Looks can be deceiving. This is Earl Parker, Vic's stunt double, in the French village area of the MGM backlot.*

B ased on the pilot episode, ABC put *Combat!* on its fall schedule along with their other World War II drama, "The Gallant Men." But ABC wanted changes, the first of which was to replace Robert Pirosh as producer. Wisely retreating to the safety of the movie wars, Pirosh was the first of many production staff that would be casualties to *Combat!*

Robert Blees was among several applicants interviewed for series producer. When offered the job, he had only one condition: that they also sign Robert Altman to direct every other episode. This was so Altman could prepare one episode while the next was being shot. Blees had worked often with Altman on the anthology series "Life in a Small Town" and been very impressed with his ability. "I think I discovered Bob Altman," says Robert Blees. "He'd never done any 'A' project up until then."

Robert Blees

Before *Combat!*, Robert Blees had received critical praise for his work on the 1961 TV series "Bus Stop." Airing opposite the ratings blockbuster "Bonanza," the series survived only one year. Also contributing to early cancellation of "Bus Stop" was the national notoriety it gained for an episode featuring singer Fabian. The episode was denounced for its explicit violence and sadism and even cited in Congressional hearings on violence in television.

Blees was proud of his artistic work on "Bus Stop" and also that "Bus Stop" was the only network series of that year that came in on budget. Blees also had experience in feature films, including the "first feature that Joan Crawford played her age."

In addition to Robert Altman, Blees also hired Robert Hauser as cinematographer, whose work he greatly admired. All three of these Roberts had been in the war. "I felt that was essential," says Blees.

But the war experiences among the new staff had been in the air, not on the ground. Blees had been a B–24 navigator in the Air Corps and Altman had joined in 1945 and become a copilot of a B–24 in the Pacific. The only infantryman associated with *Combat!* who had actual frontline experience in Europe was the show's creator, Robert Pirosh, who was no longer working on the show.

Left: Saunders' squad takes on an abandoned infant in "One More for the Road." Fletcher Fist, Vic Morrow, and Tom Lowell with one of the Monroe twins.

Right: Robert Altman insisted that German characters would speak German and French characters would speak French. In photo: Warren Spahn and Vic Morrow.

CHAPTER 2

SEASON ONE, 1962–1963

COMBAT!

Robert Altman

Robert Altman was born and raised in Kansas City, Missouri. He had a Catholic upbringing and education. He attended a military academy until he volunteered for service in 1945.

After the war, Robert Altman went to work in Kansas City for the Calvin Company. There, he developed his craft as a film maker. He took simple documentaries, employee training films, and advertisements and used them to explore creative film techniques and innovative story-telling ideas, while still bringing projects in on budget.

He left for Hollywood in 1955. After several unheralded independent films, he was given his first directorial break by Alfred Hitchcock. This led to fairly steady work directing in television, especially in action/adventure shows, such as "Bonanza," "Maverick," and "Whirlybirds." He directed the pilot for "The Gallant Men," ABC's other war series that premiered in 1962. It featured an infantry unit fighting in Italy, as seen through the eyes of a war correspondent. "I was offered 'Gallant Men,'" says Altman, "but just thought that there was more to work with in *Combat!* I think it was a well-done series. It was a think piece." Altman lasted less than a season on *Combat!*

He later went on to success on the big screen with such films as *M*A*S*H, Kansas City, The Player,* and *Gosford Park.*

War is Hell

Robert Blees and Robert Altman approached the first season with the intent to make a grittier, more realistic war story than had ever before been seen on television. Cinematographer Robert Hauser worked with them to create a distinctive look to the show. His use of hand-held cameras, cluttered foregrounds, and a *film noir*-like use of light and shadow became standard in the series. Robert Altman tried to put some unusual twists to the show. "I was trying to go against the grain of the problems that it [television] set up. For instance, you do a story about war. Your leading men, you know they'll never get killed, but the whole point of suspense is whether a person survives or not. In *Combat!*, I developed a squad and put in many, many characters. After a few episodes the audience gets used to the familiar faces. Then, I'd kill them off. Early in the episode, not making it pivotal to the plot. It kept people off-balance." He also insisted that German characters should speak German, and French characters French. No subtitles.

Robert Blees made the deal that provided *Combat!* with all the war-ravaged scenery they could use. "I knew Metro [Goldwyn Mayer] still had lot 2 and lot 3 and they're going broke. They're not shooting anything." Blees arranged to film the show on the MGM lot to take advantage of the many standing sets, with the agreement that they could use them any way they wanted. Some of the sets were so worn that they

needed little change to make them appear like war-ravaged France. The streets of the *Combat!* French village, in happier times, hosted the musical frolics of Nelson Eddy and Jeanette MacDonald. The train station the squad battles over in the episodes "What Are the Bugles Blowin' For?" and "One at a Time" once provided the tragic demise for Anna Karenina.

Next, Blees signed on Richard Caffey, who had been production executive for the pilot, as associate producer of the series. He brought Georg Fenady on board, both of whom would play pivotal roles in all five seasons of *Combat!*, long outlasting the boss who hired them. Robert Altman started bringing writers he knew to work on the series. Blees, who started out in the business as a writer, went to work making sure the right scripts were developed for the realistic, dark vision he had for the series.

Blees says, "I disliked the pilot. In fact, I called it 'The Rover Boys in Normandy.' It had no sense of reality whatsoever."

Realism would be the trademark of the show. Actual newsreel footage of the war was incorporated into the episodes. The producers worked closely with the U.S. Army to keep the stories and situations honest. The cast even endured Army boot camp in preparation for production.

Basic Training: Fort Ord

The network suggested that the cast go to Fort Ord army base for a crash course to familiarize themselves with the military. Since all the stars attending this basic training had already served in the armed forces, the ten-day trip served more for a photo opportunity than a learning experience. The training was bally-hooed in the advance press for the series.

The actors went through the same training as new recruits, with the only exception being that they could leave the post at night. They would arrive at 7:30 in the morning and work until evening.

Pierre Jalbert remembers Fort Ord fondly. "It was your usual quick indoctrination into the military and the feeling of it all. It was pleasant and the military was very nice. We got the uniform. We went to a few training sessions and learned to handle the guns."

Rick Jason was not as enchanted with the trip, thinking that basic training is something one should go through only once in a lifetime. While walking to the PX, Rick Jason had a run-in with an officer, who chewed him out for not saluting. Instead of proper military remorse, Jason just responded, "Yeah?" Unlike run-ins Jason had had with officers in his real military career, this time he knew he couldn't wind up behind bars.

The actors met many Army officers while at Fort Ord. They were looking over the new actors and new series with great interest, to see if this was a show they wanted to support.

They decided to support it wholeheartedly.

Georg Fenady recalls that, "We got incredible cooperation

from the army. We always had a cavalry officer with us — no less than a major, and maybe a colonel —for the years that we worked, as a technical advisor and liaison. Whatever we needed, I'd just call whoever was the colonel at the time and say we'd need ten tanks on this day, two half-tracks, and so on and so on. Everything we could get from the army was delivered and they were incredible."

The advisors made sure the actors and actions remained true to military life. "It wasn't objections, as much as keeping us honest, in a sense. They didn't say 'Can't do that.' It was just, 'We wouldn't do that,' and 'It didn't happen that way.' . . . One of his pet peeves, which I still hear every day, is on a radio transmission. 'Over and out. Over and out.' He would cringe. You never say 'Over and out.' 'Over' means you're going to continue the transmission. 'Out' means it's out."

Cast Changes

In addition to staff changes, the cast also changed between the pilot and the series. The Beecham character (played by Harry Dean Stanton) was dropped and, over the objections of Robert Pirosh, the name of the Cajun soldier was changed from Caddy to Caje. Pierre Jalbert says, "Caje was a contraction of Cajun. I think it was Vic that started to call me that and it stuck. I don't remember if there was any specific reason for it, it just organically took place."

Combat! went on the air with five regular cast members, three of whom would return for the following season. All the actors who eventually became regular cast members appeared in the first season.

Rick Jason's character of Hanley was promoted from Sergeant to Lieutenant, shattering Pirosh's concept of a show revolving around a small core of enlisted men. This change was made at the suggestion of Robert Altman, whose background as a flyer in the Air Corps may have made it difficult for him to imagine a war fought without officers. Rick Jason adjusted his portrayal from the devil-may-care skirt-chaser, to the cool, calm, and collected officer. The change in rank also put a professional

Combat! *became a career builder for Georg Fenady. He started in 1962 as a second assistant director and eventually became the show's associate producer. He went on to direct action television and feature films. He is pictured here (in white t-shirt) directing an episode of "Garrison's Gorillas," the series that replaced* Combat!

distance between the characters of Hanley and Saunders, dampening the budding friendship established in the pilot. Hanley still retained the sophisticated good looks, bright smile, and easy-going manner — and the hard steel behind the smile.

Vic Morrow had hoped *Combat!* was his chance to break out of his bad-guy image and change the direction of his career, but he was disenchanted with the pilot. Blees quickly set up a meeting with Vic Morrow. "I admired his work for years and thought he'd be critical to the show's success. It was apparent Vic had very strong ideas, which was fine with me. I respected that. That didn't mean I had to accept the ideas. Rick's stature was far above Vic's. Rick got more money the first year, he had the stature. On a scale of one to ten, I'd say he was about a number seven star."

Blees' first meeting with Vic lasted two hours. Vic wanted to walk away from the show after the pilot. "He thought it would ruin his career."

Far from it, Sgt. Saunders, the everyman soldier, became the defining role of Morrow's career. Morrow's powerful portrayal of this tough-as-nails leader far surpassed the simplistic press kit description of him as "strong but sympathetic." Morrow's Saunders was a man of few words, with a fierce loyalty to his men and to his lieutenant.

Pierre Jalbert was pleased to step out of the editing room to play the newly christened character Paul "Caje" LeMay. His character usually acted as the platoon's French translator, letting him script his own French dialogue. Gregarious and friendly, Caje's character goes through a series of epiphanies as the war tries to crush his spirit. Jalbert's superb performances hardly seem like the work of a newcomer. He creates some riveting moments in the pilot episode as he mourns the loss of his friend and deserts his squad under fire. He ends the season with an equally strong performance in "No Trumpets, No Drums" as he comes to terms with his accidental killing of a French civilian.

In an interview for *The Squad,* Jalbert said, "The first three months were a little scary for me, being in front of that black box. But, I had a great advantage knowing all the technicians who were working on *Combat!* I had great support from them. After about a year I was very confident. Vic Morrow helped me also by teaching me about screen presence and timing."

Shecky Greene continued his nightclub engagements while filming *Combat!* Production often was arranged around his Vegas schedule so he wouldn't have to give up any performances on the strip, for which he was receiving $150,000 per week. The directors would try to shoot his scenes on Mondays and Tuesdays, finishing in time for him to return to Vegas for the Tuesday evening show.

Blees says, "This was typical of the dedication of the guys working there. Greene would work his bit in Vegas. After Sunday's show, he'd get in an ambulance, sleep on his way to L.A., where he kept an apartment, and get ready for filming the show. We all appreciated that dedication." Such arrangements

Morrow objected to his role in the pilot but it came to define his career and create a memorable character.

weren't possible, though, when Greene was featured in the episode, such as in "The Prisoner" and "The Chateau."

Shecky Greene only appeared in eight episodes. The end came while filming, in 110-degree heat, the final scene for the episode "Far From the Brave." The many re-takes of the scene on Eucy Road (an often-filmed road on the MGM backlot lined with Eucalyptus trees) was the last straw for Greene. He had little patience for method acting and preferred the larger paychecks of Vegas.

Greene discussed his departure from *Combat!* during an interview on the Charles Grodin show. "I threw everything down and ran. I said that's the end of it. I went to Selig Seligman, the producer, and I said 'Selig, I quit.' He said, 'You can't quit 'cause the whole show's around you and I'm going to get you your own show with ABC.' ABC was nothing at the time, it was just AB, it didn't even have the C. And, I said I really don't want television 'cause this is not for me, I'm not making direct contact. Not even with the director. . . . Uh, and that smell of eucalyptus. How many times can your nose clear up?"

Though Seligman wanted Greene to stay, his character wasn't working with the new, darker concept for the show.

Steven Rogers portrayed the character Doc as a gentle, sensitive youth who is profoundly affected by his battlefield experiences. His character was the only one of the regulars to escape the show unharmed. Steven Rogers' Doc appeared in 21 episodes without a single injury. His mortal blow came not from the Germans, but from the front office.

Rogers' work and attitude didn't please the producers and he was released before the end of the first season. According to some on the set, he had expected to be noticed in his *Combat!* role and that he was going to be the star. "He thought he was going places," says Conlan Carter, "but nothing really happened. He's a good looking kid and I can see how he might have bought into that for himself."

Blees says that Seligman fired Steve Rogers because of a negative comment Rogers' wife made about Seligman at a party. But whatever the reason, this first squad medic disappeared from the show without fanfare after just one season.

Meanwhile, in Front of the Cameras

The first episode filmed for the series was "Any Second Now," directed by Robert Altman. From the start, Altman put his imprint on the series, eschewing the light-hearted banter and bright exteriors of the pilot for a darker, grittier realism. Though he directed only ten episodes, cast members credit him with establishing the look and feel of the show.

Though Saunders, Braddock, Doc, and Caje appear briefly, "Any Second Now" is primarily a solo episode for Hanley. Altman and Blees wanted to get away from an ensemble show, to feature individual stories. This was in contradiction to Executive Producer Seligman's concept of the show. He preferred to stick close to the troops. This is one of the reasons the show premiered not with the first episode filmed ("Any Second Now"), but with an ensemble show, "Forgotten Front."

Altman's early episodes featuring individual stories ruffled feathers in the front office. Seligman started vetoing anything that took the action from the squad as a whole. Altman found an unlikely ally in the ABC front office.

Despite insider predictions that Morrow would be the focus of the fans, Rick Jason scored a hit early in the show. The mail response for him took ABC by surprise. They wanted to capitalize on this unsuspected asset. So Altman directed and featured Jason in a solo episode, "Escape to Nowhere," in which none of the other cast members appear.

Producer Robert Blees cites an additional reason for doing episodes centering around only one of the squad members: "You know, we had to let our guys off every once in a while. They were going crazy, shooting these things in six days, back-to-back-to-back." In that first season, the show was shot in six days, on a five-day work week. So, if an episode started on a Monday, it would finish the following Tuesday. They often would work twelve and fourteen hour days. Today, a similar show would be shot in ten to twelve days with a production staff at least five times as large.

"Escape to Nowhere," with its solo appearance for Rick Jason, angered Seligman. When he saw the script, he told Altman that he couldn't shoot it. Altman shot it anyway. ABC put out special ads for the show that neglected to mention Morrow or the rest of the cast. This caused a barrage of agents, publicists, and managers to descend on the Selmur office.

A solo episode for Morrow, "Cat and Mouse," written and directed by Altman, was quickly added to the schedule. But because of the episode's blatant anti-war message, the episode passed without fanfare or publicity, suffering from its association with Robert Altman, whose star at Selmur Productions was fading. He was about to go the way of Robert Blees.

First Season Casualties

Blees always brought the show in within its $150,000 per episode budget, which was hard to do. "We kept a very high standard," says Blees. "Not every one of our shows was as good as I would have liked it. But it was very, very good. In fact, we were really rolling."

Blees tried to launch other shows from within *Combat!* He wanted to develop a story using Nina Foch as a war correspondent, launching a series with a slightly different flavor — one that would attract a 50/50 male/female audience, instead of the 60/40 audience that *Combat!* was attracting. ABC passed on the notion, instead choosing to produce a pilot about Alexander the Great, starring William Shatner. Though offered work on the pilot, neither Altman nor Blees wanted anything to do with it. Blees' "backdoor pilot" about the correspondent was never made, but the idea later was developed into the first-season episode "No Hallelujahs for Glory."

"He was a real nice guy," says Dick Peabody about Blees, "smart as they come. A real perfectionist." Blees was demanding of writers. He required the best scripts for the series and wouldn't accept less. Under his exacting eye, *Combat!* premiered with superior scripts and stories that rival anything written for today's television. Unfortunately, they weren't the scripts that Seligman wanted. Blees and Altman were having more and more serious disagreements with Seligman, which was becoming common knowledge around Hollywood.

Seligman replaced Blees with Altman as producer of *Combat!* Robert Altman continued to direct episodes, as well as produce. Altman's strength as a director is his ability to inspire passionate performances in actors and to create striking visuals. But his vision of *Combat!* was oppressive; he presented the show's central character, the battle-hardened Sergeant Saunders, as the perpetual victim, the ultimate martyr to war, with no control over his destiny.

This viewpoint had already gotten Altman in trouble with the front office. Altman became increasingly firm about his view of the show and the characters. At a party, he purportedly engaged in a fight with Seligman, shouting that his work was being tampered with because it didn't make kids think war was fun. Altman was dismissed as producer. Both Blees and Altman went to work on the Kraft shows after *Combat!*, until Altman was once again fired, after a well-publicized remark to the sponsors, saying their shows were as bland as their cheese.

Other First Season Influences

For most of the rest of the season, the individual directors acted as producers of their own episodes. *TV Guide* compared Executive Producer Selig Seligman to a traffic cop "directing the administrative talent in and out of offices while cutting off the press."

Amid all the tumultuous changes in staff and constant bickering among management, the cast stayed friendly and upbeat. The cameras only stopped rolling when President Kennedy was assassinated, but continued on after a three-day break. The work continued despite not knowing from day to day who was in charge.

Vic Morrow said to *TV Guide* "It's like this crazy ship, see? Half the time the sails are on cockeyed and you're never quite sure who's going to try to put 'em on next. But the wind — it's blowing fine."

One of the ablest producers to trim the sails of *Combat!* was writer/director Burt Kennedy. The combined job of director and producer suited him just fine. Vic Morrow was fond of saying that if Burt Kennedy could have written all the episodes, and Robert Altman directed them, the show would have run forever.

More than anyone, Burt Kennedy established the heart and soul of *Combat!* Kennedy instilled Saunders with an unwavering moral conviction. In a Kennedy-directed episode, even when Saunders was not in control of his situation, he was always in control of his own soul, and, ultimately, his own destiny. Kennedy's shows shine best when dealing with average men walking the line between life and death. He developed rich characterizations and relationships among the core cast, exploring themes of duty and friendship. Kennedy's strongpoint is character and character-interaction, dealing with internal conflict and the themes of duty and friendship. His scripts cemented the relationship between Billy and Littlejohn and finely honed what *Combat!* fans fondly call the Saunders' PPT (Patented Pep Talk), known to turn around the most recalcitrant soldier by the time the final credits roll.

"Bob [Altman] and Burt complemented each other on their point of view of the show," says Tom Lowell. "Bob's was very up-close and personal, like in 'Survival,' which was one man's effort to survive. He loved working with people like John Black, who wrote the script. Burt, on the other hand, loved the overview, he loved to see all of the guys interacting together. Each of his scripts always started out high angle, looking down. And that's kind of how he saw the whole thing. He always wanted to be above everything, watching the whole thing as kind of a giant jigsaw that went together. And Bob, on the other hand, loved intricate, detailed, closeup stuff."

Combat! benefited from a wealth of talent behind the camera. Established directors, such as Golden Globe-winner Laslo Benedek, and the blockbuster directors of tomorrow, such as Richard Donner, all left their imprint on the series. *Combat!*'s most prolific director was Bernard McEveety with 31 *Combat!* episodes to his credit. The only director to work all five seasons, he created the show's most spectacular action sequences. Always character-driven, his action focused on the men behind the explosions. His action sequences were often recycled and reused over and over again in other episodes.

At the end of the season, Gene Levitt was pressed into service as the new producer. He had written four of the strongest episodes of the first season: "Any Second Now," "Rear Echelon Commandos," "I Swear by Apollo," and "The Volunteer." He seemed determined to establish a new non-Altman era of *Combat!*

PERSONNEL CHANGES: The New Recruits

Dick Peabody

Richard Peabody was born April 6, 1925 in Kansas City, Missouri. His father was a writer for the motion picture trade paper "Boxoffice." Both parents were teachers.

In 1942, at age 17, he joined the Navy. Four years later, he was honorably discharged as an Electronic Technician's Mate First Class. Peabody began studying electrical engineering at Kansas City Junior College. After a year, he switched to the University of Kansas City and a liberal arts course because "I wanted fame and I couldn't find anyone who could name a famous electrical engineer."

A succession of jobs producing screen advertising and TV commercials followed. A film he wrote and directed for the Greater Kansas City Ford Dealers caught the attention of director Robert Altman (*M*A*S*H, Nashville, The Player*) who recommended that he be hired by The Calvin Company to make educational and industrial films.

On the advice of Academy Award-winning director Nick Grinde, Peabody decided to broaden his background to include performing and went to work as a TV news anchor at the NBC affiliate in Kansas City. Later, he moved to Denver to host a radio jazz show. He augmented his income with freelance writing jobs, including writing advertising copy, documentary films, radio and TV commercials, and a weekly column for a Denver night-life magazine. He also found time to produce a pilot film for television in association with orchestra leader Dick Jurgens.

Peabody formed his own radio commercial production company. In 1960, the Denver Advertising Club, awarded first, second, third, fourth, fifth, and sixth place to radio commercials written and produced by Peabody.

Two years later, he took a self-inventory and realized that he was hungry for public recognition, bored with what he was doing, and tired of moving from place to place. He concluded that acting in Hollywood would be the answer. Because he is unusually tall and considers himself homely, Dick felt his appearance would give him an advantage over other aspiring thespians. He viewed himself as an ideal Western villain type.

On his first day in Los Angeles he got a job doing the all night show at Radio Station KMPC. The next day, Robert Altman, a friend from the days at the Calvin Company back in Kansas City, offered him a small part in the first episode of the

LITTLEJOHN'S WOUNDS
Bullet Wounds:
- Left shoulder [Bridge at Chalons]
- Left shoulder [A Little Jazz]
- Lower left leg, outside [The Bankroll]
- Right side, just above waist, shot by Messerschmidt [Gulliver]
- Right shoulder [Beneath the Ashes]
- Right shoulder [Luck With Rainbows]
- Right shoulder [The Ringer]
- Right shoulder [One at a Time]
- Right shoulder [The Farmer]
- Right arm, upper [Anatomy of a Patrol]
- Right thigh [Bridgehead]
- Right thigh [Odyssey]
- Right leg just above the knee [Vendetta]

Miscellaneous:
- Injury to left side when heavy artillery piece falls on him, possibly a broken rib [The Gun]
- Twisted ankle [Ambush]
- Face bandaged at top of episode [Heritage]

Crew and Vic at Franklin Canyon.

Dick Peabody towers over dancer Donna Loren, visiting the set of the episode "The Long Wait" between her beach blanket movies.

new TV series *Combat!* and invented the character name of "Littlejohn." It stuck. Peabody was eventually signed by ABC-TV to a contract, and Littlejohn became part of the squad. His role attained new dimensions when Burt Kennedy created him a sidekick, Billy Nelson.

At six-foot, six inches tall, Littlejohn is the gentle giant of Company K. Kind-hearted and friendly, Littlejohn finds some good in everyone he meets. Though he seems a hayseed, he's perceptive about people and is hard to con. Don't ask if Littlejohn is a nickname or his last name. Even Dick Peabody doesn't know. Altman never told anyone.

Altogether, Dick Peabody has co-starred in 120 prime-time TV shows, six feature motion pictures, and has done dozens of TV voice-overs and radio spots, including an award-winning Stan Freberg TV commercial for Jeno's Frozen Pizza. In 1971, he joined KFI Radio (NBC) in Los Angeles as a talk show host in a program originating from Universal Studios. He conducted over 500 celebrity interviews with some of the biggest names in the entertainment industry.

Back surgery sidelined Peabody's acting career in 1985 and forced him to devote more time to writing — which is what he has always enjoyed most.

Peabody and his wife, Tina, a former New York and Los Angeles model, lived in the Sierra foothills until Dick's death in 1999. Their house overlooked an apple orchard and Christmas tree farm.

In the Mountain Democrat newspaper, Peabody reminisced about *Combat!:* "We were widely known in the industry as a 'happy' show. The guest stars liked to work with us because playing soldier is a lot of fun and they were under no pressure to take sides in intramural disputes. There were no disputes.

"Although none of us in the cast of *Combat!* were acquainted before the shooting started, we developed a genuine regard for each other in a short time." That affection has lasted more than thirty years.

Like his character, Dick Peabody in real life was the heart and soul of the cast. During the years of filming the series, the cast often broke up into small cliques and sometimes even rival camps, but Dick Peabody managed to be friend to all, soothing feathers and keeping people together. I never heard him utter a harsh or unkind word about any of his fellow cast members — but boy could he rail against any director or outside actor who dared to say a cross word against *his* cast. In researching this book, one constant ran through all my interviews:

everyone adored Dick. He was genuinely loved.

Together with the author of this book, he helped to reunite the surviving cast for Comboat '96 — the first and last time the cast was together (minus Vic) since the end of the series.

Dick Peabody passed away on December 27, 1999 from prostate cancer. His wife, Tina, lovingly cared for him through his protracted illness.

Tom Lowell as Billy Nelson.

Tom Lowell

Tom Lowell was born Lowell Thomas in Philadelphia, Pennsylvania. Both his parents were teachers. They moved to California in the late forties, settling in Sacramento. His father taught for 30 years as head of the Theater Department at California State University, Sacramento. His mother taught English and Speech at the same high school from which he graduated, El Camino.

Tom Lowell started his acting career on the TV show "Target the Corruptors," followed by the film *Mr. Hobbs Takes a Vacation.* Then he was cast in the picture considered by many critics to be one of the ten best films of all time, *The Manchurian Candidate,* in the role of Lembeck. He believes that this film got him the role of Billy Nelson on *Combat!*

Lowell was hired by Burt Kennedy to play a character he created for the episode "The Celebrity." The character, Billy Nelson, was a foil for Littlejohn. When Peabody as Littlejohn and Lowell as Nelson got together, it was instant chemistry.

BILLY'S WOUNDS

Bullet Wounds:
- Chest, right side [No Hallelujahs For Glory]
- Unknown location [Anatomy of a Patrol]
- Right chest [The Celebrity]
- Left arm, upper [What Are the Bugles Blowin' For 1]

Beatings:
- Blow to head with rifle butt [Eyes of the Hunter]

Shrapnel/Bomb Debris:
- Bleeding wound in thorax, left side [Glow Against The Sky]

Miscellaneous:
- Hospitalized for unknown wound [Long Way Home 2l]

Passes Out:
- [Glow Against The Sky]—three times
- [Eyes of the Hunter] Blow to head

Kennedy knew a good thing when he saw it. He built on the relationship, writing Billy Nelson into more and more episodes, despite killing off the character. "In the first episode I appeared in," says Tom Lowell, "the one with Tab Hunter, it looked as if I had died. By the time it aired, I had already shot four more episodes."

The All-American, corn-fed boy, Billy Nelson, is the squad's youngest member. He has a charming, boyish grin, and is rather gullible. So it's good he has Littlejohn to look out for him. If going by the book, this private is not a good soldier, always getting things wrong and mis-handling his equipment. But in the field, he's a man you can count on to watch your back.

The relationship between Littlejohn and Billy became a trademark of the show. Though by the end of first season he had became a major, continuing character, appearing in most episodes, Lowell wasn't signed for a long-term contract.

"My time on the show was one of the most enjoyable experiences of my life," writes Tom Lowell in a letter to a fan. "The camaraderie established in the early sixties still exists. At the end of the third season, an opportunity arrived that I could not pass up. I was offered a contract at Walt Disney Studios to do two pictures a year for the next two years. I chose to leave *Combat!* and move over to the 'Mouse Factory.' I was sad and elated at the same time. I did four pictures at Disney, which I thought would propel me into a picture career. But as we all know, the film business is a Quixotic animal — Star one day, Shlub the next! And the next few years were a struggle."

Eventually, he decided enough was enough and went behind the camera. He produced commercials for the Peterson Company in Hollywood, then moved over as head of production for a videotape production center, VCI Studios. In the early eighties, he was a senior production manager for the local PBS affiliate, KCET, working on "Cosmos," "Steve Allen's a Meeting of Minds," and others.

In the mid eighties, he formed his own production company

specializing in commercials and industrial films and videotape. He took another fling at television as associate producer on "The New Gidget Show." But when he and twelve others were fired on the same day, he decided on a career change. He went back to school, earned a B.A. in theater, then an M.A. in screen writing, and found a teaching job.

Today, he teaches Theater, Video Production, English, and American Literature and produces and directs all the plays at a California high school. He is married to his second wife, Sharon. He has three sons from his first marriage: Ian, Brady, and Chris, as well as his wife's two children, Ryan and Lauren.

Jack Hogan

Born Richard Roland Benson Jr., Jack Hogan is hard put to explain why he changed his name to something equally plain. "Maybe," he says, "I just wanted to leave home and create a new person — and maybe I did." Acting on the belief that everyone loves the Irish, he changed his name to Jack Hogan: a name that he's proudly sported for over forty years.

Jack was raised in North Carolina and studied architecture at the University of North Carolina. In 1948, bored by college life, he left the University of North Carolina and spent the next four years in the armed forces, spending two of them in the Far East. Though he never had any previous yearning for a theatrical life, during his time in the service he decided to become an actor. By the time he left his final duty station in Japan, he had made arrangements to enroll at the Pasadena Playhouse in California.

In 1955, he headed for New York to attend the American Theatre Wing and continue his training. A year later, he returned to Hollywood where a string of acting jobs, both in films and on television, followed. His first film role was playing Westin in *Man from Del Rio*. Other films include *The Bonnie Parker Story*, *The Legend of Tom Dooley*, *Paratroop Command*, and *The Burglar*.

Jack credits directors Robert Gist and Robert Altman, with whom he has been associated, for exerting great and beneficial influences on his artistic development. Another personal mentor was Anthony Quinn, under whom he has studied and who gave him his first professional role. "For some reason, Tony Quinn liked me a lot. He signed to do a western for 20th and gave me my first part. At about the same time, I was working as a lifeguard at the Beverly Hills Hotel and teaching Josh Logan's kids to swim (the director from New York), who was in town directing Marilyn Monroe in *Bus Stop*. So, he gave me two days on *Bus Stop* and it all got cut out."

Hogan had an impressive list of film and television credits when Robert Altman hired him to do a guest appearance on *Combat!* as troublesome Private Kirby in "Forgotten Front." Altman wanted a character in the show that would make trouble for Vic.

Robert Altman had worked with Hogan on the TV series "Sheriff of Cochise" and "Bus Stop." He had been impressed

---

KIRBY'S WOUNDS
Bullet Wounds:
- Right shoulder [Rear Echelon Commandos]
- Right shoulder [Bridgehead]
- Right shoulder [The Ringer]
- Creased in left temple [Nothing to Lose]
- Left shoulder, bullet passes completely through [The Long Wait]
- Left shoulder [Retribution]
- Left hand, grazed with bullet [The Convict]
- Left thigh [Hills Are for Heroes]
- Left leg, just above knee, outside [The Casket]
- Left shin, outside [Main Event]
- Right leg [Gadjo]
- [The Letter] Doc doesn't treat it, can't tell if he is limping or favoring a shoulder.

Explosion:
- Concussion from mortar burst [Next In Command]
- Concussion from German .88 barrage [Hill 256]
- Shrapnel from grenade burst, flesh wound, upper right arm [Masquerade]
- Nicked by a rock on his right temple [Decision]

Miscellaneous:
- Bandaged trigger finger, unknown cause [Next In Command]
- Twisted left ankle [Bridge at Chalons]
- Twisted left ankle [Command]
- Concussion, 2 sprained fingers, 36 stitches in head, black eye [Off Limits]
- Dislocated left leg falling down mountain [Mountain Man]
- Injured right hand at top of episode, needs rebandaging [The First Day]
- Left arm in sling at top, possibly a wound to upper arm, though no bandage seen there later in episode [Silver Service]
- Bloodied temple [The Masquers]
- Slugged at base of neck [Nothing to Lose]
- Bandage above right eye for entire episode, unknown cause [Dateline]

Passes out:
- From punch [Nothing to Lose]
- From mortar burst [Next In Command]
- From street fight [Off Limits]
- From exposure and exhaustion [Silver Service]

---

with Hogan's talent. Altman was not alone in this opinion, and Hogan was hired for several more episodes. At the end of the first thirteen weeks, Hogan had made such an impression that he was signed to a five-year contract, replacing Shecky Greene as a permanent cast member.

Tough, quick-tempered, argumentative, and a skirt-chaser, Kirby is the show's "bad boy." He's been AWOL more than any other man in the outfit and once broke up a French cafe in a brawl over a woman. Consequently, he gets most of the good

Jack Hogan played Pvt. William G. Kirby, the tough, quick-tempered, troublesome, mademoiselle-chaser.

lines. Though a wise-cracker and complainer, Kirby is a good man in a fight. Kirby is the squad's B.A.R. man (Browning Automatic Rifle).

According to his ABC bio for *Combat!*: "It's a tribute to Jack Hogan's acting ability that he is the unlikeliest of men to be cast as Kirby, the tough, quick-tempered, troublesome, mademoiselle-chaser of Sergeant Chip Saunders' squad in *Combat!* Off camera, Jack is the kind of guy Kirby just couldn't 'dig.' He's soft-spoken and serious."

After *Combat!* left the air in 1967, Jack continued to serve in uniform on several television series. His TV career included ongoing appearances as Sergeant Jerry Miller on "Adam 12" and as Chief Ranger Jack Moore in his own series "Sierra," filmed in Yosemite. In the seventies, Jack Hogan appeared in several made-for-television movies, playing Kerwin in *Houston, We've Got a Problem,* Dr. Edward Grey in *The Specialists,* and Bill Hopkins in *Mobile Two.*

In the early eighties, Jack Hogan moved to Hawaii, where he supervised the operation of his construction business. During his ten-year stay in the islands, he garnered a recurring role as Judge Smithwood in "Jake and the Fatman" and served as casting director for "Magnum P.I." He also appeared twice as a guest on "Magnum," playing well-heeled villains.

Jack, twice divorced and the father of two, retired to his hometown of Chapel Hill. Jack's favorite pursuits include painting, fishing, reading, "arguing God and politics with my friends" and taking short drives "to relieve the tension." His reading runs to Steinbeck, Hemingway, and Maugham, and he is fond of poetry, particularly the works of Carl Sandburg. His favorite painter is Gauguin, whose works he often copies.

Season One Episodes

Combat! aired Tuesday nights at 7:30 pm opposite NBC's "Laramie" and CBS's "Marshal Dillon" and "The Lloyd Bridges Show." The first season episodes show a progression of events that trace the history of the Normandy campaign. Events of season one cover D–Day, Falaise, the assassination attempt on Hitler, and the battle around Avranches. There was a time continuity to the first season as the squad drew closer to the liberation of Paris.

The show also showed a consistency of casting throughout most of the first season. The squad was not peopled with ever changing faces. Under Altman, the same actors reappeared as the same characters from week to week: Crown, Baker, Davis, and Brockmeyer became friendly faces. And others, such as Temple and Kelly, viewers came to know and then see fall to the war. It was a unique continuity for its time and helped create the feeling of a real squad.

The episodes in this compendium are listed in production order, the same order that the shows are broadcast in syndication — that is different from the order in which they were orginally aired. The three-digit number before each title is the episode number used by the syndicator. Ratings are from 0 to 4 bayonets: *Combat!* episodes are rated against each other, not against TV in general – so a 2 bayonet episode (fair) means it is an average *Combat!* episode, which some fans consider to be far above average in comparison to television today.

A Day in June (001)

Written by Robert Pirosh
Directed by Boris Sagal
First aired 12-18-62(Episode 11 of Season 1)

CAST:

Regulars: Jason, Morrow, Greene, Rogers, Jalbert (billed as "Caddy")
Pat Dahl as Hazel
Lisa Montell as Marcelle
Harry Dean Stanton as Beecham (billed as "Dean Stanton")
Henry Daniell as Minister
Brad Weston as Lt. Crowley
Max Dommar as Theo
Frankie Ray as Gardello
Jack Hogan (uncredited)
Tom Skerritt (uncredited)

Synopsis:

Rain stalls the American advance through Normandy, allowing Saunders time to reminisce with the squad about the events leading to D–Day. While waiting in England for the assault order, raw nerves among the untried troops leads to fights in the barracks. Braddock is jubilant when he learns he's won the platoon's $800 D–Day pool by drawing the June 6th date. But his happiness is brief, when he learns their platoon is in the first wave in the assault.

About Filming the Episode:

The pilot episode, with a new opener tacked on, was recycled as a flashback and originally aired as the eleventh episode. In syndication, it's always aired first. The new opening features new squad member Kirby and an uncredited appearance by Tom Skerritt. In the opening dialogue, they mention that this happened before Hanley got his battlefield commission, explaining why the Hanley is suddenly a Sergeant, but no attempt is made to explain why Caje has a different name.

Review — 4 bayonets:

Robert Blees derided the pilot as "The Rover Boys in Normandy," but I think "A Day in June" is a perfect pilot for *Combat!* Yes, the episode shows a side of both Saunders and Hanley little seen elsewhere in the series, but this was their pre-D–Day personality. As in real-life, the D–Day experience changed them all — Caje more than anyone else, since he had a total name change after that day, from "Caddy" Cadron to Paul "Caje" LeMay.

"A Day in June" offers an incredibly tight script by Academy Award–winning screenwriter Robert Pirosh, great interlacing of original footage with war newsreels, and a beautiful Omaha Beach recreation. The pilot captures the indomitable humor, spirit, and bravery of the American fighting man, along with his fears, failings, and frailty. The scenes in the barracks in England seem to ring particularly true, having been written by a man who also spent bone-chillingly boring and terrifying weeks waiting for orders that might get everyone killed. Pirosh drew on personal experience in creating the characters of Caddy and Theo, the Cajun soldiers. Pirosh's unit in France had two Cajun soldiers. Quiet men who spoke little and did their jobs well, according to Pierre Jalbert, who played Caddy in the pilot. "I played my character," says Jalbert, "as someone who did not like to kill, but who did his job the best way that he could."

Notes, Oddities, and Bloopers:

• Unlike other soldiers, Caje wears a turtleneck.
• This is the only instance where Saunders smokes a cigar (he has cigar in "The Squad," but never lights up).
• Saunders hits the beach with an M1 rifle, using it up to the end of show. In final sequence as he is marching off, he has appropriated an automatic weapon.
• The platoon wades ashore in chest deep water, but no one is wet when they hit the beach.
• Even though Hanley appears as a Sergeant, he is still billed as Lt. Hanley in the credit.

Any Second Now (002)

Written by Gene Levitt
Directed by Robert Altman
Produced by Robert Blees
First aired Oct-23-1962 (Episode 4 of Season 1)

CAST:

Regulars: Jason, Morrow, Greene, Jalbert, Rogers
Guest Stars Alex Davion as David Woodman
Ellen Willard as Anne Farell
And Special Guest Star: Donald May as Major Thompson
Emile Genest as Emile
Jacques Roux as French Priest
Felix Reinsch as Briefing Officer
Dick Peabody as Littlejohn
James de Winter as Corporal
Ned Wynn as M.P.

Synopsis:

Hanley's life is in the hands of a bomb-disposal officer who has lost his nerve. The British officer is forced to confront his fears and his "fall from grace" in the guise of a German time-bomb ticking away in the rubble of a church. Also in the church, a wounded Hanley, trapped beneath a fallen beam staring into a time-bomb ready to explode at any second.

About Filming the Episode:

Filming on this first episode of the series began on June 2, 1962. It was Dick Peabody's first Hollywood acting role. Robert Altman couldn't give screen credit to Dick Peabody for this episode unless he had at least five lines. Originally, the part was just "soldier." To get billing for his friend from Kansas City, Altman re-wrote the scenes, stealing a few lines from elsewhere in the script and merging several characters. He created a character name for this episode: Littlejohn. With his merged part,

Pierre Jalbert, Vic Morrow and Rick Jason preparing for D–Day in the show's pilot.

Dick Peabody had more lines in this episode than cast regulars Shecky Greene, Pierre Jalbert, and Steven Rogers, who appear only briefly in the teaser.

Review — 3½ bayonets:

Robert Altman directed this strong script by Gene Levitt. In "Any Second Now" Altman deals with a subject and setting he explores often in his film career: church and Catholicism. Altman revels in the stark, moody visuals of a Gothic church in ruins. By flickering candlelight, he explores the themes of a fall from grace and eventual redemption. Though his direction is firm and stirring, his symbolism gets heavy handed. This is especially evident in his choice to end the show not with a reconciliation between Hanley and his rescuer, or with a reunion between Saunders and Hanley, but with the final image of the priest returning the host to the altar.

Though fascinating in its style, its clever interplay of characters, and its brooding look into the soul of a broken man, "Any Second Now" reveals the same failings that run through Altman's other *Combat!* outings — uneven technical work. The continuity is faulty and the lighting inconsistent. I tire of seeing flashlights used in well-lit scenes and wonder at the mysterious flashlight on Hanley's chest that appears and disappears at random.

Rick Jason is in top form under Altman's direction. Though he spends the bulk of the episode flat on his back, he commands the respect of the bomb-disposal officer, commands his scenes, and commands the attention of the camera in a remarkable performance. His reactions and banter-under-stress as he

fights against the pain and fear are a pleasure to watch. I particularly like the cocky smirk as he smashes the morphine ampule and the impatient look when he's told that he's trapped underneath a time bomb.

At the top of "Any Second Now," Jason reprises that charming lady-killer of "A Day in June," an aspect of the Hanley character so rarely seen later in *Combat!* Jason puts his 200-watt smile, innocent green eyes, and a bagful of practiced pick-up lines to good use in charming a British nurse (Ellen Willard). But she's in the story only to salve the wounds and the heart of David, the bomb-disposal officer (Alex Davion). Donald May, who soap fans may remember from the "Edge of Night," appears as a Major.

Peabody was not yet being considered as a regular cast member, so his character is not shown as part of the squad. Neither Sgt. Saunders nor Hanley acknowledges him as someone they know. That will change in the very next episode.

Notes, Oddities, and Bloopers:

• I smile when the American soldier in the bar complains to the tart about the record. He whines, "You gonna play the same thing over and over again?" Get used to it, soldier, Combat! viewers will hear that same song for five seasons. It's the same record played by the women in both "Battle of the Roses" and "Weep No More."

• Morrow has a short, military haircut, the shortest he wears it in the series.

• Odd how in the bombed church everything is blown over, but many of the candles stay lit.

Just for the Record (003)

Written by William Bast
Directed by Laslo Benedek
Produced by Robert Blees
First aired 15-Jan-1963 (Episode 15 of Season 1)

CAST:

Regulars: Morrow, , Rogers, Jalbert, Peabody
Guest Star Micheline Presle as Annette
Alf Kjellin as Kurt
Edward Colmans as Andre Mallott
James Forest as Foreman

Synopsis:

While searching an abandoned French farm house, Saunders discovers a phonograph and takes a moment to play a record from home. Germans burst in and take him prisoner. The resistance rescues him and hides him in enemy-occupied Paris, where he is the unwilling guest of a French woman in love with a German officer. Her devotion to her German lover comes at odds with her sense of what is right when the fate of an American soldier is placed in her unwilling hands.

Review — 4 bayonets:

Sgt. Saunders in "Just for the Record" is not depicted as the valiant fighting soldier, but as a homesick young man lost in a foreign land. In the opening scene, Saunders searches a house for Germans. Everything is quiet. "That's where the danger is, in the quiet," says Saunders in an atypical voice-over. Alone, thinking of home, Saunders does something he rarely does in the series: he lets his guard down and makes a stupid mistake. When he finds a record player, he forgets the danger and plays a record from home. The mistake of the homesick boy gets the soldier captured. As often happens on television, Saunders escapes and finds himself in the hands (and the spare bedroom) of a beautiful French collaborator.

I adore this episode. It's on my top ten list. The strong script by William Bast provides ample moments for actors to shine. Vic Morrow as "Chip" Saunders, Micheline Presle as Annette, and Alf Kjellin as Kurt are three capable actors who find all the nuances in these complex, richly-drawn characters. Annette's tragedy is that she is not what she appears to be. She is not the collaborator motivated by greed or desires for creature comforts. She is a woman in love. Their affection is genuine. For the moments they have together, there is no war, there is no enemy.

Morrow, still new to the Saunders character when this was filmed, convincingly established the fragile side of this fearsome soldier. The scene where he listens to the message from his mother and sister is particularly well-performed. It is both subtle and moving. Alf Kjellin, as Kurt, makes it apparent why Annette fell in love with this German invader. As portrayed by Kjellin, Kurt is a man of gentle strength and quiet resolve — a good soldier and good German, afraid of what lies ahead for his country and family.

This episode was directed by Golden Globe–winner Laslo Benedek. He was an established movie director before coming to *Combat!* He directed *Death of a Salesman* with Frederick March and *The Wild One* with Marlon Brando. He later directed for "Twelve O'Clock High."

Notes, Oddities, and Bloopers:

• Opening narration by Saunders. The only other episode with a narrator is "The Celebrity." Morrow doesn't have a flair for the Sam Spade-style voiceover.

• Everyone speaks English, even the Frenchmen when speaking among themselves. This seems more natural than the extremes found later in the series, as the script is twisted trying to explain that English is the only language shared by these characters, that's why they're speaking it among themselves.

• This is one of only two times that Saunders' nickname "Chip" is used in the series. Both times it is used by family members. Despite fan-fiction to the contrary, no one in the squad ever calls him "Chip." Vic Morrow didn't like the nickname.

• This is the first appearance of the trademark Saunders' camouflage helmet, but it is used only in the teaser. The teaser was filmed several weeks after the main episode, after the camouflage helmet had been adopted.

• How did Saunders get the record back? Surely the Germans would have confiscated it.

Jonathan Bolt stars as a green recruit from Dixie in "The Squad." He says that boots "ain't made for wearin'."

The Squad (004)

Written by Harry Brown
Directed by Herman Hoffman
Produced by Robert Blees
First aired 29-Jan-1963 (Episode 17 of Season 1)

CAST:

Regulars: Morrow, Jason, Greene, Roger, Jalbert
Featuring Jonathan Bolt as Moseby
James Callahan as Reischer
Alexander Denazody as German Corporal
Harold Dyrenforth as First German Engineer
John Mayo as Lt. Peterson
Mathias Uitz as Second German Engineer

Synopsis:

In "The Squad," a Georgia boy named Moseby Lovelace becomes the first in a long line of replacements that come marching through Saunders' squad in the course of five seasons. Moseby doesn't immediately fit in. He's sorry to be part of this Yankee army and disappointed that no fellow southerners are in his platoon. He doesn't like the way Yankees fight, always hiding their heads. Saunders and Braddock try to clue him in to the rules of this war, but Moseby is determined to engage the enemy on his own charming terms. Unlike the subsequent parade of green recruits who don't want to follow Saunders' sage advice, Moseby not only lives through to the closing credits, he saves the lives of the patrol, captures several Germans, and finds some Biloxi boys to pal around with.

Notes, Oddities, and Bloopers:

• This is the only *Combat!* episode directed by Herman

Hoffman. Hoffman also directed the film *It's a Dog's Life*, which featured Vic Morrow as the voice of Wildfire the Dog.

Review — 3 bayonets:

"The Squad" is a delight. John Bolt plays Lovelace with an irrepressible charm and permanent twinkle. Like Saunders, I couldn't help smiling at him, even though I was certain that he was going to get his head blown off. Fortunately, Bolt is so charming, he rises above the failings of the script, which paints a negative stereotype of southerners. In less charming, less capable hands, Moseby would have been a slow-witted, ignorant redneck.

And why aren't there any southerners in the entire platoon? Seems an odd omission (which was corrected in later seasons).

My favorite moment in this episode is after Moseby saves the patrol by cleaning out the German machine gun nest. With his irrepressible smile fixed firmly in place, Moseby reports to Hanley. He's just pleased as punch that he's killed him a mess of Krauts. But while reporting in, his eyes wander back to the body of Private Wolensky. This subtle story-telling, through images and not words, is a gripping juxtaposition of Moseby living his fantasy of war while eyeing the reality of it. *Combat!* excelled at telling stories cinematically, rather than through dialogue. In this series, the message of the story is often found between the lines.

Lost Sheep, Lost Shepherd (005)

Written by Robert Hardy Andrews
Directed by Burt Kennedy • Produced by Robert Blees
First aired 16-Oct-1962 (Episode 3 of Season 1)

CAST:

Regulars: Jason, Morrow, Rogers, Peabody
Special Guest Star Jeffrey Hunter as Sergeant Dane
Martin Brandt as The Priest
Joby Baker as Kelly
Tony Mordente as Morello
Rex Holman as Christy
Hans Difflip as German Officer

Synopsis:

Jeffrey Hunter stars in "Lost Sheep, Lost Shepherd" as tanker Sgt. Dane, a man mad at the world, mad at the war, and mad at God. He's not too thrilled with Hanley and Saunders, either. During the breakthrough, Hanley and a squad of men become cut off behind enemy lines. They are saved from a German ambush by the unexpected appearance of Dane and his tank. Their gratitude is short-lived as Dane's recklessness and anger takes on a savage edge and they discover the secret he can't live with: that he's a failed priest now turned killer.

Review — 1 bayonet:

Jeffrey Hunter and director Burt Kennedy together create a great triumph of style over substance in this tale of a man tormented by a lost dream. Hunter plays Dane with a startling intensity. Kennedy provides moody and ethereal cinematography, highlighting Dane's wraith-like isolation as a man experiencing his own private agony (whether it's his private hell or a

private purgatory, even he doesn't know).

I enjoy watching this episode and revel in the craft of Hunter and Kennedy. In the end, though, I always feel cheated by the tale. Ultimately, who cares? Considering his actions, Dane seems ill-suited emotionally for his original chosen career. I agree with Saunders, whose long speech to Dane could boil down to one simple admonition: "Get over it." Stripped of all the beautiful camera work and acting, "Lost Sheep, Lost Shepherd" is a one-hour story about a man artfully wallowing in self-pity.

A few moments stand out. The scene between Hanley and Saunders by the fountain in the courtyard captures a camaraderie between the two seen only in glimpses in later seasons. Here, the moment is captured well. Saunders' speech to Dane is superbly acted. It is one of the first and best occurrences of a Saunders PPT (Patented Pep Talk).

This is also the first occurrence of a cute dog as a plot device: a device that will be used overly much through the series. I'll go on record now: I hate cute dogs used as plot devices. *Combat!* extras should always be leery of them. Any member of the squad who adopts a cute little puppy beware, he's just made himself a character too adorable to last to the final credits — he has become an expendable!

The final scene in the church always disturbs me. A dead body lies in the middle of the church and all the women, children, and town folk step blithely over it without a second glance. I would think that in a story dealing with the broad issues of life, death, damnation, salvation, somebody might take note of the corpses beneath their feet.

About Filming the Episode:

Rick Jason always enjoyed working with director Burt Kennedy. "He was a wonderful director. Very easy to work with."

Notes, Oddities, and Bloopers:

• The opening sequence includes fantastic footage of real tank engagements along with an overly dramatic narration.
• Trek fans will remember Jeffrey Hunter as Capt. Chris Pike in the first Trek pilot.
• Caje is conveniently absent from this episode. With him present, the squad could immediately have found out about the Germans from the priest. Where was Caje? Were he and Braddock out chasing babes together?
• Speaking of Braddock, this is the first appearance of Kelly, in a very smart-aleck, comic role that in other episodes would have gone to Braddock.
• Where did Dane get the cassock he's wearing in the final scene?
• In the final scene where Jeff Hunter, dressed as a priest, shoots it out with the Germans, one of the Germans comes through the door carrying a American Thompson.
• Doc, while holding the puppy, helps search the town for Germans. Why is the medic being used for search duty? What is Doc going to do if he finds any Germans? Throw a puppy at them?

•My favorite moment in the show: Hanley and Saunders burst into the church, teeth gritted and lead flying, spraying the building with bullets . . . . until you look closely and notice Hanley's gun isn't firing. He's just swinging that carbine back and forth, all the shots are coming from Saunders' Thompson.

"Forgotten Front." Vic with Albert Paulsen.

Forgotten Front (006)

Teleplay by Logan Swanson
From the Story by Jerome Coopersmith
Directed by Robert Altman
Produced by Robert Blees
First aired 02-Oct-1962 (Episode 1 of Season 1)

CAST:

Regulars: Morrow, Hanley, Greene, Hogan, Rogers, Jalbert
And Introducing Albert Paulsen as Carl Dorffman
Tom Skerritt (uncredited)

Synopsis:

A squad of American soldiers comes face-to-face with the enemy, only to discover that this enemy is merely a frightened little man. Worse, a nice man. Ultimately, events force Saunders to make the terrible decision that their prisoner must be killed. And a single soldier must choose between following his orders and following his conscience.

About Filming the Episode:

Robert Blees remembers the episode: "Vic was good, and the story was very, very strong. In fact, it was so strong, that before we got on the air with it, I had a Major General in my office. Since the highest rank I ever achieved in the war was 1st Lieutenant, that was very impressive. The Major General in Washington ran the so-called public relations of the armed forces through film and television. Of course, he had seen the script. It had been bucked up to him. He thought it was a little too 'honest' and he made us change the ending to a certain degree."

REVIEW :

The episode "Forgotten Front" provided America its first glimpse of the new action show *Combat!* This superb story

tells of soldiers struggling with morality in the midst of war. Those tuning in expecting sweeping action scenes and lots of bang-bang-shoot-'em ups, may have been disappointed by this intimate look at a small corner of the war and the men who fought there. Instead of blindly firing rifles, these soldier must look their enemy in the eye and knowingly make the larger choices of life and death, right and wrong.

This type of moral dilemma was at the heart of this exceptional television series. At its best, *Combat!* examined how soldiers struggle to keep (and sometimes find) their moral center.

Directed by Robert Altman, "Forgotten Front" deftly underplays the emotions and drama of this complex morality play. When death comes at the beginning of the episode, as McGraw's advance patrol is killed by a booby-trap, the emotions are fully felt, but not wallowed in. Saunders has lost a friend in McGraw. But his loss remains private and personal.

This story has no villain, except for war itself. The closest thing to a "bad guy" in this episode is Kirby acting as a surly American jerk.

In his television debut, Albert Paulsen plays a German prisoner with an endearing charm and vulnerability. Jack Hogan, as the Kirby-you-love-to-hate, lifts obnoxious to an artform.

This early episode is among Morrow's finest outings as Sgt. Saunders. Besides playing the many levels of a harried and exhausted soldier leading men who don't wish to be led, he portrays a man at odds with his own actions and with what he must ask of his command. He also shows a "dangerous" side of Saunders that's more than a little frightening, as he confronts a prisoner whose life is in his hands and, later, a G.I. who disobeyed an order.

Altman was told to add the scene that now ends the episode, where it's revealed the old man's life was spared — an ending I far prefer. I feel the producers made a good call with the alternate ending. I don't think viewers would have taken to heart a show that premiered with the willful murder of a kindly old man. And I doubt they would have accepted a character with innocent blood on his hands as one of the "good guys" among the regular cast.

Though the episode is rife with technical flaws, the acting and script are so strong these defects barely detract from the raw power of the story. The well-crafted script looks at war from the viewpoint of a medic (Steven Rogers), the only non-combatant in the story. He is a young man new to this game of war. He feels that his sympathetic reactions to the German prisoner are due to his inexperience. But, through Saunders, the audience sees that even a war-weary veteran still struggles with the larger questions of morality and duty.

Notes, Oddities, and Bloopers:

•No prologue, the show starts with theme music and credits. These credits were unique to this show: no narrator and no moving bayonet background.
•Continuity problem: in the scene with Saunders cooling him-

self under the waterpipe, Saunders goes from damp to soaking wet in one edit. Within 30 seconds he's bone-dry again.

• Lighting problems: In the night scene in the engine room, what's the source of light? It's bright as day inside. Throughout the episode, the lighting is dreadful. The squad uses flashlights in the well-lit engine room. One nice bit is, unfortunately, not possible. As Saunders is outside waiting for Caje to shoot the German, the muzzle flash brightens the side of Saunders' face. Unfortunately, Saunders wasn't in a direct line-of-sight with Caje and light doesn't travel well around corners.

• Shall we discuss how medics shouldn't be handling weapons, let alone holding prisoners at gunpoint?

• Logan Swanson, credited for the teleplay of this episode, is a pseudonym for Richard Matheson, a long-time Hollywood screenwriter and novelist. His first major film screenplay was The Incredible Shrinking Man in 1957 and he continues writing today. He was also screenwriter for all the segments of Twilight Zone: The Movie, except for segment one, that took Vic Morrow's life.

• At night, when the tank rolls up to the dyeworks, they use a stock piece of footage of a tank approaching. Unfortunately, it's a daytime shot.

• Both Kirby and Caje call Saunders "sir," a title reserved for officers.

• Why didn't the tank just move forward, block the squad's escape, and blow them to smithereens?

• This is one of the few episodes where the Germans end up ahead. Americans dead, four; Germans dead, none.

Missing in Action (007)

Teleplay by James S. Henerson and Sidney Marshall
Story by Birne Lay, Jr.
Directed by Byron Paul
Produced by Robert Blees
First aired 13-Nov-1962 (Episode 6 of Season 1)

CAST:

Regulars: Jason, Morrow, Greene, Jalbert
Howard Duff as Colonel Hobey Jabko
Maria Machado as Denise
Louis Mercier as Gallard
Glen Cannon as Tate
Michael Petit as Roger
Barton Heyman as Fergus
George Dee as Olivier (uncredited)

Synopsis:

Hanley and a small patrol must rescue Colonel Hobey Jabko, a famous aviator shot down over occupied France two months ago. While in hiding, Jabko was nursed back to health by a French couple and their beautiful niece Denise. Neither he nor she are anxious for rescue. To complicate Hanley's mission, one of his men accidentally killed Jabko's crewman, whom he had sent to them for help. This does not endear Hanley or his men to the Colonel. Denise attempts, unsuccessfully, to seduce

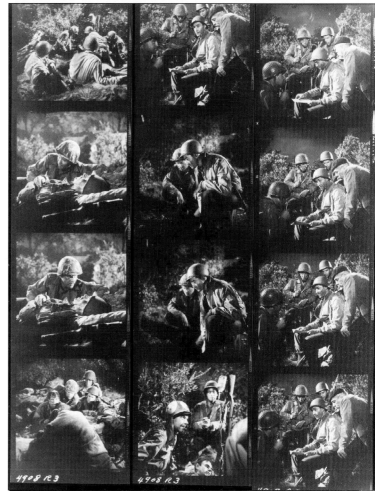

Contact sheet of photos taken for "Missing in Action."

Hanley to get him to leave Jabko behind. Denise, desperate to keep her love at her side, becomes a Nazi informer.

Review — 2 bayonets:

A story of love and betrayal, "Missing in Action" is a bit confused and cluttered. Byron Paul, in his only outing as a *Combat!* director, doesn't provide any clarity or focus to the story. Perhaps the writer is trying to tell too much. Wrenching scenes of Private Fergus agonizing over accidentally killing the American officer are mixed with comic scenes involving Braddock's personal hygiene and with an alluring scene between Jabko and the deep-voiced Denise. The script asks too much from everyone, especially Caje, who can't decide from scene to scene what his emotional state is. He runs into the barn, announces that Fergus is dead and that he's really nervous hanging around here, then runs out in an agitated state. Next scene cuts immediately to the interior of the French farmhouse where Caje is laughing and telling jokes with the farmer's wife.

Strong performances are provided by guest stars Howard Duff as Colonel Jabko and Maria Machado as Denise. The show provides interesting visual images: a weeping collaborator tripping over the corpse of a German and being left behind in the dirt; a helpless Hanley and Caje watching in silent horror as a soldier is shot before their eyes, but the episode never brings the story together to a satisfying whole.

This isn't a bad episode to watch, but it's not among the best, and lacks the flavor of a *Combat!* episode. The story centers around the guests rather than our favorite squad. This episode could have easily been shot for "Twelve O'Clock High" with no changes to the script except a character name or two.

Notes, Oddities, and Bloopers:

• Can't you shoot women on 1962 television? Denise should have gotten it between the eyes. The resistance didn't tolerate traitors.

• In 1962 couldn't you make it clear that a woman was offering her body? I wish they had clarified it a bit more. It established early in the story that Denise was willing to trade "in flesh" to keep her flyer at her side.

• Braddock shines as a soldier. In this episode the funny man does some real fighting.

• If Gallard (the resistance fighter) comes and goes easily between the farm and Allied lines, why didn't he deliver the message about Jabko to the Allies, instead of letting the poor airman struggle through the frontlines? Did the episode really need to open with a senseless death?

Rear Echelon Commandos (008)

Teleplay by Gene Levitt • Story by Richard Tregaskis
Directed by Robert Altman
First aired 09-Oct-1962 (Episode 2 of Season 1)

CAST:

Regulars: Morrow, Jason, Jalbert, Hogan, Peabody
John Considine as Temple
Arnold Merritt as Crown
Stephen Coit as Gainsborough

Synopsis:

On the frontline, the squad receives three new replacements straight from rear echelon duty in England. They are Gainsborough (a scared, overweight cook), Temple (an equally scared ex-ballet dancer), and Crown (a radio announcer whose cocky attitude masks his fear). Saunders reluctantly takes these newcomers on a dangerous recon mission and discovers that his survival depends on the ingenuity of these misfits.

REVIEW - 3 bayonets:

"Rear Echelon Commandos" is a story about the lessons a soldier must learn to survive on the front. In the episode, it is the teacher, Sgt. Saunders, who learns the greatest lesson.

Richard Tregaskis, author of the 1943 book *Guadalcanal Diary,* developed this story of Saunders at the end of his patience with war and with the stupidity of rear echelon orders. In the sixties, Tregaskis also wrote two historical war books for adolescents: *From Pearl Harbor to Okinawa* and *From Casablanca to Berlin.*

In "Rear Echlon Commandos," at first Saunders and squad are amused by the inadequacies of the replacements. But the laughter turns to anger when Hanley orders Saunders to lead these men into danger. When Saunders complains that those men don't know the difference between a patrol and a picnic, Hanley tells him what he should have already known. "Then teach them the difference, Sergeant." The lessons go badly, and

Saunders' anger subsides into apprehension as he realises his life depends on these unprepared recruits.

Vic Morrow plays the many layers of Saunders and gives a simple believability to the revelations that come to him in dealing with three people he probably never would have known in civilian life. Here is an aspect of Saunders rarely seen in the series: the defeated Saunders, the soldier who has completely given up.

When Saunders is wounded and his only experienced soldier, Kirby, is also wounded and unable to help him, he surrenders to the idea that their situation is hopeless. But his students teach Saunders that nothing is ever lost while there's still breath, and that to survive, you must use the resources you have at hand, even the unlikely abilities of a ballet-dancer. John Considine is superb in this episode as the delicate soldier who becomes a hero because of his past, not in spite of it.

Notes, Oddities, and Bloopers:

• Continuity problems: 1)After being shot, Kirby rolls over and in the next shot, the same roll-over is shown. 2) Saunders' pant leg has blood on it before he is shot.

• Jack Hogan's second appearance as Kirby, but he is not yet signed as a regular. He receives guest star billing.

• Littlejohn appears in the beginning of this episode, milking a cow. Saunders calls him Littlejohn, but Dick Peabody isn't listed in the closing credits.

• Crown appears in a later episode, "Off Limits." He also appears with Temple in "I Swear by Apollo." Arnold, the actor who plays Crown, also appears in "The Long Way Home" as Cole, a character similar to Crown.

• Helmet switch — Saunders wears his camo helmet, but loses it when rescuing Kirby. He grabs Kirby's helmet and wears that for the rest of the episode.

The Chateau (009)

Teleplay by Judith & George W. George with Jonathan Hughes
Story by Judith & George W. George
Directed by Laslo Benedek
Produced by Robert Blees
First aired 12-Feb-1963 (Episode 19 of Season 1)

CAST:

Regulars: Greene, Rogers
Co-starring Joan Hackett as Gabrielle
Frank Sutton as Corporal Cording
John Milford as Lt. Masters
Ben Wright as Count de Contran
Don Edmonds as Jackson
Ed Tierney as Friedrich
Guest Star Dan O'Herlihy as Major Richter

Synopsis:

Unable to locate the evacuation hospital, Doc takes his three wounded charges into a French chateau just behind the battle lines. The owner of the chateau, Count de Contran, wants no part of the wounded soldiers and orders them to leave. But they are captured by the Germans, who take over the chateau as a command post. While making himself at home, the

Friend or foe? Joan Hackett must decide on which side to declare an alliance when a group of wounded American G.I.s seek her aid while the Germans occupy her chateau.

German major helps himself to all the treasures of the chateau, including the Count's beautiful daughter.

Review — 1 bayonet:

In "The Chateau," the co-stars of the series are given center stage while the two stars are nowhere to be seen. This story features Steven Rogers (Doc) struggling to save the lives of three wounded men in his charge: Braddock (Shecky Greene), who has been sidelined with an injury to his shooting arm, a never-before-seen Lt. Masters (John Milford), and Corporal Cording, played by Frank Sutton.

"The Chateau" is the only episode that allowed Steven Rogers to flex his acting muscles in a leading role. His performance of Doc, though soulful and caring, lacks emotional depth. This is tolerable in a supporting role, but when his acting skills are required to carry the episode, it becomes an insurmountable problem. His challenge of conscience about stealing the German Luger is flat and his sensitivity comes across as weakness in a role that demands strength of character and will.

Guest star Joan Hackett fares better in this episode as the unwilling object of Major Richter's (Dan O'Herlihy's) lust. When placed in her moral quandry, she easily conveys to the audience the choices she faces and the difficulty of the decisions she makes. In short time, she is transformed from a mousey, scared child dependent on her father, to the strong-willed mistress of the Chateau who sacrifices her life and her heritage for the lives of the Americans and to keep her honor intact.

Frank Sutton puts in a competent, but brief, performance as Cpl. Cording. Sutton is perhaps best remembered from another military series: he played Sgt. Vince Carter for six seasons on "Gomer Pyle, U.S.M.C."

Notes, Oddities, and Bloopers:

• This is the first *Combat!* episode where neither of the two stars appear.

• Why isn't Hanley the officer in this episode?

The Prisoner (010)

Teleplay by Robert Kaufman and James S. Henerson
Story by Robert Kaufman
Directed by Robert Altman • Produced by Robert Blees
First aired 25-Dec-1962 (Episode 12 of Season 1)

CAST:

Regulars: Jason, Morrow, Green, Jalbert, Peabody
Sasha Hardin as Capt. Gemmerman
Adam Williams as Lt. Col. Nash
Richard Bakalynn as Sgt. Wolfson
John Alonzo as Bialos
Special Guest Star Keenan Wynn as Colonel Clyde
Tom Skerritt (uncredited)
Walter Koenig (uncredited)

Synopsis:

Braddock, the squad goldbrick, finagles a soft job as driver for a Colonel. But Braddock gets more than he bargained for when during their tour of the frontline positions, the jeep is overturned and Braddock is captured by the Germans. Finding Braddock in the Colonel's coat and with a Colonel's helmet, they disregard his claim that he's a mere private. And when Braddock starts enjoying the luxuries of a captured Colonel, he throws his weight around.

Review — 3 bayonets:

"The Prisoner" highlights the talents of Shecky Greene. Here, director Robert Altman succeeds in letting Greene shine. He's delightful throughout, especially in his moments with Keenan Wynn, starring as the blustery Colonel Froggy Clyde.

As to be expected from an experienced standup comedian, Greene's timing is flawless. But to anyone who would question if this king of the Vegas strip could act, this episode proved that not only could the comic act, he could act very well. He is so easy and natural in this episode that he makes it look effortless. The simplicity hides a complex craft. He carries the show easily on his shoulders, moving from light humor, warmth, slapstick, and to blustering audacity with remarkable skill.

I enjoy the episode as a departure from *Combat!* This episode originally aired on Christmas night. The censors, always leery of the violence on *Combat!,* were especially hesitant to allow any gore to be broadcast on a religious holiday.

Notes, Oddities, and Bloopers:

• Why does Braddock shower without dog tags? No one else does.

• Captain Harper is in charge of K Company.

• Altman enjoyed working on this episode with friend Shecky Greene. Shecky kept both him and crew laughing. Several of

Shecky's ad libs wound up in the final cut, including his line about capturing the German cook.

Escape to Nowhere (011)

Written by Malvin Wald • Directed by Robert Altman
Produced by Robert Blees
First aired 20-Dec-1962 (Episode 7 of Season 1)

CAST:
Regulars: Jason
Albert Paulsen as General von Strelitz
Joyce Vanderveen as Maria
Sasha Hardin as Colonel Kleist
Roger Til as French Priest
Lester Fletcher as German Interrogator
William Speckman as Bower
Lou Robb as Mueller
Hans Difflip as German Major

Synopsis:

A bewildered Hanley finds himself both the ally and the prisoner of Baron Friedrich von Strelitz, a Wehrmacht general fleeing Nazi Germany. With Hanley in German uniform, the General hopes to reach the Allied lines before the Gestapo catch up with him and arrest him for his participation in the failed plot to assassinate Hitler.

Review — 1 bayonet:

The concept of "Escape to Nowhere" offers great possibilities: a moral dilemma of a General who must choose between his oath of allegiance and the good of his country, and a daughter who chooses patriotism over familial duty. Near the battlelines, a remorseful and wounded General fears he is truly a traitor and is overcome by his shame at killing fellow Germans. At gunpoint, he tries to force Hanley to return him to Germany. But Hanley refuses, trying to convince the General that what he now views as treason is really patriotism. The General dies before reaching the Allied lines, in limbo between two great armies and still unresolved in his own mind as to whether he is hero or coward. This is the stuff of great tragedy, but "Escape to Nowhere" fails to deliver any emotional impact.

This seems Robert Altman's weakest *Combat!* episode. The direction is ordinary, matching the performances. Albert Paulsen as the General (also in "Forgotten Front" and "Retribution") looks ridiculous under a garish blonde hairpiece with matching eyebrows and moustache.

Rick Jason is very watchable in this silly story. His apprehension at passing himself off as a German at the club provide the best moments of the episode. Sasha Hardin, whose first *Combat!* appearance was in the episode "The Prisoner," is wonderfully menacing as the Gestapo agent bent on bringing the General to justice. He and Jason play off each other well in the scene in the club where they both work to not communicate the truth about themselves to the other. The scene is a beautiful study in playing around an emotion.

About Filming the Episode:

This episode is among the favorites of producer Robert Blees. "They had this wonderful train station and when I toured the lot with our art director, it was ramshackle and torn and ruined and all of the tarps had holes in them. He said we're gonna have to spend forty, fifty thousand bucks to fix this. But I said, 'Come on, this is war time. This is a bombed out station. We'll write a story around the set.'"

Notes, Oddities, and Bloopers:

• In the graveyard scene, the rain falls in front of Hanley and the General, not on them.
• In the opening scene, Hanley's pinky ring is stolen from him. He has it later.
• Among the French children is Michel Petit, who plays Bijou in "The Little Jewel" and was in "Missing in Action." And why do gun-toting tots suddenly appear, kill a priest, and depart from the storyline?

The Celebrity (012)

Story by Tom Sellers and Art Wallace • Teleplay by Art Wallace
Directed by Burt Kennedy
Produced by Robert Blees
First aired 27-Nov-1962 (Episode 8 of Season 1)

CAST:
Regulars: Morrow, Jason, Jalbert, Rogers, Peabody, Lowell
Guest Star Tab Hunter as Del Packer
Joby Baker as Kelly
Virginia Stefan as Nurse
Dennis Robertson Baker
Tony Mordente as Sgt. Kurawicz

Strange Alliance — Rick Jason and his captor, a Nazi General, portrayed by Albert Paulsen, enter into a strange pact to gain their freedom in "Escape to Nowhere."

Synopsis:

The squad is pulled back from the front for a well-deserved rest in the destroyed town of Avranches. The squad conman, Kelly, discovers that King Company's new replacement is famous baseball pitcher Del Packer. His squad members are awe struck at having the baseball star among them, unaware of his crippling fear that he might get a million-dollar-wound that sends him home and destroys his million-dollar-arm. That fear causes him to freeze when Saunders orders him to protect a buddy's flank, and Billy pays the price for Del's fears.

Review — 3.5 bayonets:

In "The Celebrity," Burt Kennedy redefined the characters and the series. Mental battles feature prominently in the story; the action and real struggle is within the soul of a man, not on the battlefield. Del Packer comes to realize that the enemy is himself and his own fear. He's got a private war to fight and it's not with the Germans. The strong script, aided by Kennedy's deft direction, reveals the dark terror of a new recruit, provides human details that round out the regular characters, and introduces Billy Nelson into the squad.

This episode provides solid entertainment, acting, and direction throughout and new insights into the characters. Defining moments include: Saunders reacting to his own self-doubt and recriminations; Hanley's great PPT (recycling Saunders' own PPT back to him); and the first showing of the relationship between Littlejohn and Billy. The show lets the audience learn quite a bit about Billy Nelson: that he has a kid brother and mother waiting for him at home, that his father died recently (rather odd, since his father writes to him the following season in "Bridgehead"), and that Billy apparently has nine lives. Though his character seems to die in the episode, the actor had filmed several more episodes as Billy by the time "The Celebrity" aired.

The scene where Saunders confesses his misjudgment about Packer captures the essence of the series. In simple, unvarnished words and in words not said, the fear of the soldier is revealed, fears that a man's decisions under fire could cost both his own life and the lives of the men he leads. The response of Lt. Hanley, though cold comfort, is the only comfort that war offers.

About Filming the Episode:

Tom Lowell auditioned for *Combat!* during his lunch break from filming an episode of "The Twilight Zone." He said, "There's nothing better for an actor than to be in makeup and costume. It makes them feel that this guy's a working actor, we don't have to teach him anything. I went over and met with Bob Blees and Burt Kennedy. I felt this automatic rapport when I walked in, especially with Burt Kennedy. Burt was a delight to work with, charming man. I just knew that I had the part the minute I walked out the door. . . . I was Billy Nelson. I was nineteen years old when I got the part. I was terribly naive, not only about show business but about life in general.

Dick loved to tease me. But he also respected my intellect and the discipline I had as an actor. We got along famously from day one."

Notes, Oddities, and Bloopers:

• The opening montage includes footage from "Lost Sheep, Lost Shepherd," "Far from the Brave," "Battle of the Roses," and "Survival."

• The winery the squad takes at the end of the episode is the same hilltop wreckage where Grady Long was killed in "Far from the Brave" and used for the destroyed convent in "One More for the Road."

• It is night when they leave for the winery and broad daylight when they arrive.

• Caje has improper grip on baseball bat in some shots. Canadian-born Pierre Jalbert had never learned to play the American game of baseball and needed to be taught the basics.

• Bernard Fox, who played Dr. Bombay on "Bewitched," is Billy's doctor. Hans Gudegast (aka Eric Braeden) plays the German leading the attack.

• Odd that Littlejohn shows no concern for Billy after his wounding and is stoic after Billy's "death."

• Nobody checks the winery to make sure all the Germans are dead.

Far from the Brave (013)

Written and Directed by Burt Kennedy
Produced by Robert Blees
First aired 30-Oct-1962 (Episode 5 of Season 1)

CAST:

Regulars: Morrow, Jason, Hogan, Greene, Jalbert, Lowell, Peabody
Joe Mantell as Delaney
Fletcher Fist as Radio Operator

Synopsis:

Private Delaney, fresh from his assignment as Army cook, is the latest green replacement for the squad. Saunders assigns him to take the Browning Automatic Rifle (B.A.R.), replacing Saunders' recently slain friend, Grady Long. As Saunders' squad is left behind to cover the main force's retreat, the soldiers look over the elderly replacement with uncertainty and hostility. Alone in a personal grief that he will not let anyone breach, Saunders faces the meaning of loss and how to measure the value of life and friendship.

Review — 4 bayonets:

In his second *Combat!* script, Burt Kennedy again nails the show's characters and the emotions of fighting men, all in a tightly crafted script. Unfortunately, this is the episode that sent Shecky Greene off the show. A shame, because he only got better and better with each episode. His scene with Delaney over the chicken is tender, realistic, and rises above the obvious humor of a soldier and a chicken.

Vic Morrow and Rick Jason both excel at acting "between the lines." Their scene after the funeral is an excellent example. More is said in the silences about what they are thinking and what they are feeling than is said in the dialogue. *Combat!* always told stories cinematically. So much of the story is in the visuals. *Combat!* dared to go long stretches without a single line of English dialogue, and often without any dialogue at all.

Burt Kennedy scripts always provide both great dialogue and great silences. The actors took advantage of both in this four-bayonet episode. Whether it is a quiet scene between Billy and Littlejohn or a brazen outburst by Kirby, this episode hits all the right marks.

As in so many of his stories, this Burt Kennedy episode celebrates the glory within the most humble person, and shows the wisdom and strength that comes from adversity. Saunders, the soldier who sets himself up as the pillar of strength to all those around him, discovers his own feet of clay and in the end, girds them in steel armor and in the fragile memories of two B.A.R. men who passed briefly through his command.

About Filming the Episode:

Tom Lowell remembers filming the escape sequence: "We were running down this street with pots blowing off, it was my first experience with that stuff. Those things were really scary, because you were right next to them when they went off. I was in fear of stepping in the wrong place and stepping on one of those things. But we had one of the best special effects crews in the business. [...] So we were running from that French town clock, down the street toward that bridge that is in just about every episode. And, just to the right, was this giant bay where they had the *Bounty*, because they were shooting *Mutiny on the Bounty* at the same time. So they had to position the cameras so they didn't hit the *Bounty*. We always tried to sneak down and watch Marlon Brando work. But he was always having a temper tantrum that day, so we never saw him."

Notes, Oddities, and Bloopers:

• Cpt. Powers is in charge of King Company, not Jampel.
• When Dick Peabody puts the pin back in the grenade, it doesn't quite fit back in the hole. Viewers who look closely, can see that he's mumbling "Son of a bitch."

The Quiet Warrior (014)

Teleplay by Gene Levitt
Story by Luther Davis and Gene Levitt
Directed by Justus Addiss
Produced by Gene Levitt
First aired 26-Mar-1963 (Episode 25 of Season 1)

CAST:

Regulars: Jason
Co-starring J.D. Cannon as Ted Slocum
Michele Montau as Lily
Brendan Dillon as Williams
Lomax Study as Andre
Charles Giorgi as Georges
Leno Francen as Marie Barole
Rolfe Sedan as Dr. Barole
Walter Janowitz as Cafe owner
Albert Szabo as Soldier
Uncredited appearances:
Hans Gudegast (aka Eric Braeden), uncredited
Barbara Babcock, uncredited, woman at Savoy Bar

Rick Jason, posing as a French civilian, and Leno Francen in the episode "The Quiet Warrior."

Synopsis:

A mud-soaked Hanley receives special orders to proceed at once to the cocktail lounge at the Hotel Savoy in London. Puzzled at his good fortune, Hanley soon finds that he has crossed over into the arena of espionage. He is tapped for an assignment parachuting into German-occupied France to rescue an important French scientist and his family. Teamed with Slocum, an experienced espionage officer (and former language teacher at a girl's finishing school), Hanley becomes entangled with the Maquis who have a traitor in their midst.

Review — 1 bayonet:

Shifting from the show's usual focus on a frontline infantry platoon, this episode instead offers a look at the workings of an espionage operation. This could have been an interesting departure if done well. But this pedantic script drags Hanley and the audience through a predictable and thoroughly dull spy story.

J.D. Cannon, as intelligence officer Ted Slocum, is charming and believable. He does a yeoman job with the heavy-handed dialog, adding a wry smirk and cocky attitude to the verbal tonnage. But even his light touch cannot save the interminable exposition scenes foisted on his character.

Rick Jason flounders in the excruciating exposition in his

interrogation by the shadowy Mr. Williams. Jason gamely tries to add a spark to this litany of background information, but he gets little assistance. The absence of movement, the static camera, unenlightening lighting, and lack of background music leave him out there to his own devices. Even his co-actor is hidden in shadows, giving no aid to poor Jason. Perhaps to his own relief, he is uninvolved in much of the rest of the story.

"The Quiet Warrior" revolves around the Slocum character. This story could easily be re-edited to fit in "12 O'Clock High" or any other WWII television series. It has nothing to do with *Combat!* The Hanley character is merely a device to link this story into the series. Once Hanley has introduced the Slocum character and met with the Baroles, he could just drop out of the episode. This was a failed attempt to launch another series from within *Combat!*

The episode works only when it lets its two capable leading actors just act. Hanley is delightful enjoying the pleasures of the Savoy — bliss at the scent of alcohol in a clean glass; confused amazement, then joy, at the sound of a woman's laughter; carefully suppressed panic at the thought of a parachute jump. The editing is unusual for the series, with some interesting effects in the scene changes. But the rest of the camera work is adequate at best and the direction uninspired. The episode is more enigma than entertainment.

Notes, Oddities, and Bloopers:
• Internal inconsistency in dates. Hanley is traveling under orders dated October 28. But Slocum says he was in occupied Paris last week; strange since Paris was liberated August 25. From evidence of other episodes, the bulk of *Combat's* first season took place prior to the liberation of Paris.
• Accessory alert: Hanley wears his ever-present ring in the beginning of the episode. He doesn't wear it once he assumes Frenchman's disguise — nice touch.
• Luther Davis, who contributed to this story, wrote the script for the Tony award-winning musical, "Grand Hotel," set in pre-WWII Germany.
• Medals: Hanley now wears four decorations: he only had a good conduct medal in "A Day in June." I cannot tell from my copy of the episode, but I guess the decorations include a campaign ribbon and purple heart.
• From telephone call Hanley receives at the Savoy: "You are traveling under special orders 107, Headquarters, 21st infantry division, date 28 October."
• Trivia: The bet that Hanley settles for Slocum: How many companies are in a German infantry regiment. Answer: 15.
• More trivia: Hanley meets Slocum at #45 Garden Court, Flat #5 in London.
• Trek connection: the woman at the bar is Barbara Babcock, who played Philana in the classic Trek episode "Plato's Stepchildren."
• For those who wonder why you hear "Forward march" clearly in the middle of orders shouted in German ... the order is the same in English as in German.
• The C–47 that delivers Slocum and Hanley to France is not painted olive drab, but a lovely AA-attracting silvery aluminum.

Cat and Mouse (015)
Written, Directed, and Produced by Robert Altman
First aired 04-Dec-1962 (Episode 9 of Season 1)

CAST:
Regulars: Morrows, Jason, Rogers, Jalbert, Peabody
Guest Star Albert Salmi as Jenkins
William Bryant as Major O'Connors
Hans Difflip as Colonel Burgen
Ted Knight as German Captain
Robert Winston German Lieutenant
Werner Becker as first German Soldier
Frank Behrens as Captain Reed
John Alonza as Bialos

Synopsis:
Saunders is one of two survivors of an ill-fated patrol into enemy territory. He must return to the blood-filled field, but now under the command of Sgt. Jenkins, an unyielding leader with little use for Saunders or Saunders' views on how to run the mission. When the rest of their patrol is slaughtered, the two sergeants become trapped inside a millhouse used by the Germans as a command center. Saunders and Jenkins find no compromise, taking opposite paths to achieve their mission. The mission is accomplished, thanks to Jenkins' sacrifice of his life. But the victory is hollow, the information bought by Jenkins' blood was no longer important to the brass behind the lines. The Allied advance rolls on, crushing all in its path.

Review — 3.5 bayonets:
Altman is quoted in articles about *Combat!* saying he is proud for creating the only anti-war *Combat!* episode, and for showing the futility of war. I am guessing that the comment refers to "Cat and Mouse," because this is the only episode that he wrote, produced, and directed. It is hard to tell for certain though, since so many *Combat!* episodes were anti-war.

I question whether a story such as "Cat and Mouse," though, truly is an example of the futility of war. It certainly shows the often futile efforts of individual soldiers and individual actions within the broad mosaic of a world conflagration. But I doubt many holocaust survivors would argue about the futility of America fighting that particular war. The effort and lives lost were not wasted. The culmination of tens of thousands of actions like those portrayed in "Cat and Mouse" and countless individual sacrifices were to a purpose, a great purpose.

That said, this is an excellent episode. Albert Salmi, as Jenkins, is a perfect foil for Morrow's Saunders. It is a pleasure to watch two pros working together under the solid direction of a gifted artist such as Altman. No false notes in this episode; no gaffs of any kind. When the two sergeants clash, Saunders is up against another Sergeant as equally stubborn, battle-hardened, and as certain that "right" is on his side as Saunders' is. Watching this episode, I cannot decide which is the immovable object and which the irresistible force.

COMBAT!

Morrow is remarkably moving in the final scene, as he reports the unneeded information Jenkins died for. I remember this scene vividly from viewing it as a child. Thirty years later, when I saw the episode again, it had lost none of its power. The story, the acting, and the message are still relevant today.

Notes, Oddities, and Bloopers:
•Saunders escapes from the mill without boots or jacket, yet has both when he reports in.
•First *Combat!* appearance of actor William Bryant. Bryant will become a semi-regular cast member by fifth season, playing Pvt. McCall.
•First *Combat!* appearance of actor Ted Knight, who played Germans in many episodes.

Reunion (016)
Written by Art Wallace • Directed by Paul Stanley
Produced by Robert Blees
First aired 01-Jan-1963 (Episode 13, Season 1)

CAST:
Regulars: Morrow, Jason, Rogers, Jalbert, Peabody
Will Kuluva as Emile Villers
Chris Robinson as Paul Villers
Angela Clarke as Claire Bouchard
Fifi D'Orsay as Mme. Fouquet
Emile Genest as Henri Fouquet
Henry Rowland as Colonel Hoffman

Synopsis:
An American soldier is reunited with his estranged French father after a seventeen-year separation. The meeting is happy for both, with the bonds of love easily re-established despite the passage of time. But the war intervenes to separate them once again. The French resistance arrests his father as a suspected collaborator just as Paul must return to his unit to face a German advance. Later, when Paul is trapped in the German-occupied town with a wounded Saunders, he turns to his father for help. At first his father refuses, but ultimately accepts the soldiers and treats Saunders' wounds. As Paul waits in hiding, he begins to question whether his father really is a collaborator and if he has risked both his and Saunders' life in trusting to this father he barely knows.

Review — 3 bayonets:
"Reunion," by Art Wallace, is the type of plot rare in *Combat!* — a love story. "Reunion" tells a story of love, trust, suspicion, betrayal, and forgiveness.

Guest stars Will Kuluva, as Dr. Emile Villette, and Chris Robinson, as Paul Villette, both give excellent performances. Their scenes together are touching and poignant, especially their first meeting. Actors could easily overplay such juicy, emotionally charged scenes and make them maudlin, but these two portray the levels of emotion with dignity and strength. Morrow is also superb as Saunders in this episode. Wounded for much of the story, he still offers support to this soldier under his charge. No PPTs here, just quiet strength from Saunders, even when he's about to pass out on his feet.

How interesting that one of the few times the word "love" is used in this strongly male-oriented show, the love expressed is a son's love for his father.

Notes, Oddities, and Bloopers:
•The character names in the closing credits do not match the names spoken in the episode. This problem occurs several times in the first season. Here, the character names are "Villette" in the show, but are listed as "Villers" in the closing credits. The credits also list a Colonel Hoffman. But no Colonel appears in the episode, though a lieutenant and a Captain have featured speaking roles. Which of these is the actor credited as Colonel Hoffman is anyone's guess.
•Why does Paul leave his M1 behind to pick up the wounded Saunders? He should have been carrying both Saunders' Thompson and his own rifle.
•Nice fog all around the squad that's dug in . . . but the fog doesn't get to the squad, it's just all around them wherever they look, but not in the low ground of their foxholes.

I Swear by Apollo (017)
Written by Gene Levitt
Directed and Produced by Robert Altman
First aired 11-Dec-1962 (Episode 10 of Season 1)

CAST:
Regulars: Jason, Morrow, Jalbert, Rogers, Hogan, Peabody
Gunnar Hellstrom as Dr. Belzer
John Considine as Wayne Temple
Arnold Merritt as Jerome Crown
Eugene Borden as Bresson
Maya Van Dorn as Mother Superior
Betty Tessman as Nun
John Neris as Frenchman
Philip Abbott as Capt. Correm

Synopsis:
The squad infiltrates German lines to locate Bresson, a Frenchman with vital information on German troop movements. But Bresson is critically wounded by a mine while still in German territory and cannot be moved. They take refuge in a convent. Saunders and Caje abduct a German doctor to treat Bresson, but they fear the doctor will let their patient die under his knife to keep his deadly information out of Allied hands.

Review — 3.5 bayonets:
Screenwriter Gene Levitt brings *Combat!* into an alien world far stranger than most visited by your standard science-fiction series. In "I Swear by Apollo," the squad takes refuge in a cloistered convent inhabited by specter-like nuns who take little notice of the mortals passing among them. As directed by Robert Altman, these silent figures are unworldly creatures. They are beyond the understanding of these fighting men who temporarily share their space. The war moves around these sisters, but never touches them.

Whether these men stay or go is of little concern to the nuns, just so long as they keep their war outside. Robert Altman's direction emphasizes the alien quality of the sisters.

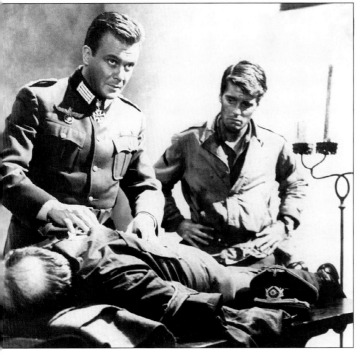

Steven Rogers and Gunnar Hellstrom in "I Swear by Apollo."

He hides the nun's faces in shadow. They come and go silently, with barely a whisper of feet on stone. The near absence of *Combat's* usual background music in the convent scenes helps set this world apart from the usual war-time settings our squad encounters.

The story by Gene Levitt has mythic qualities. A mighty wind snatches papers from a Frenchman's grasp, bringing him into harm's way. A man is struck down by an unseen force en route to the convent. The squad, not knowing where to turn for help, follows the paths of the holy women to a place of safety. Within the convent walls, beneath the overbearing presence of the crucifix, Altman reveals death threats, lies, and even the theft of light from the altar. The sisters continue their duties, oblivious to the drama of men-at-arms and to the mortal struggle of two wounded men. In the end, one life is saved, another is lost, and the sisters' existence continues unchanged, except for a fresh grave in their cemetery.

Altman is inventive throughout with his direction, but the surgery scene goes on overly long and is terribly "showy," with an excess of nicely framed shots of determined men spying through dripping candles, interspersed among closeups of crucifixes. Though the use of soft breathing under the scene until the drop in blood pressure is quite effective. The long, Boticeli-like shots around the surgical "altar" were quite pretty — but enough already! Too much style.

The acting in this episode is consistently strong. Morrow has a particularly gripping scene as he explains to the doctor the price of a less-than-successful operation. Gunnar Helstrom portrays Dr. Belzer as a creature almost as alien as the sisters. His German doctor is devoid of emotion, even as he finds himself in the hands of the enemy. Helstrom appears later in the first season in "No Time for Pity." John Considine, in his

second and final outing as Private Temple, plays the dying soldier with a bittersweet calm. Simple moments and single lines have surprising power. Hanley's simply stated "I'd almost forgotten there were natural ways to die," makes the heart attack sound as alien as the sisters who move among them between life and death.

Notes, Oddities, and Bloopers:
• If the Frenchman had had a decent briefcase, this episode never would have taken place.
• These credits list Crown and Temple's first names, though they are never used in the episode.
• How does Caje have such detailed knowledge of the inner workings of a convent?
• If I were a captain, I definitely wouldn't want to go out in the field with Hanley or Saunders. Captains never come back alive once they leave with one of these two. A heart attack this time? Sure! I'm beginning to suspect coverup.
• Neither Temple nor the Frenchman are anywhere near the mine to trip it when it explodes.
• This is Altman's first *Combat!* screen credit as producer.
• Not a single firearm is discharged in this episode. The only wounds are inflicted by an inanimate object (a mine) and by nature (a heart attack). There are no person-on-person injuries in this episode—though threats galore from Saunders as he bullies the doctor, the Frenchman on the bicycle, and even Kirby.
• Hanley uses his name over an open radio. Definitely against standard operating procedure, King Two!
• The medal worn at throat of German doctor (Knight's Cross) has the oak leaves and swords upside down.

The Walking Wounded (018)

Written, Directed, and Produced by Burt Kennedy
First aired 30-Apr-1963 (Episode 30 of Season 1)

CAST:
Regulars: Jason, Morrow, Rogers, Jalbert, Peabody
Special Guest Star Gary Merrill as Capt. August
Co-starring Geraldine Brooks as Lt. Ann Hunter
Steven Joyce as Jones
George Davis as Old Frenchman
David Manley as Tanker
Berkeley Harris as Pvt. John Lee

Synopsis:
Saunders becomes one of "The Walking Wounded" and falls under the mercies of three broken souls more deeply wounded than he. Captain August is a doctor no longer dedicated to the living; Lt. Ann Hunter is the nurse whose love for Hunter isn't enough to save him; and Steven Joyce is Jones, an ambulance driver who is hiding his cowardice behind a red cross. They are caring for a critically wounded soldier, but when the ambulance is caught in an air raid, they abandon the patient to his own fate. Saunders recovers the ambulance and the patient, and refuses to allow any of them to give up on their patient or on themselves.

Review — 3 bayonets:

"The Walking Wounded" shows Saunders' almost messianic drive to get others to not just live up to their potential, but to exceed their own expectations. Here Saunders is at his most evangelical, forcing a trio of broken souls to meet his exacting moral standards. In the process, they heal their own wounds.

"The Walking Wounded" is a simple and moving morality play. The bulk of the credit for its success goes to Burt Kennedy, who wrote, directed, and produced the episode. The three *Combat!* scripts by Kennedy ("Far from the Brave," "The Walking Wounded," and "Next in Command") deal with the theme of coming to grips with living and dying. The episodes show soldiers walking the edge, determining for themselves whether they will be destroyed or strengthened by war.

When in command, Saunders is always certain of his own moral rectitude — he's right, you're usually wrong, and there's no middle ground. His is a world of moral absolutes, and woe to the soldier not living the gospel according to Saunders. He will insist a soldier do what is right, even if it means risking his life on a hopeless quest. Saunders is an impossible creature! And just the type of man I would want leading me if I was ordered to take a hill. Certainly the man I would want driving my ambulance when a know-it-all doctor has written me off.

The lighting throughout is rich and sumptuous, especially the scene in the hayloft and any closeup of Geraldine Brooks. Kennedy films her beautifully, always with a halo effect about her face, to the point of being distracting. About as annoying is the little dog. Saunders is noble enough for four sergeant in this episode, did he have to prove he's nice to dogs, too?

But those are minor distractions from a thought-provoking story. Morrow portrays Saunders (who possesses a moral code more unwavering than any old testament prophet) with an all-consuming and terrifying tenderness. No velvet glove softens his steel fist, yet he conveys compassion behind each brutal act of kindness.

About Filming the Episode:

Dick Peabody says of director Burt Kennedy, "He was probably the best writer the show ever had. And Burt was a very good director in getting very warm performances out of the actors. I think he brought out the goodness in the character. There's something he did with never raising his voice, kind of whispering."

Notes, Oddities, and Bloopers:

• Saunders rolls downhill into barbed-wire and doesn't get scratched.
• Why does the burning truck carrying the fuel barrels not explode?
• Continuity problem: after the driver changes the tire, he gets in the front of the truck with Saunders; next scene Saunders is driving alone.
• Saunders is wet before he steps out of the ambulance into the rain.

• Saunders removes his jacket to cover the dog at bedtime. When he wakes in the morning, Saunders is wearing the jacket.
• Toward the end of the episode, when Saunders is filling the radiator with water, he complains that "The radiator's all shot up." Yes, and Saunders is the one who shot it.

The Medal (019)

Written by Richard Maibaum • Directed by Paul Stanley
Produced by Richard Maibaum
First aired 08-Jan-1963 (Episode 14 of Season 1)

CAST:

Regulars: Morrow, Jason, Rogers, Jalbert, Peabody, Lowell
Guest Star Frank Gorshin as Wharton
Co-starring Joseph Campanella as Vincent D'Amato
Edward Knight as Lt. Kohrs
Dennis Robertson as Baker
Fletcher Fist as Brockmeyer
Tom Troup as Medic
Clegg Hoyt as Cook
Gordon Bruce as German

Synopsis:

The squad is pinned down by a tank and it is up to two close friends, Wharton (Frank Gorshin) and D'Amato (Joseph Campanella), to free them. In a selfless act of bravery, D'Amato takes out the tank and guns down a platoon of German infantrymen at the cost of his own life. Hanley and Saunders mistakenly credit Wharton with the heroic action. When Hanley recommends Wharton for a Silver Star, Wharton keeps silent, knowing the medal will impress his girlfriend, who has just sent him a Dear John letter. He becomes torn over his need to be a hero and his guilt at robbing a dead comrade of his deserved glory.

Review — 2.5 bayonets:

Writer Richard Maibaum provides fans a true squad story in "The Medal." In its first season, *Combat!* showed whole-squad interaction at its best, and "The Medal" is the best example of that first season dynamic. The concepts of friendship, loyalty, and heroism are tested to their limits and redefined within the heart of a man torn by loyalty to a woman who abandoned him and to the comrade-in-arms who never did.

The relationships are key to this story. "The Medal" explores the special kinship that develops between soldiers who face death together, with no one to depend on but each other. The banter between D'Amato and Wharton hides the strong bond that sustains them through their ordeals and terrors. It is the same teasing banter shown between Littlejohn and Nelson, and, as it developed later in the series, between Caje and Kirby, and even between Saunders and Hanley, shown briefly as they discuss how the army and Saunders have disagreed in the past.

"No one's in this for the glory, unless he's a psycho," says Saunders. "They're just doing their job." In the end, Wharton's real act of bravery is done for all the squad to see — he confesses to them how he had cheated his buddy. This act finally restores to his fallen friend the honor that was his due.

Notes, Oddities, and Bloopers:
- In battle with German 58th Grenadiers regiment (same as they fought against at St. Lo).
- D'Amato's tank charge is reminiscent of real-life Audie Murphy's medal-winning act of heroism.
- Incorrect POV shots whenever anyone surveys the carnage around the tank and very erratic lighting in the night scenes.
- So nice to know there are other platoons around who occasionally help 2nd platoon win the war.
- Baker's back awfully soon after getting hospitalized in "Reunion."
- Caje does a lousy job of keeping guard. He is busy butting into Wharton's private life when he should be watching for Germans.
- Saunders is "barbed-wired" on the same street where he was shot in "Reunion." He should avoid that corner in the future.
- All the letters that the squad receives are addressed in the same handwriting.
- Saunders' hands are covered with blood while on the barbed wire, but are clean a minutes later when he brings in Wharton.
- All that screaming on the barbed wire and Saunders only winds up with one band-aid on the face?
- It's somewhat poetic that it's a "boutique" sign that proves to be Saunders' downfall.

The Volunteer (020)

Written by Gene Levitt
Directed and produced by Robert Altman
First aired 22-Jan-1963 (Episode 16 of Season 1)

CAST:
Regulars: Jason, Morrow, Jalbert, Rogers, Hogan, Peabody
Introducing Serge Prieur
Ted Knight as Kurt
Kurt Levin as Karl
Ed Gilbert as Herman
Veronique as Hilda
Nadine Arlyn as Ilsa

Synopsis:

In "The Volunteer," written by Gene Levitt, a young French orphan tries to join the squad as a soldier, but ultimately finds the game of war not to his liking. Unbeknownst to the squad, the kid follows them into action. When Hanley is wounded, Saunders orders the kid to help the lieutenant to the rear. But Hanley collapses en route. A German patrol on the move puts the young volunteer's ingenuity to the test.

Review — 2 bayonets:

Serge Prieur plays the orphaned, thirteen-year-old Gilbert Barole with angelic earnestness. A strikingly beautiful boy with soulful eyes, Prieur conveys the hopes, fears, and desires of a boy alone in the world — all without speaking a word of English.

Robert Altman directed and produced this engaging story. The episode has all the visual hallmarks of the Altman *Combat!* style: cluttered foregrounds, hand-held cameras, a lot of play with sunlight and shadow, excruciating close-ups, scenes obscured by dust and smoke.

It's interesting watching "The Volunteer" back-to-back with "Survival," also directed by Altman. Directorially, "The Volunteer" is a dry run for "Survival." The sharp-eyed viewer will note many filming locations repeated from one episode to the next. Prieur in "The Volunteer" and Morrow in "Survival" travel the same roads, climb the same hills. Prieur wanders through charred woods that are still smoking after a barrage. A week later Saunders finds his "brother" in the same charred forest (freshly smoking). But more than just locations, Altman repeats camera shots between the two episodes: closeups of shadows of running feet, dappled sunlight streaming through overhanging trees, the same spinning point-of-view as both Morrow and Prieur run through the woods.

Portions of the drunken liberation scene at the opening are re-used in "The Sniper" and "Ambush," though the racier moments do not repeat. These later episodes don't repeat views of Lt. Hanley, surrounded by his carousing men, carrying a babe in his arms through the village streets; or of Saunders also carrying off a young woman and later familiarly slapping her on the rear as he leaves town.

Rick Jason has some wonderful moments as Lt. Hanley in this episode. His relationship with his "volunteer" is delightful, as Jason alternately treats this boy with sympathy, frustration, anger, and finally desperation as he must entrust the lives of the advance force of the American army into the hands of a child. Most *Combat!* scripts rarely give Hanley a chance to behave as an officer. Usually, that side is shown only in brief flashes, and less of that as the series progressed. But in this episode (when Hanley's not copping a feel on the streets of the village), he's definitely the officer struggling to keep his men alive and to accomplish his mission, even after being seriously wounded.

Notes, Oddities, and Bloopers:
- This episode features a slightly different version of the opening theme music.
- Uncharacteristically, Saunders takes up the rear in all the marches in this episode.
- Ten Germans encounter Gilbert in the woods, but this patrol has twelve men when they take the village.
- Walt Davis performed the downhill fall as the double for Rick Jason. But, there is a continuity error in the stunt. Hanley is lying in the opposite direction than the stuntman landed in.
- When Gilbert is running from the German patrol, he alternately is without a rifle, then has it, then doesn't. His lunch pouch also is mysteriously present, then not.
- Continuity: Saunders' cigarette in the final scene changes length between cuts.
- Two women are in the credits, though no women have any dialog or featured roles. So, if Dick Peabody needed five lines of dialogue for screen credit, what did Veronique and Nadine Arlyn do to earn their listing?

Survival (021)

Written by John D.F. Black
Directed and Produced by Robert Altman
First aired 12-Mar-1963 (Episode 23, Season 1)

CAST:

Regulars: Morrow, Jason, Jalbert, Peabody, Lowell
John Seigfried as Kurt
Donald Ein as Sergeant
Mike Murphy as 1st tanker
Matty Jordan as 2nd tanker
Joby Baker as Kelly

Synopsis:

Outnumbered and out of ammunition, Hanley, Saunders, and the squad must surrender to the Germans. In the confusion of an artillery barrage, Hanley and the men escape, not noticing that Saunders is trapped behind in a burning barn. Alone and in agonizing pain, Saunders wanders helplessly through German-held territory.

Review — 4 bayonets:

When Vic Morrow received his Emmy nomination for Outstanding Continued Performance by an Actor in a Series (Lead), he credited his performance in "Survival" for earning him that honor. Morrow delivers an outstanding performance, as mesmerizing and terrible as a roadside wreck that drivers can barely stand to view, yet cannot turn from. To enhance the realism, Vic Morrow did extensive medical research on burns.

"Survival" is the zenith of Altman's vision of Saunders as a living martyr to war. Altman heaped harrowing images on an already brutal script by John D.F. Black. The episode is uncompromising in its look at agony and despair, and flaunts a shocking grimness, rare even by today's TV standards.

Altman offers up some powerful images in this episode, shots that linger in the mind long after viewing:

•helpless mortals pulled through dust and dirt, harnessed to an all-powerful symbol of war and destruction
•a man writhing impotently in pain, bound and abandoned to flames
•a young man struggling to put on boots, looking up into certain death: a completely pointless death, that didn't progress the plot but merely added another layer of despair and hopelessness
•shot after shot of help and succor just out of reach, from the moonlit crossing of Saunders and the squad in the stream, to the agonizing nearness of a golden apple dancing beyond reach in the sunlight

About Filming the Episode:

"We didn't have a script for it," remembers Altman. "We had the situation and how he got burned and separated. But then it was just working with Vic and figuring out the things a man does when he's out of his mind in pain. The surrendering to a dead German just happened. It seemed right." This was Robert Altman's last work on Combat! "They didn't feel we should make this episode. I got fired over it."

Notes, Oddities, and Bloopers:

•This is the only episode to have music not by Leonard Rosenman. Music in this episode is composed and conducted by George Bassman.
•The last appearance of Joby Baker as Kelly.
•In the opening, Morrow's helmet appears on and off his head in no particular pattern, and is finally off when he surrenders.
•Tanks were too important to use for prisoner transport. But it makes a great visual!
•After the explosion involving a stunned Sgt. Saunders, the crew found an 18-inch long shard of real glass sticking out of the ground near Vic; it just missed him.
•For the river night-time shoot, all the actors wore wet suits under their uniforms. Tom Lowell says that "the water out on lot 3 was always ice cold, even in the middle of summer."
•For further information about this episode, read the Combat! chapter in the Altman biography, "Jumping off the Cliff."

No Time for Pity (022)

Written by Steven Rich • Directed by Bernard McEveety
Produced by Robert Blees
First aired 26-Feb-1963 (Episode 21 of Season 1)

CAST:

Regulars: Jason, Morrow, Hogan, Jalbert, Peabody, Lowell
Co-starring Denise Alexander (pre-show credit only)
Guest Star Gunnar Hellstrom (pre-show credit only)
Michael Davis as Jean
Robert Winston as Hoffman
William Phipps as Captain Witlow
Guy de Vestel as Marcel
Paul Busch as Mueller
Dennis Robertson as Baker
Andrea Darvi (uncredited)
Raymond Cavaleri (uncredited)

Synopsis:

Hanley and men discover German paratroopers in an observation post, where they're holding a young girl, old man, and five children as hostages. The town is about to be bombarded, giving Hanley only three hours to rescue the hostages. Hanley sneaks into town alone and finds the German soldiers in the town library. Their lieutenant spends time between spotting targets for his artillery by trying to seduce the beautiful town librarian, Annette.

Review — 3 bayonets:

This episode is my guilty pleasure for season one. It is phenomenal: it has phenomenally abysmal dialog and phenomenally unbelievable action — all presented in a fast-paced, strongly directed episode that overcomes all its defects with verve. I adore it. The episode is out-of-character with such flair and confidence that I enjoy watching it more each time. It is a triumph of strong directing and crisp acting over bad writing.

Steven Rich wrote this, his first and last, Combat! episode. It features Hanley in a characterization that makes this suave, educated gentleman sound like one of the Bowery Boys. This script gifts us with such delightful moments as Hanley talking about "the entire enchilada," "get a layout of the place and flash it back," and proclaiming that "this joint would be rubble if it wasn't for those children." Even in his angriest PPTs (patented pep talks), Hanley used the grammatically correct phrase "if it weren't." Perhaps Rich had a G.I. slang dictionary when he wrote this episode. Hanley refers to the field radios alternately as chatterbox, handy-talky, and squawk box.

Bernard McEveety made his *Combat!* directorial debut with "No Time for Pity." Saddled with a goofy script, a roomful of child actors, and an amazingly bad day-player portraying the Captain, McEveety zeroed in on his assets. A great action director, McEveety opens the show with an exciting battle sequence, focusing on hardware and men. Watch those shots, they'll become part of the package of standard action footage shown again and again in the next three seasons.

He doesn't linger long on the bad dialog, but moves quickly to Hanley infiltrating the German-held town. With excellent pace, McEveety covers the fact that nothing much happens for about a half hour in the middle of this episode. He creates tension focusing on Hanley scurrying about the dark corners of this town, narrowly avoiding detection. And he creates moments of sexual tension between Gunnar Hellstrom as the German officer and Denise Alexander as the repressed town librarian. Hellstrom does great seduction, with confidence and an unrepentant hedonism.

Time is used to good effect in the script and in the filming. Once Hanley is in the town, the episode proceeds in real time: the minutes left to the barrage are the minutes left to the end of the episode. With the recurring closeups on clocks and watches, and poignant dialogue about lost moments and wasted years, this episode moves despite its lack of action.

The plot is a rehash of "The Chateau," with a beautiful, innocent young woman held captive by an amorous German officer. The innocent uses her feminine wiles to bring about the German's destruction in a thunderous barrage (at the sacrifice of her own life).

Besides McEveety, the episode introduces some other *Combat!* firsts. This is the first featured appearance by Paul Busch, who spends five seasons of *Combat!* as the German most likely to be killed. He has all the good German dialogue in this episode and is amusing fumbling through a German/French dictionary. He lurks outside the wine shop, trying to get a glimpse of the German Lieutenant entertaining the librarian. Despite being a voyeur, he turns out to be a good guy who is unwilling to slaughter fleeing French children.

Portraying captured French children are: Andrea Darvi ("Gitty") in her first *Combat!* appearance, and Raymond Cavaleri (Michel from "The Casket").

Rick Jason, when he is not spouting inane drivel, is wonderful in this episode. Especially the scene with Annette in the basement as he tries to comfort, soothe, and coerce the frightened librarian into helping him. The scenes between him and Saunders are somewhat out of character — it is a throwback to

Gunnar Hellstrom as an amorous German officer who uses a young librarian and a group of French children as a shield in "No Time for Pity." Hellstrom appears twice as a German officer in the first season.

their characters from "A Day In June" though, so I don't mind.

Notes, Oddities, and Bloopers:
• Kirby's got that M1 again.
• Can't those Germans hear Hanley talking on his squawk box?
• In this episode, Hanley's call sign is "Badger." Saunders takes on the King Two call sign when the lieutenant goes off on his own to badger.
• Starting a fine tradition, Paul Busch dies in his first appearance. Though this time the kill goes to a German, Gunnar Hellstrom, not to an American.
• Cpt. Witlow in charge of K Company. Still no sign of Jampel.

Next in Command (023)
Written, Directed, and Produced by Burt Kennedy
First aired 05-Feb-1963 (Episode 18 of Season 1)

CAST:
Regulars: Morrow, Hanley, Hogan, Jalbert, Rogers, Peabody, Lowell
Guest Star Ben Cooper
Fletcher Fist as Brockmeyer
Bill Harlow as Davis
Dennis Robertson as Baker

Synopsis:
Ben Cooper plays Corporal Cross, the newest addition to the squad. For once, the new boy is a seasoned veteran. But he is tormented by a fatal mistake he'd made on another hill. That mistake has crippled him, stripping away not just his ability to fire a rifle, but his ability to be a soldier.

Review — 2.5 bayonets:
"Next in Command" is the last of the trio of *Combat!* scripts by Burt Kennedy. As in "Far from the Brave" and "The Walking Wounded," the show presents a morally unwavering Saunders faced with a soldier spiritually broken by the war. This time, Saunders' second-in-command battles his own inner war.

A hallmark of a Kennedy script is the relationship between Billy and Littlejohn. In "Next in Command," the comraderie between the two goes over the top and enters dangerously into the land of cute.

Jack Hogan's Kirby is deliciously obnoxious in this episode, retaining the edge he had in "Far from the Brave." Here, the Kirby-as-troublemaker character is firmly established, along with the introduction of his history of being demoted. Antagonism between Littlejohn and Kirby is strongly evident.

Character-wise, this is a strong episode, with inter-relationships between squad members a vital part of the story. But the plot is weak. Saunders messes up uncharacteristically while dealing with Cross. When the Germans arrive, why take Cross to dispatch those soldiers? Cross has already demonstrated his unreliability. Also, why would the first-in-command take only the next-in-command on a dangerous outing? And why did Saunders take Cross's word that he'd killed the German? I would want to see a body. Better yet, Saunders ought to want to BURY the body; they had already buried the bodies of the Germans killed earlier.

The ending of "Next in Command" comes out of nowhere. How were they tossed off the hill? In the previous scene, they had destroyed the mortar and the squad seemed victorious.

About Filming the Episode:

During the *Combat!* reunion, Tom Lowell said that "Burt Kennedy developed Billy's relationship with Littlejohn along the lines of my relationship with Dick Peabody ... Well, that was the relationship Peabody and I had. He has the most subtle humor of any person I have ever met. And he was constantly doing these things. Now, you have to realize I was 20 years old at the time and I was the kid of the outfit. Burt just used that, writing that into the characters. You can see that in the bicycle scene and the grenade scene."

Notes, Oddities, and Bloopers:
•Interesting that Hanley withheld information from Saunders. It seems that Hanley protects the privacy of all his non-coms, not just his favorite.
•Davis and Baker again part of the squad.
•Brockmeyer has been demoted in this episode. He's a private, though in his last episode, "The Medal," he was a corporal.
•Odd that Cross can disappear the whole night and nobody notices. Worse yet, when Cross runs out of the house during a firefight into certain death, Saunders follows after him, abandoning his squad while they fight the enemy.

Night Patrol (024)
Teleplay by Frank Jesse • Story by Quentin Sparr
Directed and Produced by Burt Kennedy
First aired 05-Mar-1963 (Episode 22 of Season 1)

CAST:
Regulars: Morrow, Hanley, Hogan, Jalbert, Peabody, Lowell
Co-starring Skip Homeier as Billy Joe
Bill Harlow as Davis
Hans Gudegast, aka Eric Braeden (uncredited)

Synopsis:

"Night Patrol" is a confused story about a mysterious lieutenant the squad encounters while out on night patrol. It's a tale of fear and suspicion, of dark secrets hidden and revealed in the confines of a cavern. This story is stylized, moody, and mysterious — none of which is handled particularly well in director Burt Kennedy's last *Combat!* episode.

Review — 1/2 bayonet:

The plot of "Night Patrol" suffers from multiple personality. It cannot quite decide what it wants to be from scene to scene. In the end, I am not sure of the point, or really who the character Billy Joe was or why anyone should care. Perhaps the poor plot had too many writers mangling it: the story is by Quentin Sparr, the teleplay by Frank Jesse, and with so many Kennedy story touches, I'm assuming Kennedy had the red pen out quite a bit on this script. Kennedy's strength is character development, but the character-oriented scenes seem out of place in this quasi-ghost story. The banter between Billy and Littlejohn is adorable (and unnecessary); as usual, I like the Kirby presented by Kennedy, but the goofy line about Kirby not knowing when 0700 hours was? Just a cheap shot at humor.

The story begins well, with cross-cut scenes of both a German platoon and Hanley's platoon preparing for night patrol. The usual Kennedy banter works well here. The final scene is also effective; it starts with Saunders giving his less-than-truthful report to Hanley and ends with a beautiful dolly shot of Hanley on the phone reading names off dog tags. But in the middle, once Skip Homeier appears as the mysterious lieutenant, the story is pretty hopeless.

The interior sets for the cave are magnificent. The scenes are beautifully lit. Light dances off the water, painting ghostly images on the damp walls. But where did the light come from in this underground cavern?

About Filming the Episode:

Tom Lowell gleefully recalls "the bats in the batcave scene. We had an absolute ball. Burt gave us those pages — it was like five pages of dialogue that morning — and said 'Here, I wrote this for you guys last night.' Like Jack said, it was so wonderful when these writer/director/producers could do their own shows, because they could change, or add, or whatever they wanted to, there on the spot. So we had a great time, especially in the batcave scene, I loved doing that scene."

Notes, Oddities, and Bloopers:
•Kirby with that M1 again. By episode #024, the B.A.R. is not yet his full-time weapon.
•Kudos for avoiding the standard Hollywood cliche . . . actors in distress actually enter a cave that DOESN'T cave in.
•As the actors rush into the cave, they bump against the stone wall and it moves.
•Recurring squad members: Baker and Brockmeyer are mentioned by name, but they do not appear in this episode, though Davis has a minor scene with Hanley. Davis appears often in season one and occasionally in season two.
•Skip Homeier (a Trek alum) appears later in "The Impostor" and "Entombed," where Homeier also plays a character trapped in a cave.

Off Limits (025)

Written by George F. Slavin
Directed and Produced by Robert Altman
First aired 19-Feb-1963 (Episode 20 of Season 1)

CAST:

Regulars: Morrow, Hanley, Hogan, Jalbert, Peabody, Lowell
Jeremy Slate as Cpl. Andy March
Peggy Ann Garner as Lt. Amelia March
Arnold Merritt as Crown
Mark Ryan as Hanson
Andre Phillippe as Andre
Marie Gomez as Claire
Maxine Arnold as 2nd Nurse
Betty Tesman as 1st Nurse
William Windom as Captain Lew Anders

Synopsis:

Jeremy Slate and Peggy Ann Garner guest star as Cpl. Andy March and his wife, Army nurse Lt. Amelia March. In "Off limits," March meets his wife while returning from a mission. Hanley promises to arrange a short leave for March to spend with his wife. But when Kirby's temper lands him in the stockade, March takes his place on a dangerous mission.

Review — 3 bayonets:

In his farewell directorial assignment for *Combat!*, Robert Altman assembled a fine cast of actors for a story of infidelity, betrayal, and loyalty. William Windom is properly attractive and fatherly as the doctor who tempts the married nurse. Though the character seems untroubled by his own relationship with a married woman, he finds *her* moral behavior inappropriate when he meets the husband. Oh, well, it's the sixties, after all, so it should be the woman's fault, and Windom pulls it off with such confidence that it barely detracts from the story. Peggy Ann Garner, who first came to prominence as a child actress playing the young Jane in the 1944 *Jane Eyre* and the leading role of Francie Nolan in *A Tree Grows in Brooklyn,* plays the very adult, adulteress wife.

The highlights of this episode are Saunders' two speeches: one to Kirby, who, though his own actions lead to March's wounding, still has the gall to look down on March's wife, and the second to the wife. Saunders' words are reminiscent of Bogart's classic *Casablanca* speech at the airway to Ingrid Bergman. Hanley also shines in all his officer glory as he dresses down Private Crown for being AWOL.

"Off Limits" is a fine episode, with strong acting, and an interesting look at people exploring the limits of loyalty in their relationships. Crown, Kirby, and Lt. March must all redefine for themselves what will be off limits for them in the future.

Notes, Oddities, and Bloopers:

•Kirby has a bandaid on his right hand, on the pinky, during scene where he's over the side of truck talking to March.
•March's wife is with the 325th evac hospital.
•This episode gives Jack Hogan a solo credit card.
•No closing credits for Jeremy Slate or Peggy Ann Garner.

*Kirby loses a bar fight in the episode "Off Limits."
Pictured here is Jack Hogan in makeup and his
stunt double Fred Dale.*

No Hallelujahs for Glory (026)

Teleplay by Luther Davis and Mort R. Lewis • Story by Luther Davis
Directed and Produced by Paul Stanley
First aired 19-March-1963 (Episode 24 of Season 1)

CAST:

Regulars: Jason, Morrow, Hogan, Peabody, Jalbert, Rogers, Lowell
Guest Star Elizabeth Allen as Eleanora Hunt
Angela Clarke as Mme. Michelin
George Petrie as Captain Smith
Charles McDaniel as Bearded Correspondent
Garry Walberg as Thin Correspondent
Maurice Marsac as Jacques
James Goodwin as Mike

Synopsis:

An arrogant female photojournalist visiting the front puts the squad and a group of French civilians in unnecessary danger. In her quest to garner the sensational type of images for which she is famous, Eleanora Hunt slips past the American lines to a German-held town. The squad is ordered to rescue her, but their intrusion ahead of the main line makes the French villagers believe that the liberation has arrived.

Review — 1.5 bayonets:

I grit my teeth through much of this episode. The portrayal of Eleanora Hunt, a professional female journalist, is so condescending and negative. She's grating, bitchy, ignorant about the military, and difficult to believe as a real character. Incompetent as a reporter and uncooperative with her sources, I don't understand how she achieved success in her chosen profession. She is looked down upon by all the men in the show, who do everything short of saying that what she needs is a good roll in the hay. The moral of the story seems to be that if women would just remember their place and stop trying to prove they are better than men, then innocent people won't get killed.

This story can be blamed on Luther Davis, who also devised the lackluster episode "The Quiet Warrior." Paul Stanley, as director and producer, salvages this episode with some stark visuals and memorable images. The opening sequence showing Eleanora's photos of men on the front is charming. The final sequence showing Saunders reading her photo-article is devastating. In between, Stanley lets viewers be more horrified by their own imaginations, rather than by anything graphic that he can show on screen. He does not show the audience the corpses in the room after the S.S. has finished their interrogation, only the reactions of Saunders and Hunt to seeing them. The shadow of the gallows, with its three victims and the anguished reactions of the crowd, speak volumes more than any explicit shot of corpses dangling by their necks.

Jason and Morrow interact nicely in this episode. Both have strong scenes with Elizabeth Allen (Eleanora): in the town Hanley is forceful with her, about to throw the uncooperative reporter over his shoulder and carry her off. Saunders is particularly abusive (verbally) with her. No PPT, just derision. The character, as written, deserves the abuse.

About Filming the Episode:
Dick Peabody recalls working with Elizabeth Allen: "She was a wonderful lady. And every night, after putting on our civvies, we'd go to The Retake Room and she and I would sit there for three or four hours. And this lady, this beautiful lady, could match drink for drink with me." That, according to Tom Lowell, is an incredible feat for anyone.

Notes, Oddities, and Bloopers:
•Saunders is introduced as Hanley's platoon sergeant. Must have been a temporary assignment.
•Often in two-shots with Saunders and taller guest stars, or even two-shots with Saunders and Littlejohn, Saunders is eye-level with the taller actor. You rarely catch him in the act. In the briefing scene, however, you see him walk to his mark and step UP on a rock (and later step down when scene is over).
•Another Canadian character spotted. That makes two. Not much to represent the efforts of Canadian forces in WWII.
•Some unusually graphic one-on-one killings as squad re-enters the town, except for Billy, who is not shown doing the act.
•Times change: Caje mentions that Eleanora would have gotten ten years back in the states for stealing the jeep.
•Caje appears wounded when the jeep is attacked. But he's perfectly fine in the next scene.
•Kirby with that darned M1 again.
•I like Hanley trying to hide his laughter at Saunders' crack to the Captain about "No submarines around here."
•An annoying flashback in the final scene. Were they afraid their audience was not paying attention and needed the message beaten into their heads?

Battle of the Roses (027)
Written by Rik Vollaerts • Directed by Sutton Roley
First aired 02-Apr-1963 (Episode 26 of Season 1)

CAST:
Regulars: Morrow, Jason, Hogan, Jalbert, Rogers, Peabody, Lowell
Guest star Antoinette Bower (front credit only)
Fletcher Fist as Brockmeyer
Bill Harlow as Dorsey
Penny Santon as Celeste Fourant

Synopsis:
Saunders finds a beautiful walled garden untouched by war, and in its center a childlike woman (Jeanine) lost in a private island of peace. Saunders fails to convince Jeanine that they must flee before the German bombardment. She won't leave the garden, thinking it has the power to protect her. Eventually, he and the girl's governess force her to leave, but she escapes back her garden walls, that continue to shield her.

Review — 2 bayonets:
Jack Hogan, Rick Jason, and Vic Morrow provide some nice moments in "Battle of the Roses," discovering an island of serenity in their violent defense of a French village. I enjoy the looks of complete incredulity and awe as Kirby and Saunders find the garden. Hanley finds his little corner of peace in a quiet discussion in the night with Saunders. Guests Antoinette Bower is a woman whose mind has been shattered by the war she refuses to acknowledge. The final images in "Battle of the Roses," where the camera shows us Saunders through the idylized vision of Jeanine, are quite lovely. In those shots, director Sutton Roley brings viewers briefly into Jeanine's world of beauty, closing off all the destruction, and focusing only on the man and the rose and the kiss. For that flash, all the ugliness of the world and the war are gone.

About Filming the Episode:
This is the first of fifteen episodes directed by Sutton Roley. The camera is very mobile when Roley is behind it. He eschews the hand-held camera in favor of the fluidity of movement offered by the dolly. He brings much motion to the visuals even within very cramped stories, such as "Glow Against the Sky" and "A Rare Vintage." Peabody recalls that "Sutton Roley was a good lens guy. He had very inventive ideas about where to put the camera and how to move it and how to block a scene. As good as anybody in the business."

Notes, Oddities, and Bloopers:
•Kirby with M1, Caje with turtleneck. Saunders has no need of his Thompson, he is just as lethal with garden implements.

Hill 256 (028)
Written by David Moessinger • Directed by James Komack
First aired 09-Apr-1963 (Season 1, Episode 2)

CAST:
Regulars: Morrow, Hogan, Jalbert
Guest Star Robert Culp as Sgt. John Metcalf
Curt Conway as Capt. Dugan
Liam Sullivan as Maj. Hendricks
William Zuckert as Col. Veach
Walter Friedel as German Prisoner
Clegg Hoyt as Technical Sergeant
Conlan Carter as M.P. Corporal
Alan Caillou as British Lieutenant
Richard Peel as British Sergeant
George Keymas as Maj. Daggett
Bill Gaskin as Sgt. Kaufman
John Shay as Maj. Canfield

Synopsis:

Kirby is separated from the squad during a barrage. Staff Sgt. Metcalf finds him unconscious in a ditch, revives him, and takes him on the assault of Hill 256. But Kirby runs, claiming he was taking cover from a machine gun — a gun only he saw. Metcalf charges him with running from the enemy. On a 48-hour pass, Caje and Saunders attend the court-martial; visiting Kirby in the cell, they see him put up a brave front to cover his fear that he will be found guilty and executed. They go in search of the proof that Kirby, for once, is innocent of misconduct.

Review — 3.5 bayonets:

This taut courtroom drama pits the trouble-maker Kirby against war hero Sergeant Metcalf. It's a foregone conclusion who the court will believe when stalwart Metcalf accuses Kirby of cowardice — until Saunders intervenes. Writer David Moessinger has crafted a great story, made more interesting by a lack of villains. Everyone is doing his duty, everyone is behaving honorably, and Kirby may lose his life over it. When first aired, this episode probably had a level of tension that has been lost in re-runs: Kirby was still a new member of the squad, not a "regular" to most of the audience. There was the possibility that Kirby might be convicted. Now, watching the episode, viewers know that Saunders will ultimately save the day. But the possibility of failure, at the time, was quite real.

Robert Culp is magnificent as the battle-hardened veteran; Vic Morrow's Saunders is, as always, superb. His struggles to save his man in the face of insurmountable odds is fascinating

to watch. The interplay between Culp and Morrow is the highlight of the episode. Curt Conway as the defense lawyer also puts in an enjoyable performance.

About Filming the Episode:

Conlan Carter: "I had three lines and stood behind Jack Hogan for five days. And that had nothing to do with me being hired. My shining moment of glory was when they posed me in the photo behind Jack."

Notes, Oddities, and Bloopers:

•Trek fans will note that Liam Sullivan (Maj. Hendricks) starred in the classic Trek episode "Plato's Stepchildren."
•Conlan Carter makes his first *Combat!* appearance as an M.P. corporal in this episode.
•Kirby got front billing on separate card.
•Details about Staff Sgt. Metcalf: John C. Metcalf, Fox Company, 361st infantry. In army three years, served in Europe and Africa. Bronze star, Silver star, three purple hearts.
•The hill used as Hill 256 is used in "One More for the Road."

The Sniper (029)

Written by Edward J. Lakso • Directed by Ted Post
Produced by Gene Levitt
First aired 16-Apr-1963 (Episode 28 of Season 1)
CAST:
Regulars: Jason, Morrow, Hogan, Jalbert, Rogers, Peabody
Guest Star Gail Kobe [listed only in the opening]
Jordan Grant as Marks
Fletcher Fist as Brockmeyer
Bill Harlow as Davis
Michel Petit as 1st Boy
Phillipe Chappele as 2nd Boy
John Newton as Fisher
Maya Van Horn as Woman
Athan Karras as Carot
Walter Kohler as Man
Guy de Vestel as Villager
Alex Dunand as Bistro Man
Arlette Clark as Old Woman
Hans Gudegast as Hans Grubber

Synopsis:

A freshly liberated French town, exuberant villagers, free-flowing wine, lots of young women longing to express their gratitude to the brave American liberators, and several days off duty — what could possibly arise to spoil this idyllic picture? A sniper, of course. This never-say-die German stays behind after the German withdrawal to wage his own private war, aided by a beautiful but bitter Frenchwoman who has her own reasons to hate the town that her German lover terrorizes.

Review — 2 bayonets:

This first *Combat!* story by Edward J. Lakso shows little of his later fire. Though a solid script, the characterizations are shallow. Saunders' dialog with Gail Kobe (the embittered French barmaid) is stilted and lacks the usual Saunders conviction. He seems almost a busybody, prying into affairs that are none of his business.

Hans Gudegast, as the sniper, is appropriately sly and sexy

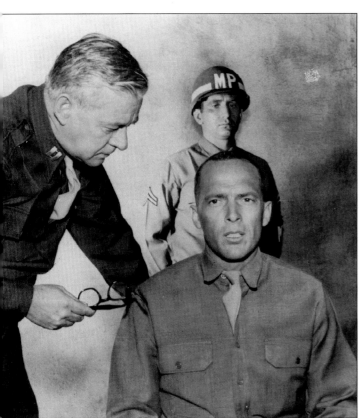

Curt Conway interrogates Jack Hogan in the episode, "Hill 256," while Conlan Carter as the MP looks on.

as he seduces Kobe and slithers freely about the village. But the story offers no look inside this character; we never even hear him speak. Why did he stay in the village? Why is he waging this one man war? And why, when Saunders is wounded, nearly blinded, and has plenty of help within easy calling distance, does he stumble off alone in pursuit of the sniper? Saunders is always heroic, but he is usually not stupid and heroic.

The liberation of the village in the beginning has some charming moments. I love Littlejohn strutting like a peacock with two tiny girls on his arms. Female fans enjoy hunky blond Fletcher Fist stretching out for some R&R. Kirby provides his usual salacious and inappropriate behavior around anything in skirts. Directed by Ted Post, the episode is peppered with delightful visuals. Post teases his audience in places, putting many characters in the sniper's sights, and making us guess who will be the next to fall to this predator. But the first victim was a gimme. The moment the G.I. said he was going to forego the partying and write that long letter to his wife that he's been putting off . . . you knew he was a goner.

About Filming the Episode:

Dick Peabody: "Hans [Gudegast] was doing a scene on lot 2 in the French village. And Ted Post said, 'Damn it, come on give me something. Cut! Prove you're an actor, Hans.' And this is in front of the whole cast and crew. I'm paraphrasing what he said. It was very insulting. And I think it was Hans' first job and it destroyed him. This is a young guy, he's 19 or 20, and so he came up to me and he was so disconsolate. And I said don't listen to that asshole, because you've got a helluva lot of talent and he doesn't have any. Just think about that when you do the next scene with him."

Notes, Oddities, and Bloopers:
• Caje wearing that turtleneck again and Kirby again carries M1.
• First mention of Jampel, referred to as a Major in this episode. Later in series he is a captain.
• Semi-regulars Brockmeyer and Davis appear.
• The two children at the window in this episode appear later in Combat!: Michel Petit stars as Bijou in "The Little Jewel" and Phillipe Chappele plays the haunted boy seeking his sister's murderer in "What Are the Bugles Blowin' For?"
• Hans Gudegast was in college when he worked on *Combat!*

One More for the Road (030)
Written by Kay Lenard and Jess Carneol
Directed by Bernard McEveety
First aired 21-Apr-1963 (Episode 29 of Season 1)

CAST:
Regulars: Morrow, Kirby, Jalbert, Rogers, Peabody, Lowell
Fletcher Fist as Brockmeyer
Don Edmonds as Stroback
The Monroe Twins as The Baby

Synopsis:

While behind enemy lines, the squad discovers an orphaned infant boy. Against the objections of his men (and his own con-

science) Saunders orders the squad to leave the baby behind. Everyone complains that Saunders is "going by the book" at the expense of a baby. Saunders finally gives in, but comes to regret his change of heart. Saunders loses a man because of his failure to follow the book.

Review — 3.5 bayonets:

In "One More for the Road," Saunders' authority is undermined by the presence of a small baby. This is the only episode where he completely loses control of both the squad and the mission. This tightly written and directed episode offers a look at a Saunders struggling, and failing, to reconcile the necessities of wartime command with his own moral integrity. Even the devoted Billy joins in recriminations against Saunders' orders.

This episode shows something never seen again in the five seasons of *Combat!* — Saunders buckling to pressure. When he changes his mind and retrieves the baby, his good intention becomes the first paving block in this episode's road to hell. He loses control of the squad and loses their respect. They question, ignore, and even disobey Saunders throughout this episode. The baby is in command; he commands the attention of the squad, to the exclusion of their duty. Saunders fights a losing battle to get his squad back, trying to get them to remember they are soldiers, and trying to keep them all alive.

Yet, when the squad almost abandons the child when they find out "they've been had" in protecting a German baby, it is Saunders who brings both his squad and himself back to their moral center. The ending is bittersweet. Though the baby has been brought to safety, Saunders' decision cost a man his life.

The episode loses half a bayonet for the sequence of Caje passing himself off as a civilian (and the too convenient earlier discovery of all the items he would need for this deception), plus another loss for the too clever title of the episode.

Notes, Oddities, and Bloopers:
• Fortunately Caje wears a turtleneck under his uniform in this episode. It looked nice with the civilian clothes, but out-of-place with his field garb.
• The apple orchard is used in "A Day in June" and "Survival."
• Same pontoon bridge used in "Bridge at Chalons," "Command," and other episodes.
• Continuity problems: As Saunders leaves baby behind, he lowers the helmet over his eyes, in next cut it's high on forehead.

High Named Today (031)
Written by David Z. Goodman • Directed by Paul Stanley
First aired 07-May-1962 (Episode 31 of Season 1)

CAST:
Regulars: Jason, Morrow, Hogan, Jalbert, Peabody, Lowell, Rogers
Guest star Dean Stockwell as Rob Lawson
Lew Brown as Pratt
John Apone as Soldier #1
Steve Gaynor as Wounded Soldier
Burt Berger as Corporal

Synopsis:

Private Lawson, a reputed "one man army," joins the squad. His displays of recklessness puzzles and angers Hanley and the squad, and he ignores threats from Saunders and Kirby. Lawson is frightened neither by the enemy nor by his fellow soldiers. He is certain nobody will get killed because of him; just as he is certain he is not going home: his mother told him so. Lawson's father and grandfather both died in previous wars, and she has convinced her son that it is also his destiny.

Review — 2 bayonets:

Dean Stockwell (Al of "Quantum Leap") puts in a terminally ethereal performance as Rob Lawson, a young man convinced he has one foot in the afterlife. I find it difficult to feel anything for this soldier who is untouched and unmoved by the actions around him. The meandering, script doesn't help. Too much time is spent establishing Lawson's reputation before he appears. So there is no surprise that he charges the sniper. The third time he rushes into danger is not dramatic, only redundant.

The best moments in this episode occur during the night scene in the barn. In the quiet darkness, the script brings us close to the characters of Doc, Kirby, Nelson, Caje, and Littlejohn. I wish the director had also allowed the audience to get close to Lawson. But he simply presented the motivation for Lawson's behavior, not the emotions and conflict behind them. With Lawson unconcerned whether he lives or dies, I was equally uninterested in the resolution of the story — except in a clinical fashion. And how did the story end? Did Lawson have a revelation? Will he be a good team member from now on? I guess so. The script leaves these questions unresolved. But since Lawson is absent in future episodes, Lawson's Mom was probably right.

Notes, Oddities, and Bloopers:
• When Lawson is firing on the barn, a man in white shirt sleeves peeks his head into the frame for a moment.
• No one in the squad is wounded or killed in this episode
• The only bit of personal information about Doc is revealed in this episode: his mother is dead.

No Trumpets, No Drums (032)
Written by Edward J. Lakso • Directed by Richard Donner
Produced by Gene Levitt
First aired 14-May-1963 (Episode 32 of Season 1)

CAST:
Regulars: Jason, Morrow, Jalbert, Hogan, Peabody, Lowell, Rogers
Jean Del Val as Marceau
Ted Roter as Frenchman
Billy Beck as Dubois
Nicky Blair as Johnson
Andrea Darvi as Micheline

Synopsis:

Caje cracks after accidentally killing a French civilian. Saunders, acting as a friend, is unable to convince Caje that he is blameless for the disaster that orphaned a little girl. Both Saunders and Caje learn hard lessons about war and about distancing themselves from their hearts.

Review — 3.5 bayonets:

In the first aired episode of *Combat!* ("Forgotten Front"), Caje follows the dictates of his conscience and refuses to kill an innocent man. "No Trumpets, No Drums," the final episode of the first season, opens with Caje killing an innocent man. I rather doubt this was planned, but I appreciate the symmetry. Not for the first time, Caje falls apart, broken by war. But in this instance, it takes more than a few sips of wine and the smile from a pretty girl to put the shattered pieces of this soldier back together again.

This is only the second *Combat!* script by Edward J. Lakso, *Combat's* most prolific writer, but he has captured the essence of these characters. The dialogue is crisp and strong. The scene in the barge between a belligerent Caje and an oddly tentative Saunders provides a harsh contrast to later scenes where Saunders is again the hard-nosed, unforgiving Sergeant. At first, Saunders reacts with sympathy and understanding (like a civilian) and Caje fails to respond. Saunders has to admit to Hanley that he has handled the situation wrong. Only when Saunders returns to being a soldier, forcing Caje to remember that his duty is to the larger cause, not just to one small child, does Caje redeem himself. In fighting the larger battle, the smaller battle is also won.

In this Lakso script, the interactions between squad members are right on target: Littlejohn's offer to stand watch for Caje, Saunders' refusal to know which one squad member saved his life, Kirby's unwavering self-interest, Hanley's regret at dressing down both Caje and Saunders, and Doc ... Well, Steven Rogers' Doc never did have much character development, and Lakso didn't broaden the character's range in Doc's final appearance.

This is director Richard Donner's only *Combat!* credit. He leads the characters gently through the episode, letting the drama of the words do their magic. Andrea Darvi, as the waif that Caje orphans, adopts, abandons, and eventually rescues, is heartbreakingly wonderful.

Notes, Oddities, and Bloopers:
• Patton would have approved of Saunders. He slaps Caje twice!
• The in-town battle sequences are re-used in "The Little Carousel" and many other later episodes.
• Caje puts on his helmet backwards when he runs after the armored car. In the next scene, it is on correctly.
• The boat is tied up at the same dyeworks used in "Forgotten Front." The lake there was used in the musical Show Boat, and many other MGM extravaganzas that required waterfront.
• Doc is offered wine in the final scene, but refuses it. He seems to be the only squad member who took the pledge.
• Kirby uses both an M1 and a B.A.R.
• As a little girl, I fell in love with Caje from this episode. I wanted him to take care of and protect me. I never thought it through to realize that for him to take care of me, as he had with Micheline, that first he would have to kill my father.

Combat! was ABC's highest rated new show of the '62–'63 season. In addition to fan praise, the show garnered critical acclaim by receiving two Emmy nominations: Vic Morrow for Outstanding Continued Performance by an Actor in a Series (lead) and Robert Hauser for Outstanding Cinematography.

ABC felt confident enough in the show to finally assign the stars permanent dressing rooms with complete furnishings. They decorated the rooms at studio expense. Rick Jason had an MGM set designer plan his decor. Vic Morrow created his own — the kindest description of it is "garish." The love nest was upholstered in red velvet, with black velvet lamps that had heart-shaped cutouts in the shades with crystals hanging from each and gold interiors. Vic's trailer for location shooting had an open door policy, with drinks usually flowing freely after filming had finished. His velvet dressing room at the studio was by invitation only.

Tom Lowell had been working for Combat! on a show-to-show basis. Gene Levitt offered him a contract going into the second year, but at less than he was making as a freelance artist. At the time, he was making about $1,200 a week on his other projects, but Combat! only offered him $750 an episode to be under long-term contract, the same that he was paid for each individual show. He opted to continue on a show-by-show basis.

Jack Hogan was signed to a five-year contract. "I was first hired to be a bad guy," says Hogan. "We'd be in a script, pinned down by the Germans for ten pages, and they had to have somebody to argue with Vic to create a little conflict. After they decided they wanted me, I decided I better clean up that act if I was going to last five years. Then, from that point on, it sort of evolved into playing with Peabody. That was the fun part, while it was developing. After awhile though, toward the end, it got to be he was 'good ol' Kirby' and you could always count on him. And they gave all the good lines to somebody else and all I would say was, 'What are you gonna to do now, Sarge?'"

Dick Peabody signed a five-year contract during Robert Altman's reign. Now that Gene Levitt was the producer, Dick worried about being released from the show. Neither he nor Tom Lowell felt that Gene Levitt wanted them on the series. Before production ceased for the summer, Dick went to the main office and asked to borrow several thousand dollars to buy a car. He figured they would refuse to loan money to someone they were planning to fire. He got his loan, and had a worry-free hiatus.

New Season, New Faces, New Battles

Robert Hauser, after receiving an Emmy nomination for his work on Combat!, left the series and was replaced by cine-

Conlan Carter joined the team to play Doc as the second season opened in September, 1963.

CHAPTER 3

SEASON TWO, 1963–1964

matographer Emmett Bergholz. The new producer, Gene Levitt, brought in new directors and writers.

The second season was marked by battles over script quality, hard-ball salary negotiations, and the occasional actor walkout. Using his Emmy nomination as leverage, Vic Morrow went into heated contract negotiations, asking for more money and the right to direct.

Seligman's offices were at ABC. He rarely came on the set unless there was trouble, such as when Vic went on strike in season two. Seligman reached Rick Jason at home, telling him to get on the set immediately. That week's episode was supposed to feature Saunders, so Rick Jason was looking forward to a week off. Instead, Rick filmed two weeks of unplanned Hanley episodes.

Vic Morrow soon got his raise and directorial commitment. When the producers finished negotiating with Vic, Rick Jason's agent reminded them of the "favored nations" clause in Rick's contract. "We got alternate first billing. And what he got, I got," says Rick. "They had forgotten they had given me a favored nations clause. So they wanted to know if I wanted to direct. And I said, 'No, I'm still learning how to act.'"

Pierre Jalbert also went on strike. Into the second season, he still had no drive-on pass (a pass so that he could park near the dressing rooms, instead of using the outside parking lot where the crew parked). Pierre had been an editor with MGM for years, so some staff continued thinking of him as a technician, not an actor. Eventually, Pierre had enough. During a heavy rain one morning at 5:00 am, when the guards refused him entry, Pierre just went home. He told the guard, "Tell my show I'm leaving. I'll be back when I can drive on." This was on a day he was scheduled to be in every shot.

He got his pass that day.

With Robert Altman gone, the timeline and character continuity disappeared from the show. Though the character of Davis, who had been a semi-regular of the squad, survived briefly into season two, most of the recurring characters, including Baker, Brockmeyer, and Crown, just disappeared from the storyline.

Quality scripts, however, remained. And, if quality scripts were not delivered, the actors could wait. Rick Jason and Vic Morrow held up filming on one episode as they rewrote a scene on the set, removing extraneous dialogue. Both are actors that perform as much between the lines, as during them. They preferred the style established in season one, where the story is told more cinematically than verbally.

When Gene Levitt came to find out why production was halted, the actors handed him the revised script and said that was what they would film. Levitt said they couldn't do it that way because it knocked twelve minutes from the show. Jason and Morrow just said that he had better write twelve more minutes of script. They would wait.

None of the backstage battles affected the onstage camaraderie. Though the actors all came from diverse backgrounds, they had a working chemistry that sizzled on camera. The whole production staff could be at each other's throats, but the actors would just keep acting and having a good time. This friendly atmosphere attracted an impressive roster of guests to the series. "We were widely known in the industry as a 'happy' show," says Dick Peabody. "The guest stars liked to work with us because playing soldier is a lot of fun.'

"A lot of people wanted to work with Vic," says Dick Peabody about Vic Morrow. "The actors would do the show even if they weren't doing television, just to work with him. That's what Lee Marvin told me. He said, 'I don't do television anymore, but I wanted to work with Vic.' He was an actor's actor."

Sportsmen and Generals on the Set

More than just actors wanted to appear on *Combat!* Several sports celebrities made their TV acting debuts on the show. Ex-heavyweight champion Rocky Marciano appeared briefly as a G.I. in "Masquerade." Cy Young Award-winner Warren Spahn makes a cameo appearance as a German soldier in "Glow Against the Sky." Baseball's winningest left-handed pitcher has no lines in the episode, but has a great closeup that ends the teaser. U.S. Olympic ski coach Bob Beattie brought his skiing skills to the third-season episode "Mountain Man." He plays a German soldier pursuing Caje (by ski) down a mountainside. *Combat!* made the most of these sports celebs for photo opportunities, heavily promoting their cameo roles.

During the second season, a delegation from the Department of Defense visited the set. They presented the cast and crew with an award for being the best recruiting tool the army had had since World War II.

When congressional medal of honor winners convened in Los Angeles, the cast was flabbergasted that those heroes wanted the actors' autographs. Pierre Jalbert felt it should be the actors asking them for autographs. One of the medal of honor winners gave Dick Peabody the ribbon from his medal. He kept it all his life. Another gave him one of his purple hearts.

Personnel Changes: Conlan Carter

To replace Steve Rogers, Conlan Carter was hired to play the new medic. "It helped that my agent was a good friend of Selly Seligman," says Conlan.

Conlan Carter was born in Center Ridge, Arkansas on October 3, 1934. A son of sharecroppers, he was raised on a farm near Matthews, Missouri. In 1951 and 1952, while at Matthews High School, he was Missouri State Champion in the pole vault and was elected to Missouri's All-State Track Team.

He attended Missouri State College at Cape Girardeau for two years on an athletic scholarship. In college, he became conference champion in pole vaulting for Missouri Interstate Athletic Association and competed in high jump, low hurdles, and broad jump. Carter was invited to the 1954 Olympic trials, but could not attend because of finances.

He began his life-long love affair with flight when he joined the US Air Force in 1954. In August of 1956, after two years in the Air Force, Carter hitchhiked to San Francisco, where he

Makeup man John Truey applying Fuller's earth to pitcher Warren Spahn.

found work with the Southern Pacific railroad. There, Conlan joined a musical theater group, studied voice, and won an acting scholarship to the Bay City Actors Lab. He concentrated on musical comedy and appeared in many productions. While studying, he also worked as a field auditor for an insurance company to support himself and his new wife.

Carter moved to Hollywood in 1959. Within two months, he was signed as a regular on the television show "The Law and Mr. Jones." Carter also made guest appearances on several hit television shows, including "Twilight Zone," "Beverly Hillbillies," "Dr. Kildare," "Rawhide," and "Gunsmoke." He even guested on an episode of *Combat!* (as the M.P. in "Hill 256") before joining the show's cast in the role of Doc. "I didn't come in with a contract in the beginning," recalls Conlan Carter. "They signed me to do two or three shows. They kind of weren't sure what to do with the character. So they wrote this stuff and then just kind of waited to see what would happen with it. After the third or fourth episode they said, 'well, looks like it's gonna work,' so they signed me."

He received an Emmy nomination as best supporting actor for his outstanding work in the second-season episode "The Hostages." During the show's 1964 summer hiatus, Conlan garnered his first movie role in the comedy *Quick Before It Melts*. Between acting gigs, he also enjoyed flying. Both he and his wife had their private pilot's license and spent much of their off time above the clouds. Conlan Carter's post-*Combat!* career included frequent appearances on television and several feature films. During this period, he acquired his commercial pilot's license, splitting his time between acting and the wild blue yonder. Conlan was divorced in 1970 and remained a bachelor for nineteen years.

In 1976 he traveled to Kano, Nigeria in West Africa to do a geological survey for oil exploration. He worked for Beech Aerospace Service in 1985, doing secret airborne electronic surveillance. This was a particularly interesting time for him, since the hush-hush work required high-level security clearance and a national security briefing. His last showbiz appearance was in a "MacGyver" episode in 1986. Later that year, he took a job in Florida, as a private pilot flying for a client and his family. In 1989, Conlan wed his high school sweetheart, Betty Murphy. They lived in a home adjoining the airport and he flew a Dassault Falcon Jet for the family, flying them within the continental United States, Canada, the Caribbean, and Europe. He is now retired.

Carter has four children: Christopher Conlan, Tracy Lynn, Heather Dawn, and Jonathan Patrick.

About his character on *Combat!*, Conlan says, "He never had a name. It was just always 'Doc.' It was always assumed that he was from the mid-West, but that was because of the way I talked." He researched medics for his role. "I figured out how to bandage a little bit and things like that. I just practiced so it wouldn't look like I was a total nerd. Mostly, you didn't see me doin' it, anyway. And the only people I ever was able to save

On a break from Combat!, *Conlan Carter organized a celebrity air race to promote the Reno National Air Races. Celebrity pilots included Jackie Cooper, James Franciscus, Susan Oliver, director Sydney Pollack, Cliff Robertson, and Conlan Carter. "All stock airplanes, all the same kind, from L.A. to Reno in a cross-country race. All of the pilots had a celebrity aviation pilot with them and I had a gal named Edna Gardner White who was a very famous woman aviator from the twenties and thirties. All the passengers were significant to aviation, but not show business. We had a ball," said Carter. Susan Oliver, the only woman pilot in the race, won the event.*

were the squad. But anybody that carried the radio, you knew he was going to get killed. That was a given. I never could save those guys. . . . On the balance, they didn't do a lot with the stuff that I did. Mostly I just stood around. I'd say, 'Sarge. I don't think he's gonna make it, Sarge.' And, of course, the Look. You don't say anything, just shake your head. Everybody knows what you mean."

Gene Levitt

Gene Levitt started working as a writer for *Combat!* He was an experienced screen writer, having scripted the films *Underwater Warrior* (1958) and *The Night Runner* (1957), among others, as well as writing many television shows. He

```
┌─────────────────────────────────────────────┐
│  DOC'S WOUNDS                                 │
│  Bullet Wounds:                               │
│  •  Outer right thigh [Encounter]             │
│  •  Outer right thigh [A Walk with an Eagle]  │
│  •  Right abdomen [Operation Fly Trap]        │
│  •  Left side of chest [Cry For Help]         │
│  •  [Little Carousel]                         │
└─────────────────────────────────────────────┘
```

wrote the script for "Any Second Now," the first episode filmed after the pilot. He became producer of the series starting with the episode "Battle of the Roses," replacing the dismissed Robert Altman. He had a tough job to fill; *Combat!* was an extremely complicated show to film, especially at the budget the cash-strapped ABC allotted them. And there was friction with the cast: many of them had been hired by Altman, felt loyalty to him, and had respected his work.

Dick Peabody says of Gene Levitt, "He was a writer, and a good writer. I loved 'The Volunteer,' which he wrote. He and I never really hit it off. The day he walked on the set, I was leaning on a wardrobe rack, just sort of watching him approach. I'd never met him, but I knew who he was and he knew who I was. He came up to me and said, 'You know, you just gave me a look like Who the hell is this sonofabitch. What right does he have to take over the show?' Now, come on. Can you get convicted for just an expression on your face? Of course, that's exactly what I was thinking. He knew that I was Altman's friend. But Altman had told me, he said this guy, as soon as he takes over, he's going to hire somebody to do everything for him. He'll get a script consultant so somebody else can decide what scripts they're going to use. And he'll get people to do his job. And that's exactly what happened."

Gene Levitt clashed with Vic Morrow, especially over the coerced directing assignments. Rick Jason remembers that "Vic would do a show and he didn't care if he went six, seven, or even eight days. And it drove Gene up the walls, because Gene is the one who got the heat from it."

After leaving *Combat!* in 1966, Gene Levitt went on to write, direct, and produce in television and feature films. He directed the film *The Phantom of Hollywood,* whose plot centered around the demolition of a major studio and used the actual demolition of the MGM lots as its centerpiece. The movie includes the final screen appearance of the *Combat!* French village.

Season Two Episodes

All the action of season two takes place after the liberation of Paris. Any attempt to trace historical events in a straight timeline collapses in the second season. Though the war in Europe only lasted a year after D-Day, the cast of *Combat!* fought for five years and never battled their way out of France.

Combat! returned to its 7:30 p.m. time slot on ABC, opposite "Marshal Dillon" and the first half of "The Red Skelton Hour" on CBS, and "Mr. Novak" on NBC. *Combat!* was followed at 8:30 p.m. by ABC's WWII comedy "McHale's Navy."

Ambush (033)

Written by Edward J. Lakso
Directed by Sutton Roley
First aired 03-Dec-1963 (Episode 12 of Season 2)

CAST:
Regulars: Jason, Morrow, Hogan, Jalbert, Lowell, Peabody, Carter
Guest star Marisa Pavan as Marie Marchand
Charles Macaulay as Capt. Baumer
Michael Pataki as G.I. Radio Man
William Speckmann as 1st German Soldier
Kort Falkenberg as Hans
Guy de Vestel as Uncle Henri
Maurice St. Clair as Andre
Steven Landers as German #1
Edgar Ritscher as German #2
Billy Beck as French Priest
Francis Ravel as Man
Gabrielle Rossillon as French Girl
Mignonne Gret as Girl

Synopsis:
"Ambush" brings Saunders, Hanley, and the squad into a peaceful village torn apart by hate. The pleasures of a liberation celebration are cut short by the murder of a doctor whom the town thinks was a Nazi collaborator. The squad later learns he was a U.S. intelligence agent. Saunders must enlist Marie Marchand's unwilling help to find a German tank even though she blames them for not protecting her father.

Review — 2 bayonets:
With orders not to interfere in local affairs, the squad must ignore a young woman's pleas for help and are unable to intervene to prevent her father's murder. Marisa Pavan, as Marie Marchand, is superb as the daughter consumed by bitterness. She speaks only French, yet conveys the depth of her anger and hatred for the Americans who failed her. Pavan began her film career in the John Ford WWI film *What Price Glory?*

Pierre Jalbert features prominently in this episode as the only bridge between Saunders and the girl. His moments with her are touching as he bears the burden of putting into words the importance of her helping those who would not help her. The lingering closeup of Caje whispering in her hear and pleading with her is beautifully photographed.

Sutton Roley nicely merges Altman's street scene from "The Volunteer" with new footage, including a delightful segment of a buxom woman leading Kirby a merry chase. Unlike in "The Volunteer," Saunders and Hanley separate themselves from the festivities, remaining aloof while the squad chases babes and frolics in the fountain. Director Roley provides some stunning long shots through the village at the end of the episode. Roley's action sequences are riveting, with the Americans and Germans fighting nearly on top of each other. No background music punctuates the big battle, so the audience hears the footsteps

In "Ambush," Marisa Pavan is a French girl harboring a bitter hatred for the Americans.

Bridge at Chalons (034)

Written by Bob and Esther Mitchell
Directed by Ted Post
First aired 17-Sep-1963 (Episode 1 of Season 2)

CAST:
Regulars: Morrow, Jason, Hogan, Jalbert, Lowell, Peabody, Carter
Guest Star Lee Marvin as Sgt. Turk
Lee Kreiger as Capt. McQuillan
Rudy Hanson as German Leader
Peter Helman as German
Kurt Landon as Other German
Donald Ein as German Corporal
Mathais Uitz as 1st German Cyclist
Heinz Sadler as 2nd German Cyclist
Chris Anders as 1st Bridge German
Dieter Jacoby as 2nd Bridge German

Synopsis:

On a mission with a hard-nosed demolition expert, Sgt. Turk, Saunders mother-hens his men, and in the end, even Sergeant Turk. While behind enemy lines, Turk shows his contempt for the squad's ineptitude and a mutual hatred develops between the sergeants. Saunders' men are picked off one by one, until only the sergeants remain to complete the mission.

Review — 3.5 bayonets:

Guest Star Lee Marvin is superb as the sergeant-with-an-attitude who makes Saunders' life miserable. Marvin was larger than life both on camera and off.

Rick Jason was surprised to see Marvin do a guest stint. After a three-year run as star of the series "M Squad," in which he was to share in the profits, Marvin should not have needed the money. But Marvin confided to Jason that the books for the series showed no profits, so Lee Marvin was again working series, but trying to select only good shows.

An ex-Marine, Lee Marvin brought touches of realism to his role. Marvin saw action in WWII in the Pacific and was wounded in the battle of Saipan. In "Bridge at Chalons," he is completely natural as a man of arms. He holds his weapon like someone familiar with the feel. He added the rubber inner tube around his helmet, just as he had done with his own helmet in the Pacific.

About Filming the Episode:

"I always thought Lee Marvin was so cool," says Tom Lowell. "The way he came in and had his rifle slung that way. Remember the way he had his elbows looped through the strap? That was so cool. I tried to do that for every show after that and Dick would look down at me and say, 'Don't even try it.' After Lee Marvin came on, everyone wanted a rubber band wrapped around their helmet."

"Lee Marvin was a kick in the tail," says Conlan Carter. "The fun part of him was not so much in the acting, though he was good and he did what he did well. But he was a hard drinker. After the shoot was over for the day, man could he put them down. Tell the stories! And he had incredible recovery."

"Georg Fenady says, "That man had a hollow leg. At two

---

through the brush and waits anxiously as a German moves towards Saunders.

Saunders tactics are questionable. After bringing his squad almost on top of the tank, only then does he call in a barrage, forcing his men to run like mad. If he had called in the barrage from a distance, he would not have lost any men and could have avoided dodging American shells. The last run, though, is spectacularly filmed, with shells exploding in the river and the dock blasted into splinters just as the squad rushes past it.

About Filming the Episode:

Tom Lowell says: "This was one TV show where there were so few women. I mean, it was really like the army or a giant male fraternity. Even the script supervisor was a male. So, when a woman would visit the set or was a guest star on the show, it was a major event. We just followed her around like bees, wherever she would go."

Notes, Oddities, and Bloopers:

•One of the dead Germans lying face down in the water lifts his head to take a breath, then returns to playing dead.
•The first shot of the artillery piece shows a man in civilian clothes following behind the German soldiers. The civilian is also in a shot of the soldiers setting up the camouflage.

Lee Marvin in "Bridge at Chalons."

Synopsis:

On patrol looking for the German gun known as "Big Frieda," Saunders is captured by Phil, an old doughboy trapped in the past. Reliving the first World War, he captures Saunders, who he thinks is a German. Within his confused memory, Phil knows the location of the big gun. And the lives of the Americans moving up depend on Phil's failing mind.

Review — 1 bayonet:

"Doughboy" features strong acting from an exceptional cast, marred by hokey cinematography and a weak script. Eddie Albert does a star turn as a veteran suffering the lingering effects of shell-shock. In a montage of vintage war films, trench warfare, and new Franklin Canyon footage, the audience enters Phil's nightmare and relives his tragedy from the first world war of watching all his men slaughtered.

A veteran of many war films, Albert played Colonel Newton in *The Longest Day,* released a year before this episode, and played Colonel Bliss in 1963's *Captain Newman, M.D.*

Italian actress Alida Valli (often billed in films simply as Valli) plays Marie, who nursed Albert's character to health in the first war and is now his wife. Both actors were Hollywood veterans at the time, having started their careers in the thirties. They are still active today. Vic Morrow more than holds his own in this lofty company. Tom Gries, the director, would go on to create the TV show "Rat Patrol" (1966).

But all this fine talent is wasted on this lightweight script that can't quite decide what it wants to be: psychological drama or action saga.

About Filming the Episode:

Georg Fenady remembers "We didn't have many actresses on the show. But a few. Great ones, too. I remember Valli. A sweet, sweet lady. Beautiful woman. She was a big star." Valli appeared in 113 films. In an international film career encompassing six decades, Valli is perhaps most fondly remembered for the 1949 thriller *The Third Man.*

Notes, Oddities, and Bloopers:

•Eddie Albert's rifle is an authentic WWI era Springfield.
•During the firefight on the farm, the horses, chickens, and goats are unflustered by guns blazing around them.
•The railway gun fires as fast as a 105; a gun of that size could only fire about three times an hour.

o'clock in the morning I'm staggering out to my car and he says 'Where are you going? I know a place to go.' I said, 'Lee, we have to get up in two hours.' I left him, and he went wherever he went. The next day, at seven in the morning, he put on all of his equipment — backpack, helmet, and rifle — and stood three feet from the camera all day, standing tall."

Notes, Oddities, and Bloopers:

•Sarge starts with a holstered .45 and a sheathed bayonet on his belt. Later the bayonet has disappeared.
•While carrying Turk back on the stretcher, Sarge's Tommy gun is on his left shoulder. After he sets the stretcher down, it's on his right shoulder.

Doughboy (035)

Teleplay by Bernard C. Schoenfeld
Story by Gene Levitt
Directed by Tom Gries
First aired 29-Oct-1963 (Episode 7 of Season 2)

CAST:

Regulars: Morrow, Hogan
Guest star Eddie Albert as Phil
Paul Busch as German Sergeant
Hans Gudegast as German Vehicle Commander
Michael McDonald as Ed
Bill Harlow as Nick
Special Guest Star Alida Valli as Marie

The Long Way Home (036, 037)

Written by Edward J. Lakso
Directed by Ted Post
Part 1: Aired 08-Oct-1963 (Episode 4 of Season 2)
Part 2: Aired 15-Oct-1963 (Episode 5 of Season 2)

CAST:

Regulars: Morrow, Jason, Hogan, Jalbert, Lowell, Peabody, Carter
Guest star Richard Basehart as Capt. Steiner
Co-starring Simon Oakland as Sgt. Tom Akers
Woodrow Parfrey as Pvt. Gates
Sasha Hardin as Lt. Brummel

Vic Morrow finds himself held prisoner by Phil (guest star Eddie Albert), a man who fought in World War I and still believes he's fighting the same war, in "Doughboy."

Glenn Cannon as Rankin
Arthur Batanides as Nader
Jim Sikking as Lyles
Michael McDonald as Wilson
Arnold Merritt as Pfc. Cole
Walter Linden as German Compound Guard - day
Norbert Meisel as German Compound Guard - night
Rudy Dolan as 2nd German Guard - day
Robert Fortier as Captain Jampel (in part 2 only)

Synopsis:

(part 1) Caught in an ambush, Saunders and his men surrender. In a temporary compound, they are brutally interrogated by S.S. Cpt. Steiner. Sharing their prison camp is Sgt. Ackers and three other American prisoners. Steiner's been working them over. Saunders devises a plot to sneak Billy out of camp. Steiner vows a terrible punishment, born by the timid grocer-turned-soldier, Gates. In a second failed escape attempt, one of Saunders' men is killed and Saunders is beaten.

(part 2) A wounded Billy reveals the squad's predicament to Lt. Hanley, who can offer no help. With Caje under a death sentence for attacking a German guard, Saunders must quickly devise a new escape plan. As a diversion, the soldiers start tunneling, but the real plan involves a faulty circuit, water, and a wire fence. In the end, the grocery clerk slays the "Superman," saving Saunders and the squad.

Review — 3 bayonets (both parts):

A strong script by Edward J. Lakso shows the squad tested to the limits as they face death and torture at the hands of S.S. Captain Steiner, played by Richard Basehart. Always a superb actor, Basehart is excellent portraying this icy villain so sure of his own superiority. In a battle of wits with Saunders, he wins the first rounds.

"The Long Way Home" is a squad episode, letting all the cast shine. As each is called to face Steiner, they show both fear and bravery, often simultaneously. Carter, Peabody, and Jalbert make the most of these moments. Hogan is excellent during his "panic attack" as he is dragged screaming to the interrogation — craftily managing to turn on the faucet in the struggle. Morrow underplays the emotions, still conveying that Saunders is torn apart at each cry from his men.

Guest star Simon Oakland plays Akers, a man whose spirit has been broken by Steiner, until Saunders shows him the light. Woodrow Parfray plays the frightened grocery clerk with a gentle touch, making him a convincing hero. The show ends with a quiet moment between friends, as Saunders and Hanley avoid the celebration, and instead drink to those who were lost.

About Filming the Episode:

Jack Hogan recalls "Ted Post [the director] would sit there as you're doing the scene, reading the newspaper in his director chair. One time someone came up and told him, that there was a plane in the shot and Ted shouted, 'Hold the plane!' as if we had any control over LAX."

Tom Lowell: "We filmed some of it, including the shower scene, up at Franklin Canyon. I shot *Manchurian Candidate* there, too. For the second part, I had to come back and sit around, watching everybody shoot the rest, because I was finished."

Notes, Oddities, and Bloopers:

• Where were all the German guards when the squad escaped?
• The opening of part two re-uses the elevated shot from "Bridge of Chalons" with Caje, Littlejohn, and Kirby walking towards Saunders. Of course, none of these actors can be in the scene, since they're all still prisoners.
• Odd the Germans allowed prisoners to keep cigarettes and lighters; when the prisoners were searched, everything else of value was taken.

A Distant Drum (038)

Written by Kay Lenard and Jess Carneol
Directed by John Peyser
First aired 19-Nov-1963 (Episode 10 of Season 2)

CAST:

Regulars: Jason, Morrow, Hogan, Jalbert,
Guest star Denise Darcel as Annette
Sasha Hardin as Keppler
Charles DeVries as Buehler
Ed Knight as German Sergeant
Ray Baxter as German Soldier
Bill Harlow as Corp. McGill
Introducing Holly McIntire as Louise

COMBAT!

Synopsis:

In "A Distant Drum" a wounded Hanley, separated from his platoon, forces a reluctant French woman to give him aid. In the tradition of hurt/comfort stories, Hanley suffers, bleeds, drags himself through the underbrush, plays dead, fords streams, and passes out at appropriate moments, until a beautiful woman arrives to remove his clothes, bind his wounds, and offer supportive backrubs. In return, Hanley saves her daughter from an attempted rape, bestows mother and daughter with a kiss, and then exits into the night with a dead German across his shoulder.

Review — 1 bayonet:

Though Hanley is my favorite character, "A Distant Drum" is not among my favorite *Combat!* episodes. The writing team of Kay Lenard and Jess Carneol wrote this, their second script for *Combat!* (the first being the brilliant "One More for the Road"). This writing team had a good grasp of Saunders' character, but had no notion what to do with Hanley (though getting his shirt off was a step in the right direction, as far as his female fans were concerned). The plot is thin, with far too much time spent watching Hanley in distress.

Sasha Hardin plays Keppler, a German scavenger who steals from the dead, the living, and seems to rape young women with the knowledge and consent of his squad leader. His sergeant seems bothered by Hardin's actions, but puts up with it. Keppler, and how he interacts with his squad, is unbelievable.

Why is Sasha Hardin's hair bleached in this episode? With lush black hair framing blue eyes, Hardin was menacing as the Gestapo colonel in "Escape to Nowhere" and the Lieutenant in "Odyssey." As a short-haired blond, he looks like a geek.

French-born actress, Denise Darcel plays the frightened French mother who is forced to aid Hanley. She is a woman torn, desperately wanting to do the right thing for this man and the right thing for her daughter. But to offer safety to the one, puts the other in danger. Her scene alone with Hanley, after bandaging his wounds, is touching and poignant. She gives comfort to this wounded man, despite her misgivings, and finds herself drawn to the helpless soldier that fate brought to her door. Her actions, her looks, and her touch are simultaneously maternal and sensual. Darcel played Denise in Robert Pirosh's *Battleground*.

The conclusion to this episode is rushed and unnecessary. Caje, Kirby, and Saunders race through the dialogue. The tight shot, as they all gather into the frame above Hanley's stretcher, looks hokey. And I would have thought Hanley knew better than to tell Kirby where he can find a farmhouse with two lonely, defenseless Frenchwomen in it.

Notes, Oddities, and Bloopers:
•Why is Hanley on a stretcher in the last scene?
•Hanley accessories: He is conveniently wearing no undershirt and is without the gold ring he usually wears, which the scavenger would have pinched.

Denise Darcel provides wounded Rick Jason a pretty shoulder to lean on when and refuge from his German pursuers in "A Distant Drum."

•An early ground-level shot of Hanley reveals the camera moving through the grass.
•American-born Holly McIntyre spoke flawless French in the episode, without an accent, according to Denise Darcel. Holly is the daughter of Jeanette Nolan, who plays Sister Terese in "Infant of Prague."
•The credits incorrectly list Bill Harlow as playing Corp. McGill. He plays Davis.
•When Hanley is crawling through the front yard toward the door, one of the chickens keeps pace alongside him.
•The title of the episode is a quote from the Rubaiyat of Omar Khayyam.

Bridgehead (039)

Written by Edward J. Lakso
Directed by Bernard McEveety
First aired 09-24-63 (Episode 2 of Season 2)

CAST:
Regulars: Morrow, Hanley, Hogan, Lowell, Peabody, Carter
Nick Adams as Pvt. Mick Hellar
Noam Pitlick as Pvt. Gene Scott
Paul Busch as German Sergeant
Joey Walsh as Pvt. Jack Johnson
Richard Jury as Pvt. Wayne Shrope
Fred Harris as Cole

"Come and get me!" Nick Adams shouts his challenge to the Germans, as the lone survivor of a squad sent out to establish a "Bridgehead."

Synopsis:

In "Bridgehead," Saunders must take a German-held bridge against nearly insurmountable opposition, including resistance from private Hellar (Nick Adams). As squad members fall to enemy fire, Hellar's attitude toward the mission and to Saunders' leadership grows more hostile.

Review — 3.5 bayonets:

"Bridgehead" has all the elements of a great *Combat!* episode, plus the benefit of a script by Edward J. Lakso and direction by Bernard McEveety. Well-acted, carefully crafted moments abound: a genuine Saunders' patented pep-talk to a new squad member, Littlejohn's agonizing self-recrimination over a fatal blunder, Billie's fear under fire, and Doc's impassioned desire to shed his non-combatant role and seek vengeance. With all this going for it, "Bridgehead" should be top-notch. But these moments exist in isolation, never gelling into a cohesive whole.

This *Combat!* episode takes place in real-time (the action of the show takes approximately 55 minutes, the episode is approximately 55 minutes long). Saunders' mission must be completed within a set time. This should add tension, create a sense of urgency. But director McEveety, usually so skilled at developing pace, inexplicably lets the action meander from one corner of the battle to another.

A major detriment to the episode is the character of Hellar,

portrayed by Nick Adams. Adams' performance is fine. He ably embodies this jazzman's arrogance, ego, and wise-cracking insubordination. He is a laid-back shirker, which makes keeping an intense pace difficult. Nothing makes this character move fast, so scenes with him break the tension. His eleventh-hour redemption and self-sacrifice are predictable. He is a distraction from what might have been a breath-taking episode, a story as moving as "Hills Are for Heroes," whose plot is similar.

Doc and Billy have the best moments in this episode. Tom Lowell embodies the fear of a young man facing certain death. He is compelled to fight on, not by duty or honor, but by the sheer will of an angry Sergeant. Despite uncontrollable shaking and tears, he does his job. His fellow soldier, older and more mature, fails the same challenge, spending the episode huddled in a corner. Conlan Carter gives us a Doc that dispels any lingering memory of Steven Rogers' sensitive, introspective medic. Carter's Doc rails against the non-combatant role imposed on him by regulations. Not a passive man by nature, in this episode he has reached his limit, unable to sit and watch the casualties mount. He wants a weapon, he wants to fight back. Carter convincingly shows the mixed desires and fears of this complex character: tender and compassionate as he deals with Littlejohn's wounds (physical and emotional), then vengeful as he craves blood for blood. It's a great scene, for awhile; but it is weakened by Doc's quick acquiescence to Hanley's pep talk. How real was his anger when just a few sentences from Hanley can restore his reason and good nature?

About Filming the Episode:

"I want a rifle. That was my big line," says Conlan Carter. "Me, I didn't care about shooting a gun. I'd never played a medic before. I'd done so many westerns and got to shoot a gun a lot."

Tom Lowell: "Nick Adams was very nice, easy to work with. Working with Adams and Vic Morrow was a real treat. They were, to a degree, similar in their acting styles. You're talking about television series acting. You don't get a lot of rehearsal time, so there's not a lot of time to really develop your character. You have to do that all on your own. But it's obvious that people like Vic and all those guys really did their homework."

Notes, Oddities, and Bloopers:

• Though Billy's father was dead in "The Celebrity," he talks about a recent letter from his father.
• Doc bandages a wounded Kirby before Kirby is wounded.
• Hanley talks about the other squads' activities; finally, there's another squad! I was beginning to think that this was the most understaffed platoon in the US army.
• Would someone please get Saunders a knife! He often mooches blades from his men and in this episode mooches a bayonet from Hanley.
• Joey Walsh, who plays Johnson, returns in fourth-season's "Hills Are for Heroes." Noam Pitlick (Pvt. Scott) appears in third season's "Beneath the Ashes."

Masquerade (041)

Written by Anthony Wilson
Directed by John Peyser
First aired 01-Oct-1963 (Episode 3 of Season 2)

CAST:

Regulars: Jason, Morrow, Hogan, Jalbert, Peabody, Carter
James Coburn as Cpl. Arnold Kanger
Norman Alden as PFC Cooper
Rick Traeger as German Colonel
George Keymas as Captain Simms
K.L. Smith as 1st G.I.
Jacque Shelton as 2nd G.I.
Bruce Watson as Sentry
Alex Burke as 1st Man
and Dan Stafford as Lt. David Comstock
Rocky Marciano (uncredited)

Synopsis:

Two Germans, dressed as G.I.s, try to infiltrate battalion headquarters under the pretense of escorting a "captured" German Colonel. Their plans are complicated first by a land-mine that disables their jeep and then by a suspicious Saunders. In a clever script by Anthony Wilson, Kanger matches wits with Saunders in a deadly game of survival.

Review — 4 bayonets:

In "Masquerade," James Coburn plays the infiltrator Kanger with a mesmerizing menace and a keen, predator's gaze. His manner is as easy as his smile. He deftly turns away suspicions and turns on the offensive when the questioning takes a dangerous turn. My favorite scene is between him and Saunders; Coburn turns the tables on Saunders' interrogation, questioning both his actions and his manhood. The tension of this verbal duel is heightened by body language. The two constantly shift to attack positions as they speak; the threat in their physical movements is in sharp contrast with their banter.

Morrow's Saunders is a match for Kanger, meeting every deft ploy with his own wit and cunning. Ultimately, Kanger is defeated by his own arrogance.

Dan Stafford plays Lt. Comstock, an infiltrator not quite up to the task. Though his "American" passes muster, he is betrayed by his humanity. He blanches at the sight of a dead German in the street; he is unwilling to sacrifice his commanding officer for the sake of the mission; and when Germans attack the town, he is unable to fully play G.I. to gun down a fellow German soldier. Kanger is unbothered by such moral dilemmas. This predator has no veneer of civilization. When Comstock endangers Kanger's survival, Kanger dispatches him without hesitation.

Notes, Oddities, and Bloopers:

- The platoon is very familiar with battalion medical staff. Hanley knows who the best surgeon is; all are old friends with the ambulance driver (even though he says he never comes to the front). Just how much time do these soldiers spend back in the hospital?
- Coburn blooper: in the scene after Comstock's death, Coburn hands a cigarette to Saunders, who ignores it until Caje smiles

and says, "No thanks." Then Saunders says "thanks" and takes one.

- Badly crafted exposition as Saunders tells the squad about Kanger. Kirby and Littlejohn whine about Krauts not playing fair. Then after Littlejohn asks about Kanger (while standing next to Caje), Caje asks the same question.
- Saunders says he's from out west when talking with Kanger, says he's from Illinois when questioned by guards.
- The 361st was stationed outside Sheffield before D–Day. Infiltrators claim to be from the 594th.
- Lt. Comstock should recheck his facts: St. Paul is not the Gateway to the West.
- The interplay between Saunders and Hanley is interesting, especially how Hanley officially dismisses Saunders' concerns while still contacting battalion.
- "Masquerade" was originally titled "Operation Grief," perhaps an Americanization of the German operation "Greif," known to the Allies as the Battle of the Bulge.
- Rocky Marciano makes his TV acting debut as a G.I.

Infant of Prague (041)

Written by Rik Vollaerts
Directed by John Peyser
First aired 14-Apr-1964 (Episode 31 of Season 2)

CAST:

Regulars: Jason, Hogan, Jalbert, Peabody, Carter
Guest Star Jeanette Nolan
Jeanne Rainer as Mlle. Solere
Pamela Branch as Mlle. Mornay
Leigh Chapman as Mlle. Bochard
Harald Dyrenforth as Panzer Captain

Synopsis:

While on patrol, Hanley's squad is saddled with an elderly nun and three postulants. The nuns are helpless and cute while the squad is alternately enchanted and befuddled by them. Hanley and the squad endeavor to shepherd the sisters to safety, but the eldest escapes to search for a religious statue.

Review — 0 bayonets:

The Easter episode "Infant of Prague" should be viewed as a comedy, as it was intended. Viewers who are looking for drama will find much at fault with the story. If you are not in a mood to smile at the nuns, you will find them annoying. The sisters could not be cuter if they had started flying and singing "Dominique."

Rik Vollaerts, the writer that penned "Battle of the Roses," devised the repetitive plot for "Infant of Prague." The elderly Sister Therese, in a chain of foolish decisions following the death of Reverend Mother, behaves in a manner inconsistent with personal survival and common sense (but appropriate for comedy). Jeanette Nolan plays Sister Therese with gusto and a devilish twinkle in those angelic eyes. Against military procedure, Hanley and squad rescue her, instead of abandoning her to the protection of the Infant of Prague.

This story has much momentum, but nobody gets anywhere. They start in town, try to leave town, then hide in a barn. They return to town, try to leave town, then hide in the woods. For a third time, they return to town (following the dictum of comedy in threes). Neither the plot nor the actors get anywhere. The episode is padded with much WWII archival footage. And great footage it is, very watchable — one of the best aspects of this episode.

Kirby's character shows the first signs of softening in this episode. He is concerned about the nuns, even offers to risk himself to find food for these women who chose self-starvation. The first-season Kirby would have hoarded his chocolate bars and made a pass at the postulants.

Notes, Oddities, and Bloopers:
•The sisters are rather partisan. No sympathy for the death of German soldiers. When a German captain is killed before her on holy ground, Sister Therese doesn't notice.
•In action with the 103rd Panzers.
•When the postulant nearly faints, Doc is looking at her, but ignores her. Moments later when she really faints, he rushes over.
•Dick Peabody is charming in the scene in the culvert under the roadway.
•This was the show's Easter episode.

The Wounded Don't Cry (042)
Written by James Landis
Directed by James Komack
First aired 22-Oct-1963 (Episode 6 of Season 2)

CAST:
Regulars: Morrow, Jalbert, Hogan, Lowell, Peabody, Carter
Guest starring Karl Boehm as Carl Bauer
Oscar Beregi as Schiller
Leonard Nimoy as Neumann

Synopsis:
A German field hospital, filled with wounded men and cut off by the American advance, becomes the squad's observation post. An embittered Saunders turns even colder when an S.S. patient critically wounds one of his squad. Bauer, a German orderly in the field hospital, pleads with Saunders to allow him to take a truck to recover the plasma desperately needed by both the wounded American and the German casualties.

Review — 2 bayonets:
The war has taken its toll on Sgt. Saunders. In "The Wounded Don't Cry," Saunders has become an embittered soldier, untrusting and unwilling to treat the enemy as human beings. This is a marked contrast to the Saunders of just two episodes ago in "Masquerade," where he argues for compassion for a wounded German. No longer is he one of Kanger's "American suckers."

This emotional state, though, does not survive to the closing credits. When Saunders must travel with a German prisoner on a mission of mercy, it becomes a journey to recover not just plasma, but Saunders' humanity. The instrument of change is

Bauer — an introspective former school teacher who is charming, harmless, hates the S.S., and is nice to birds.

The plot is thoroughly predictable. Though the premise should allow opportunity for soul-searching and analysis of the human condition, writer James Komack does not let such matters interfere with his simplistic tale. Instead of writing Germans as human beings, he separates them into good Germans and bad Germans.

Wehrmacht good. S.S. bad.

Makes life so simple. And how does the script reveal this dichotomy? By showing S.S. soldiers killing an innocent school teacher and a Wehrmacht soldier returning a cute bird to its nest. Later, this nice Wehrmacht soldier guns down the evil S.S., his fellow countrymen, without any remorse or hesitation. "The Wounded Don't Cry" is mindless, action/adventure masquerading as drama.

Morrow's acting is more multi-facetted than the script. Morrow plays a Saunders at odds with own beliefs. His hard, unromanticized description of watching his soldiers die because they trusted a flag of truce is so revealing in its simplicity. It shows how Saunders changed from the wise-cracking scamp of "A Day in June" to this war-weary creature who sees plots in a simple act of mercy.

Saunders is distrustful of all Germans — even the saintly Bauer. Unfortunately, there is little chemistry between Morrow and German-born actor Karl Boehm (playing Bauer). Boehm struggles valiantly with the role, but perfect characters are hard to relate to; and the script allows nothing of human nature to intrude into this German paradigm of virtue.

Under Komack's direction, the action never flags long enough for the audience to think too deeply. Forget about the unexplored possibilities in this episode, just enjoy it for escapism. As a piece of adventure fluff, "The Wounded Don't Cry" is an enjoyable, light romp through the countryside with our favorite Sergeant. Watching Morrow emote for an hour is rarely a waste of time. This episode is a solid, middle-of-the-road, two-bayonetter.

About Filming the Episode:
Dick Peabody recalls working with Leonard Nimoy, a close friend of Vic Morrow's, who recommended Peabody for Nimoy's acting workshop. "I was with Leonard about six months, every Saturday for about three hours. And he was a wonderful teacher. I learned a lot from him."

Notes, Oddities, and Bloopers:
•The two-story field hospital set is also used in "The General and the Sergeant."
•First time the squad encounters the German 241st Infantry, who they will chase across France for the next two seasons. Fighting takes place around LeMans.
•The bird in the nest looks terrified. It flaps its wings and tries to get out of the nest, but its leg looks tied down.
•Saunders and Caje have a close encounter as the Sarge rolls

over him, avoiding the grenade blast.

• When Bauer shoots one of the Germans, his weapon has no magazine.

• Vic didn't get along with German-born Karl Boehm. One actor noted that Vic was often reserved with the native-born Germans who appeared on the show.

The Little Jewel (043)

Written by Shirl Hendryx
Directed by John Peyser
First aired 12-Nov-1963 (Episode 9 of Season 2)

CAST:
Regulars: Morrow, Jason, Hogan, Jalbert, Lowell, Peabody, Carter
Michel Petit as Bijou
Mindas Masuilis as German Machine Gunner #1
Dieter Jacoby as German Machine Gunner #2
Heinz Sadler as German Machine Gunner #3
Ed Tierney as Scarface Sgt.
Paul Busch as German Sergeant

Synopsis:

When the squad feeds a starving orphan, they acquire a permanent shadow. But is the adorable waif tagging along only out of gratitude and for a quick hand-out? Suspicions run high when the kid's information leads the squad into an ambush and gets Caje captured. Redeeming himself, Bijou gets the Germans hidden in a bunker to reveal their location, and leads the squad in a raid to destroy an oil refinery and rescue Caje.

Review — 3 bayonets:

Bijou (English translation: The Little Jewel), as played by Michel Petit, is charming, precocious, and calculating. He will look you in the eye and smile while stealing your wallet. He plays equally well on the sympathies of Americans and Germans. All who view this appealing child are enchanted, except for Kirby. Not only is he immune to Bijou's charms, but when he has had enough, he picks up the kid, holds him upside, and shakes him.

Saunders displays his soft spot for children. When Kirby tries to convince him that the kid has sold them out to the Germans, Saunders dismisses Kirby's concerns. He trusts the kid. Usually cautious in giving his affections and trust to adults, Saunders is defenseless against children. Morrow is chilling in the moment when he believes that Bijou betrayed him and the squad. The rage is barely suppressed, as he nearly strikes the boy.

This first *Combat!* script by Shirl Hendryx is well-crafted, without any extraneous filler, except for the teaser. "The Little Jewel" has one of the longest teasers, lasting over six-and-a-half minutes; it mostly consists of the squad walking through a rain-soaked village. ("The Letter" has the longest teaser.) It is an tedious opening for an otherwise well-paced episode. Fine performances by Jalbert, Hogan, and Lowell. I can even forgive the forced happy ending as Kirby gets sentimental, walking into the sunset hand-in-hand with Bijou.

About Filming the Episode:

"Peyser was one of our more practical-joke-inclined directors," remembers Tom Lowell. "Once, we were out on one of the berms. There was a shot of Vic coming over the hill, and he was supposed to go by camera, and then two Germans are supposed to come over the hill soon after. 'The Travels of Jamie McPheeters' was shooting on the next hill behind us, which was a western, and Royal Dano was the guest star. Peyser asked Royal to do something, so in the shot, you see Vic coming up over the hill and he goes by camera. And two seconds later, instead of the Germans, it's this Indian who pops up."

Notes, Oddities, and Bloopers:

• Lowell carries Saunders' .45 through most of the episode, after losing the B.A.R. in the river.

• The squad wears insta-dry uniforms that aren't even damp after the squad takes refuge in the river.

Beau Vanden Ecker costumes Warren Spahn as a German for the episode, "Glow Against the Sky."

Glow Against the Sky (044)

Written by Kay Lenard and Jess Carneol
Directed by Sutton Roley
First aired 05-Nov-1963 (Episode 8 of Season 2)

CAST:
Regulars: Morrow, Hogan, Jalbert, Lowell, Peabody
Bill Sargent as Huffman
Brian Avery as German Soldier
Bobby Hyatt as American Medic
Carl Carlsson as German Sergeant
Kurt Landen as German Sentry
Addison Meyers as German Medic
Kurt Kreuger as Capt. Neubauer
Warren Spahn (uncredited)

Synopsis:

Saunders' squad, with a critically wounded Billy Nelson, is trapped in the cellar of a destroyed house in a town taken over by Germans. With the German field hospital in view, Littlejohn and the squad helplessly watch Nelson suffer. Saunders decides to deliver Billy to the Germans so his life may be saved.

Review — 3.5 bayonets:

Fans who enjoy hurt/comfort stories will adore "Glow Against the Sky," the show's most excruciating example of this delightfully painful story type. Billy is wounded in a German barrage in the teaser. Throughout the rest of the show he is gang-comforted by Littlejohn, Saunders, Caje, Kirby, and even the Germans.

This episode features standout performances by Tom Lowell, Dick Peabody, and Vic Morrow. Tom Lowell's Billy Nelson is the All-American kid — and how difficult it is to watch this boy-next-door suffer. With a perfect sense of timing, Lowell switches easily from pained screaming to delirious humming, knowing just how far he can go before it becomes too much. "That was the most satisfying show for me, dramatically. In that scene where I was going nuts and Vic and everybody was trying to keep me quiet, I remember I got applause on the set for the first time ever. That was a thrill. That didn't happen very often."

This is Peabody's best work on *Combat!* Playing against Tom Lowell brought out a charm and honesty in his portrayal, and created a permanent place for "the big lug" in the squad. "Glow Against the Sky" is the big payoff for Peabody in his on-screen relationship with Lowell. No flaws or gaffes from Peabody, just consistent concern, tenderness, and a gnawing guilt. Beautifully acted, his, "Please, Sarge. I don't want you to do this," is so plaintive in its sincerity and pain. Lowell's face disappears in Peabody's massive hands as he tries to give a comfort beyond their ability.

Amidst all this artful suffering, Morrow manages to also pull out the stops. His emotional pain at watching Billy suffer is devastating. The end of act three is silently eloquent, when,

after surrendering Billy, Saunders discovers that he has Billy's blood on his hands and that an angry Littlejohn is looking daggers at him.

Director Sutton Roley brings this tiny tragedy of a dying boy into intimate focus. Grueling close-ups of Billy writhing in pain are cross-cut to views of three powerful men struggling impotently to provide him relief. Roley crams four-shots into a camera frame that can only comfortably hold one close-up. This harrowing proximity of camera lens to monumental pain and suffering draws the audience frightfully close to the action.

About Filming the Episode:

Tom Lowell remembers: "So much of it was studio stuff. We were out on location only a couple nights. I worked harder on that ['Glow'] than any of the other ones, because I wanted it to be a good performance. Most of the time, we'd get scripts the week before and everybody'd go in and see how many lines they had next week. Everyone would rag on each other, saying stuff like 'Hey, I only got three lines, what is this, your show?' So, when this one came along, I thought, 'Oh, wow.' I really jumped in with both feet."

Dick Peabody was unhappy with his work in this episode. "I think I was sort of insecure for the whole five years, in some respect, because I knew I didn't have the background. I had never done a play in my life, even in school ... And, of course, Lowell, whose father was head of the drama department at Sacramento State College, had been imbued with it from an early age and had done millions of plays and so forth. So he had the good sense just to play it the way he wanted to and ignore Sutton Roley [the director]. But everything Sutton Roley told me to do, I did, to my detriment ... He was a great lens guy, but I don't think he was very good with actors."

Notes, Oddities, and Bloopers:

- The pot that blew up in front of Tom Lowell in the opening segment was "a pretty good blast," Lowell recalls. "It knocked my helmet off."
- Saunders still needs to requisition his own knife; he several times borrows Kirby's in this episode.
- Saunders' aim is remarkable. He sprays a room of Germans, striking only the soldiers and missing the non-combatant medical staff.
- Continuity: Close-ups show Littlejohn hovering inches above Billy's face. The long shot, from over Saunders' shoulder, has him standing upright.
- When Saunders jumps in the truck, his helmet falls to the ground and is left behind. Next shot of Saunders in truck, he has his helmet.
- Famous pitcher, and Cy Young Award-winner, Warren Spahn makes his acting debut as a German soldier.

The Party (045)

Written by Edward J. Lakso
Directed by John Peyser
First aired 24-Dec-1963 (Episode 15 of Season 2)

CAST:

Regulars: Jason, Hogan, Jalbert, Peabody, Lowell
Guest Star Danielle DeMetz as Angelique
Biff Elliott as Rafferty
Terry Becker as Claybourne
Nick Georgiade as Londos
Monique Lemaire as Roxanne
Daniele Aubrey as Renee
Charles Kuenstle as Driver
Robert Sorrells as Reeves
George Davis as Old Man
Andrea Darvi as Jeannine

Synopsis:

Enjoying a pause in the American advance, Caje, Kirby, and Nelson try to advance themselves with a trio of French beauties. They clean themselves up to no avail — the ladies have planned a special party with three grim Sergeants. Though outranked, Caje, Kirby, and Nelson are not outmaneuvered. The would-be Lotharios scheme to separate the sergeants from the ladies.

Review — 3 bayonets:

The 1963 Christmas Eve episode, "The Party," is a delightful romp. As a change-of-pace, the squad are engaged in the war between the sexes. In the end, the ladies are victorious.

Hogan, Jalbert, and Lowell show their flair for comedy as they plot against the sergeants who would steal the objects of their desire. Hogan and Hanley play a charming comedy scene where Kirby unsuccessfully tries to con the lieutenant.

Andrea Darvi, last seen as the sorrowful orphan Micheline in "No Trumpets, No Drums," now plays it for laughs as a larcenous orphan who uses her smile to get into Billy's heart (and wallet). The three older orphans also use their smiles to good advantage, conning the sergeants and Saunders' men into providing a feast for their orphanage. Veteran character actors Biff Elliott, Nick Georgiade, and Terry Becker play the sergeants who dig themselves into a hole. George Davis, a semi-regular on the show playing French villagers, has a charming mime routine.

A highlight of the "The Party" is the guys' attempts to make themselves presentable. Their frolics in the river are joyous and rowdy. This is a rare episode in that the actors are clean for most of it. Much time was usually spent in makeup to get that proper grimy look. This week, the three soldiers look great in their $200 haircuts and clean, pressed, undamaged uniforms (where they got either on the frontlines is not explained).

Director John Peyser keeps the pace of this episode fast, never letting viewers pause to examine the plot or remember that somewhere a war is going on.

About Filming the Episode:

"The Party" was Tom Lowell's first on-screen kiss. "I had forgotten to tell my wife at that time about it. When she saw the episode on Christmas Eve, she was so mad. She would not speak to me for two days." Lowell is the only actor who got to kiss one of the female guests in this episode. Pierre Jalbert had to settle for stealing a kiss from the goose, which is in the background of one of the shots in the jeep.

Anatomy of a Patrol (046)

Written by Bob and Esther Mitchell
Directed by Bernard McEveety
First aired 26-Nov-1963 (Episode 11 of Season 2)

CAST:

Regulars: Morrow, Jason, Jalbert, Peabody, Lowell, Carter
James Caan as Sgt. Beckman
William Sargent as Blocker
Bill Smith as Richter
William Wellman as Woody
Kort Falkenberg as Meitner
Jeff Davis as Johnson
Juergen Seifert as Bernsdorf
Mark DeVries as Holweg
Bobby Hyatt as Gray

Synopsis:

Saunders' squad and a German patrol race to recover the pilot and reconnaissance photos from a downed American plane. Saunders engages in a battle of wits with his counterpart: another sergeant, similar to Saunders, who cares deeply for his squad. Each tries to accomplish his mission while keeping his men alive. But for one to succeed, the other must fail. Ultimately, Saunders outsmarts the German, but at a cost in both American and German lives.

Review — 4 bayonets:

"Anatomy of a Patrol" shows Saunders sublimely fulfilling his duty as the perfect squad leader. Combat! shows surprisingly little of Saunders commanding his men through a structured plan and engagement. In this episode, the audience is allowed inside the mind of Saunders as he leads his men on patrol. "Anatomy" shows Saunders not as the man or as the G.I., but as the squad leader. The story contrasts and compares him with his nemesis (German Sgt. Beckman played by James Caan).

The plot of this episode is indistinguishable from the 1957 submarine film The Enemy Below, right down to the use of a corpse as a diversion; the story is used in many television series, including classic Trek. Script writers Bob and Esther Mitchell make this tried-and-true story seem fresh.

The action sequences are especially exciting. The most spectacular fire fights filmed for Combat! were shot by director Bernard McEveety, and the best of them are in this episode. The same shots are used again and again in dozens of episodes that follow.

William Smith puts in a good job as Caan's right-hand-man (and the corpse that Caan must sacrifice for his mission).

Notes, Oddities, and Bloopers

• William Wellman, Jr., son of Hollywood maverick director "Wild" Bill Wellman, appears as Woody.

• The action sequences are especially exciting and are used again and again in dozens of episodes that follow.

What Are the Bugles Blowin' For?
(047 & 048)

Written by Edward J. Lakso
Directed by John Peyser
Part 1: Aired 03-Mar-1964 (Episode 25 of Season 2)
Part 2: Aired 10-Mar-1964 (Episode 26 of Season 2)

CAST:

Regulars: Morrow, Hanley, Hogan, Jalbert, Carter, Peabody, Lowell
Guest Star Ronald Howard as Captain Johns
Philippe Chapelle as Robaire
William Beckley as Corporal Joyce
Michael St. Clair as Marcher
Terence Mitchell as Newsy Meggs
James Forest as Giles
James Wixted as Mason
John Orchard as Robin (1st part only)
Richard Peel as Bolt
Eric Micklewood as Deeds
Richard Chambers as William
Erik Holland as German Lieutenant (2nd part only)
Norbert Meisel as German Corporal (2nd part only)
John Alderson as Sergeant Rawlings

Synopsis:

(part one) When Hanley orders an exhausted Saunders to hand carry a retreat order to a British unit whose radio is dead, Saunders tries to leave the squad regulars behind for a well-deserved rest. The squad opts to stay by him, unwilling to trust the Sarge's safety to green recruits. When told of the retreat, British Captain Johns refuses to abandon his position, and orders Saunders to help him hold his ground. Saunders knows staying means that the comrades who came to protect him, might die beside him.

(part two) Saunders wants to get his squad out from under the command of a stubbornly courageous British Captain who finds his command surrounded by Germans. Saunders also faces opposition from the British regulars, who blame him for the death of one of their own.

Review — 3 bayonets (both parts):

A story of obsession, "What Are the Bugles Blowin' For?" pits Saunders against a British officer (Capt. Johns, played by Ronald Howard) who is fixated on holding his ground, at any cost. Also in the mix, a French child determined to find his sister's assailant.

Actors and production staff most often mention the two-parter "What Are the Bugles Blowin' For?" as a favorite episode (right after "Hills Are for Heroes"). Both parts were filmed on MGM lot 2 at the old English train station.

Veteran British actor Ronald Howard gives a superb performance as the oh-so-proper British officer. He was the son of film great Leslie Howard (Ashley Wilkes in *Gone with the Wind*). "Nice man," recalls Carter. "I liked him very much." The scenes between Carter and Howard are excellent, as are all the scenes in the makeshift hospital. Vic Morrow, comforting a wounded and delirious Caje, is moving as the Sarge tries to be confident in a hopeless situation, and fails to hide his guilt over bringing Caje to this place.

About Filming the Episode:

Pierre Jalbert rates this episode highly. "I'm talking about texture, physical application, the story was also rather fascinating. I think it was done excessively well. The texture of it felt really real. When you can imagine that this was done in about ten days, it's mind-boggling."

Director John Peyser worked closely with special effects master A.D. Flowers to create the sensational pyrotechnics. Tom Lowell says, "That was fun. A lot of night shooting. Setting up the explosives, watching that all go off, was really a trip. Massive explosions. Went down the whole train. And I remember John had this big long dolly shot with cranes and everything, the train blowing up, and Vic running. It was a very well-done show."

Notes, Oddities, and Bloopers:

• At the end, while Saunders is walking the French boy toward Hanley, in the background, above the fence, sixties-style traffic whizzes by.

• The opening barrage is the final barrage from "Far From the Brave," with rain overlaid on it.

• This episode re-uses the stunt from "Glow Against The Sky," where the stunt double for Billy performs a backflip into an existing crater.

• The episode title is the opening line of the Rudyard Kipling poem "Danny Deever."

Saunders' squad aids a trapped British unit in "What Are the Bugles Blowin' For?"

COMBAT!

Barrage (049)

Written by Edward J. Lakso
Directed by Sutton Roley
First aired 10-Dec-1963 (Episode 13 of Season 2)

CAST:

Regulars: Jason, Morrow, Hogan, Jalbert
Guest Star Alf Kjellin as Hans
Ed Deemer as German Soldier #4
Peter Hellman as German Soldier #3
Frank Killmond as Clark
John Rayner as American Sergeant
Horst Evers as German Soldier #1
Tom Pace as German Soldier #2
Dieter Jacoby as Machine Gunner #1
Mathias Uitz as Machine Gunner #2
John Crawford as Gunnar

Synopsis:

After failed night patrols, the squad is ordered to try by daylight to find the artillery that's tearing apart the American lines. In a suicide mission, all are hurt or killed. A wounded Saunders crawls into a cave, where he finds Hans, a German deserter, who binds Saunders' wounds. When Hans' sergeant arrives, he convinces them he captured Saunders. When the cave collapses, trapping everyone, the deserter must decide on his loyalties.

Review — 3 bayonets:

The episode opens with the squad returning in defeat from a night patrol. Hanley delivers the bad news that they have to go back. When he says "if one of us makes it, our mission will be a success," few viewers will be surprised to discover that the one who makes it is Saunders.

Originally titled "The Deserter," this episode shows a man too scared to run and too scared to stand and fight. Swedish actor Alf Kjellin makes his second *Combat!* appearance as Hans, the German deserter. This role of a cowardly ex-musician, afraid of war and of his sergeant, is a sharp contrast to the confident officer he played in "Just for the Record."

Kjellin and Saunders work well together, creating a fascinating chemistry in their scenes in the cave. Morrow turns in his usual strong job as he makes Saunders carefully exploit Hans' doubts and fears, to Saunders' advantage. Alternately cajoling and commanding, Saunders plays on the musician's emotions.

John Crawford, who plays the German sergeant, is a longtime character actor, working in Hollywood since 1945. He was Sheriff Bridges on "The Waltons" and guested on "Star Trek," "Charlie's Angels" and others.

Thunder from the Hill (050)

Written by Edward J. Lakso
Directed by John Peyser
First aired 17-Dec-1963 (Episode 14 of Season 2)

CAST:

Regulars: Jason, Hogan, Jalbert, Peabody
Peter Whitney as Massine
Robert Carricart as Diebold
John Neris as Jean
Ben Wright as Boulange
George Sawaya as Pierre
Jacques Sorel as Andre

Synopsis:

Hanley and men are sent into German-occupied France to meet with the leader of the Free French Guerrillas. But their guide, Massine, refuses to lead them to their rendezvous unless Hanley helps him raid a German depot. Succumbing to the military blackmail, Hanley helps the resistance fighter procure weapons for his own private war.

Review — 1 bayonet:

One bayonet for this slow-paced episode that saddles Hanley with another irrational outsider (played by Peter Whitney). Hanley's supposed ally becomes the major obstacle to completing the mission. For the plot to work, the audience must feel sympathy toward Massine, an annoying character behaving irrationally. I get as frustrated as the Hanley character when I watch this episode.

In the technical aspects, the show is adequate. Some of the camera work in the rock quarry is remarkable. The actors and camera crew set up on a hillside, with lots of loose shale and pebbles for effect. These scenes were shot in a rock quarry at Bronson Canyon.

By second season, director John Peyser has yet to hit his stride as a *Combat!* director. This show needed a firmer hand behind the camera. Edward J. Lakso's script is atypical for him. His usual strength is squad interactions, but character development is nearly non-existent for the show's regulars in this story.

Notes, Oddities, and Bloopers:

- One small pigeon makes a meal for four soldiers? Must not be very hungry.
- The World War II-era truck is authentic, including the wood-burning engine.
- When Hanley puts his mind to it, he organizes a great midnight requisition expedition.

The Pillbox (051)

Teleplay by Don Tait
Story by Ted Pettus
Directed by Vic Morrow
First aired 07-Jan-1964 (Episode 17 of Season 2)

CAST:

Regulars: Jason, Hogan, Carter
Henry Horman as Meisner
Glen Cannon as Runner
Paul Busch as German Lieutenant
Ray Baxter as German Trucker #1
Ed Deemer as German Trucker #2
Joseph Turkel as Klimmer
Guest stars Warren Oates as Stark
and Albert Paulsen as Dorfmann

Synopsis:

Pausing to help a wounded G.I. from L Company, Hanley is separated from his retreating troops. Caught behind the German offensive, Hanley and the wounded soldier take refuge in an abandoned pillbox. Hanley, after unwillingly capturing three Germans, is wounded and unable to control his prisoners. Partially crippled, the captor Hanley is as trapped as his prisoners. Stark must have medical care, but the only way Hanley

Albert Paulsen and director, Vic Morrow, in "The Pill Box."

can get that help, is to leave behind three murdered prisoners.

Review — 3 bayonets:

Vic Morrow's first directing project for *Combat!* was a solo acting effort for Hanley, "The Pillbox." Morrow did an excellent job directing this taut morality play. He shows the influence of Altman's directing style and tips his hat to the classic war film *All Quiet on the Western Front.* He also shows an interesting personal directing style just developing.

He uses little background music inside the pillbox. Leonard Rosenman's themes merely lead in and out of commercials. Instead of music, Morrow relies on natural sounds for the background: thunder, rain, trucks, and labored breathing, something he owes to Altman's style.

Rick Jason is superb in "The Pillbox" playing the multi-layered dilemmas tearing Hanley apart. Warren Oates (as Stark) is outstanding as a soldier wanting to live at any cost. Director Morrow weaves a bond between Hanley and Stark that is both tender and grueling. Albert Paulsen, as the opportunistic Dorfmann, makes his third appearance on *Combat!* in two years. In his first appearance in "Forgotten Front," he also

played a prisoner (named Dorfmann), whose fate Saunders had to decide.

By following the book and taking charge early in the episode, Hanley boxes himself into a corner (both literally and figuratively). He creates the moral quagmire and finds no satisfactory solution. Unlike Saunders in "Forgotten Front," Hanley makes no decision. He waits. A well-timed artillery barrage eventually takes the choice out of Hanley's hands.

About Filming the Episode:

Rick Jason remembers: "I have to pick up Albert Paulsen and open up this big, heavy door, and walk away with him. That was the closing shot of the show, walking into the distance carrying this guy who weighs about 190 pounds. As I walk away from the camera, I'm mumbling 'You heavy son-of-a-bitch . . .' It's the only thing that gave me the strength not to drop him in the middle of the shot . . . I loved working with Vic as a director. He was so considerate of his fellow actors. Always knew what he wanted from you and how to get it."

Notes, Oddities, and Bloopers:

•*Combat!* often goes to extremes to deprive actors of weapons, but this is the most extreme: a tank to take out one carbine.
•Lovely shot of Hanley flinging rain cape over the camera. Vic wanted that particular shot to give a black screen for a cut.

Gideon's Army (052)

Written by Charles B. Smith
Directed by John Peyser
First aired 31-Dec-1963 (Episode 16 of Season 2)

CAST:

Regulars: Morrow, Jason, Hogan, Jalbert, Lowell, Peabody, Carter
Milton Selzer as Colonel Glinski
Albert Szabo as Karacz
Reggie Nalder as Man With One Eye
Ray Baxter as Cougher
Marc Cavell as Jan
Peter Hellman as German Sergeant
Dean Heyde as German Soldier
Lou Robb as German Lieutenant
Richard Jaeckel as Sgt. Buxman

Synopsis:

Saunders and his squad liberate a concentration camp of sick and starving Polish laborers. Unwilling to leave these helpless men behind, Saunders lies to Hanley in order to buy time and get transport for them. When a German column approaches, Saunders enlists the aid of these unarmed men in convincing the enemy that they are outnumbered.

Review — 1.5 bayonets:

"Gideon's Army" is Combat's only venture into the holocaust — pity they did it so tentatively. The episode starts out well: the first act is rather excellent, the second act still above average, but then it slides rapidly downhill.

This story avoids the ethnicity of the prisoners, simply referring to them as D.P.s (displaced persons), just off-the-street Poles, not Jews or members of any of the other groups that the Nazis targeted. The likelihood of finding Polish D.P.s in France at the time was low. The death trains ran from West to East. The Nazi-labeled "undesirables" from France were shipped to Poland, not from Poland. This labor camp (and there were lots in France) should have been peopled with Frenchmen.

What rescues this story, as usual, is Saunders. Some excellent moments as he tries to win an unwinnable situation (with an off-stage assist from Hanley). That radio call between Hanley and Saunders is classic, epitomizing their relationship caught somewhere between friendship and duty.

Director John Peyser creates some beautiful visual images in this episode. He has great long shots from the top of the guard tower and across the prison yard. One sweeping shot going from a closeup of a nervous Billy high in a tree down to a stoic Littlejohn on the ground is magnificent.

About Filming the Episode:

Conlan Carter did the Bible reading scene in one take. "We didn't even rehearse it. I just took the Bible and said 'Why don't we shoot this thing. Cause it's gonna be tough to get it. You might as well run the camera and if it works, fine, and if not . . .' And it just rolled out. I'll never forget that. It was one of the few shows they did that with, the voice-over thing."

Notes, Oddities, and Bloopers:
•Richard Jaeckel enters battle with an MP40, but surrenders with a 98K rifle.
•Saunders asks an awful lot when he orders the squad to let one German survive the shootout. With all the lead flying, how did they decide which one would survive?
•Watch at the top of act two when two Germans burst into the house between Billy and Saunders; they both open up, killing the Germans, but should also have killed each other in their cross-fire.

The General and the Sergeant

(O53)

Written by Gustave Field
Directed by Bernard McEveety
First aired 14-Jan-1964 (Episode 17 of Season 2)

CAST:
Regulars: Morrow, Jason, Hogan, Jalbert, Lowell, Peabody, Carter
Guest Star John Dehner as General Armand Bouchard
Christian Pasques as First Young Man
Lucien Lanvin as Second Young Man
Maria Schroeder as Young girl #1
Gabrielle Rossillon as Young girl #2
Renaud Villedieu as Boy
Mathias Uitz as German Soldier #1
Denise Alexander as Jacqueline

Synopsis:

In a newly liberated town, a former French general tries to usurp command of Saunders' squad. Saunders takes pity on this old man and plays along. The squad continues on to a destroyed French castle. They are caught inside when a German armored convoy stops to refuel. They are saved from discovery by the general. But his next assistance proves not so

useful, as he gives the squad instructions that walk them into an ambush. Eventually, the general redeems himself, the squad wins the day, and the episode ends with the squad and the lieutenant on military parade through town.

Review — 2 bayonets:

"The General and the Sergeant" is a solid, middle-of-the-road entertainment. John Dehner as an over-the-hill general gives a touching performance. Dehner is perhaps too good in his scenes where he makes a fool of himself. These are uncomfortable to watch. Denise Alexander (the charming-and-sensitive French girl from "No Time For Pity") puts in a good show again as a charming-and-sensitive French girl.

When this story strives for pathos, it falls short. This episode works best where the script, direction, and the omnipresent background music is applied with a light touch. Nice directing, nice acting, a fun script that, though on the saccharin side, still delivers entertaining moments. Forget the bulk of the episode, the best bits are watching Saunders try to keep a straight face with the antics of an old man trying to save face. Dick Peabody's grin during the inspection is also priceless. From the first meeting where Saunders endures being kissed in public on both cheeks, to the end where the squad parades by in tribute, it is obvious that Dehner and Morrow are two pros who know how to get the most out of their camera time. Except for a scene where Hanley ribs Saunders, but then must play bad cop to Saunders good cop, the rest of the episode is just filler to hold together an hour of film.

Dehner was a TV and Hollywood staple for fifty years. A great character actor, he was a regular on "The Betty White Show," "The Westerner," "The Virginian," "The Doris Day Show," "The Don Knotts Show" and several other TV series, as well as appearing in over seventy films.

Notes, Oddities, and Bloopers:
•Lovely short scene between Saunders and Hanley on the road. One of the nicer moments where their friendship shows. Hanley actually teases Saunders.
•This episode was originally titled "La Retread."
•Poor Saunders, he gets a kiss from the general, but only a handshake from the beautiful girl. Kirby, as usual, has his priorities. His only interest in the town is the caliber of its ladies.
•This is the most restrained (cheap) liberation scene in *Combat!* No flags, flowers, wine, or extras. This village only has a dozen citizens.
•In the map scene, the general is placing pins indicating that the Allies are still on the beaches at Normandy, but discussing the war as if the Americans have advanced far into France. When saying that Patton is striking straight at the heart of the enemy, at Berlin, he's pointing to Belgium.
•The cemetery the general visits is the same cemetery used in "The Furlough."
•The tombstone for the General's wife reads "R.I.P. Elizabeth Ashley Bouchard." This episode came out the same year as

The Carpetbaggers, which launched Elizabeth Ashley's career.
•Saunders wears a bayonet scabbard on his pistol belt during the town scenes. But later in the chateau, it is gone. When Saunders grabs the German from behind, he must twist him around toward Caje where Caje can then knife him.

The Hostages (054)

Written by Richard Adams
Directed by Ted Post
Produced by Richard Goldstone
First aired 28-Jan-1964 (Episode 20 of Season 2)

CAST:
Regulars: Morrow, Carter, Jalbert
Guest Star Mark Richman as Capt. Aptmeyer
Dick Patterson as Barnarbo
Hans Gudegast as Ecktmann
Ken Berry as Motor Sgt.
Tom Peters as Commo Man
Lew Gallo as Mororcycle MP
Joseph Perry as 1st Sgt.

Synopsis:

With Caje and Saunders held hostage by Germans in an American-occupied town, Doc must use his wits to deceive both Americans and Germans in an effort to save the lives of his friends. Helping himself to an ambulance, Doc provides the Germans an exit from town, only to discover that the German wants to use the Americans to trip a mine field.

Review — 3 bayonets:

Conlan Carter shines as the focus of this story. If anyone still questions how this second medic differs from Steven Rogers' Doc, this episode provides the definitive answers. No sensitive, introspective, reluctant warrior here.

Conlan Carter's Doc takes charge from the get-go. When Saunders orders Doc to abandon both him and Caje to their fate, Doc ignores the order and finds his own solution. With cool eyes, he stands up to a German officer who has a machine gun trained right on him. With a pleasant grin, this Arkansas boy looks his fellow soldiers right in the eye and lies through his teeth — with unquestionable sincerity. When scheming, wits, charm, and lies fail to free the hostages, the medic must become the soldier. He well deserved his Emmy nomination for this episode.

Guest star Mark Richman is appropriately oily as the German aristocrat who treats the Americans as beasts. Hans Gudegast puts in a fine supporting role as Ecktmann, who keeps Saunders and Caje at bay, and dies for his efforts.

The show features a large supporting cast, giving some great moments in small scenes. Ken Berry's motor pool sergeant is charming and Tom Peters plays an exceptional mooch as the comm man.

About Filming the Episode:

Conlan Carter was surprised by the Emmy nomination: "I woke up one morning with the telegram and I called my agent and he said 'What? Read me the telegram.' Cause he thought a friend of mine might be playing a joke on me . . . I didn't win,

of course, but it was a nice thing and I still have the little plaque."

Notes, Oddities, and Bloopers:

•While Doc is driving the ambulance through the countryside, one shot shows tall buildings through the window of the ambulance.
•Continuity errors: as Saunders exits the shower with unfastened boots, he enters the barber shop with perfectly fastened boots; Caje buttons his shirt in the shower room, but when he exits the shower room the shirt is unbuttoned.
•Again, those wonderful insta-dry, one-size-fits-all uniforms.
•Doc tightens lugnuts on the American ambulance counter-clockwise (should be clockwise).
•The "gunshot" through the windshield of the ambulance: unfortunately, the later camera shots through the windshield show it up to be what it is, a Vaseline smear on the windshield. Nice effect from the outside, not from the inside.
•After the ambulance crash, when Richman gets up, he has no pistol in his holster. A second later, there's a .45 in the holster.
•Saunders is shot with his own Thompson.

A Silent Cry (055)

Written by Edward J. Lakso
Directed by Bernard McEveety
First aired 18-Feb-1964 (Episode 23 of Season 2)

CAST:
Regulars: Morrow, Jason, Hogan, Jalbert
Jacques Roux as Fontaine
Lili Valenty as Renee LeClair
Titus Moede as Marks
Guy deVestel as Andre LeClair
Ed Deemer as German Lieutenant
Ed Gilbert as German Captain
Robert Crawford, Jr. as Jaques
Richard Anderson as Sergeant Perkins

Synopsis:

A sergeant specialist with an attitude is once again attached to Saunders' outfit. Radio technician Sgt. Perkins is a pacifist/philosopher who finds Saunders and all soldiers incomprehensible. Saunders must take Perkins behind the lines to deliver radios to the French underground. When Perkins stops at a French farmhouse to repair the master station, the Germans take a fix on their location and surround the house.

Review — 1 bayonet:

Once again Saunders is saddled with a mission he doesn't want, troops that should be resting instead of marching, and a brilliant but obnoxious Sergeant with unique technical expertise. Lee Marvin did it better earlier in this same season in "A Bridge at Chalons." And Jack Lord will do it marginally better later in "The Linesman."

In this incarnation of the well-explored plot, the epiphany of Richard Anderson's obnoxious sergeant comes in the guise of a young boy who shares his interest in radios and Shakespeare. Perkins (played by Richard Anderson, later of "The Six Million Dollar Man") turns around his life when he meets a French boy just like him, but one willing to fight.

This one-bayonetter has a pedantic script, lackluster direction, and another cute French kid. This is a some-things-are-worth-fighting-for story that does not convince.

Notes, Oddities, and Bloopers:
•The Germans' radio direction-finder vehicle is an American ambulance.
•The episode was originally titled "The Formula." I'm not sure "A Silent Cry" is an improvement.
•Footage is re-used from "Hill 256" and the well-trodden wooden footbridge makes an appearance.

Eyes of the Hunter (056)
Written by Esther and Bob Mitchell
Directed by Bernard McEveety
Produced by Richard Goldstone
First aired 21-Jan-1964 (Episode 19 of Season 2)
CAST:
Regulars: Morrow, Jason, Hogan, Jalbert, Lowell, Peabody
Co-starring Ed Nelson as Burgess
Erin Holland as German Corporal
Joe di Reda as Sergeant Calder
Hans Difflip as German Lieutenant
Ed Deemer as Machine Gunner
Joseph Sirola as Casper
Bill Smith as German Sergeant

Synopsis:
Burgess is the only survivor of an earlier patrol to knock out a German observation post. He volunteers to show Saunders and his men the way. But Littlejohn suspects that this fearless soldier has an objective other than the OP. When Caje and Billy fall into German hands, Burgess is ready to write them off.

Review — 1.5 bayonets:
Director Bernard McEveety excels at action sequences, so this episode low on action and high on dialogue gives him little to work with. This script by Esther and Bob Mitchell is a confused tale of a mysterious survivor who has a reputation for no good. The character development is confused, as is the plotting.

As usual, the squad rescues this episode — not their actions, but their acting. Morrow, Jalbert, Hogan, and Lowell show the great teamwork that made this show so watchable. Peabody especially provides some excellent moments, showing the best aspects of this good-natured, decent character.

About Filming the Episode:
Rick Jason shared that Dick Peabody is as decent, humble, and self-effacing as the character that he played. "He cannot come to grips with the fact that he is special. ... He considers himself lucky to even have been employed and never considers to this day the impact he had on the show. And the impact that he continues to have on the show."

Counter-Punch (057)
Written by Kay Lenard and Jess Carneol
Directed by John Peyser
First aired 11-Feb-1964 (Episode 22 of Season 2)
CAST:
Regulars: Morrow, Jalbert
Co-starring Steve Gravers as Martinez
and Malachi Throne as Moorwood
Anthony Holland as Cutner
George Savalas as Cooper
James Davidson as Bowers
Eugene Borden as Roget

Synopsis:
When battalion headquarters is overrun, Saunders and Caje pick up rear-echelon stragglers, including a technical sergeant who clashes with him over strategy and command. With a motley assortment of unmilitary soldiers, Saunders decides to commandeer a train loaded with Germans to make a break for the American lines.

Review — 2 bayonets:
Whenever I watch this episode, I can't quite remember how it ends. The second half hour does not quite match up with the first. Both are good "episodes," but darned if I can figure out why screenwriters Kay Lenard and Jess Carneol went from point A to point B.

The beginning deals with Saunders gathering the misfits under his wings. Steve Gravers is properly grating as the know-it-all, and Malachi Throne is excellent as the bindlestiff Moorwood. When this ragtag team encounters a French train filled with Germans, the story takes on a new direction, turning into a story with similarities to Von Ryan's Express, a best-selling novel released the same year as this episode.

"Counter-Punch" takes advantage of the availability of MGM's classic steam engine. This historic steam locomotive, old No. 11, originally served the Virginia and Truckee Railway, running on the Reno-Carson City-Virginia City circuit. Bought by MGM in the forties, the locomotive appeared in many classic MGM films. It now has an honored place in Old Tucson.

About Filming the Episode:
John Peyser had the prop department provide him a holster and pistol that fired blanks. He would wear the pistol on his hip when filming and used to fire it at planes flying overhead.

Notes, Oddities, and Bloopers:
•Great archival footage use. Planes strafing the train are P-51s.
•While squad is walking down road, the sound of a propeller-driven airplane cuts in and out underneath the music.

Mail Call (058)
Written by Arnold Belgard
Directed by Bernard McEveety
Produced by Richard Goldstone
First aired 04-Feb-1964 (Episode 21 of Season 2)

CAST:
Regulars: Jason, Morrow, Hogan, Jalbert, Peabody, Carter, Lowell
Ray Fulmer as Holmes
Fred Harris as Smitty
Ed Deemer as German #1
Mike Masters as Non Com
James Best as Trenton
Paul Busch (uncredited)

Synopsis:

The squad is concerned over Saunders' depression after receiving a letter from home. They are surprised to see him take his frustration out on Pvt. Trenton, the new recruit. Saunders sees past Trenton's good-natured act and faked injuries, and forces him to face his own fears. Saunders is fearful too, of the fate of his brother, who he learns is MIA at Okinawa.

Review — 4 bayonets:

The script for "Mail Call" is the epitome of what makes *Combat!* work: squad interactions, personalities, the human interest into the lives and characters of the soldiers themselves, not just the blood-and-guts realities of war. To survive on the front, soldiers only had each other to depend on. Frontline squads survived as a team, or they didn't survive at all. In "Mail Call," the squad closes ranks to protect one of its own.

This episode underscores the cohesiveness of the squad, that they genuinely care about each other's welfare. They may have been clumsy in their attempts to help Saunders, but they do try. Thankfully, these manly men of the sixties do not sit around and discuss their inner feelings, as is common in nineties TV shows. They instead take action.

Combat!, too, survives today because of the teamwork of its cast. This strong ensemble acting is very evident in "Mail Call." Each character has his place in the squad and in the story. The opening sequence is particularly delightful to watch, as the squad gathers round the jeep, sharing equally in each other's mail and in their joy. But not in their problems. Saunders keeps all at a distance, even Hanley, who fails to draw him out by reminding him of their long-term friendship.

Guest star James Best has been a staple on TV since the sixties. Including his work as Sheriff Coltrane on "The Dukes of Hazzard," he has appeared in over 600 television shows.

About Filming the Episode:

Guest star James Best recalls, "Vic was a very nice guy, really friendly. It was a pleasure to work with the whole cast. A very congenial shoot. Some of 'em aren't that congenial. On those shows, you'd really look forward to going to work. Of course, the *Combat!* thing was interesting to me, because I was in WWII. I was a radio gunner in a B-17."

Notes, Oddities, and Bloopers:

• The squad fights 10th regiment, 25th Panzers.
• During exchange between Saunders and Billy, while Caje is in the doorway, his boots are unbuckled. When Caje comes up to Saunders, the boots are buckled.
• The driver of the jeep in the opening sequence has an appearing/disappearing helmet.

• In scene in Hanley's office, Hanley wants to send out Saunders' patrol in two hours, but Saunders buys them extra time. But when Saunders sees his men, he says they're moving out in two hours.
• The battle for Okinawa was in '45. Since the Americans are still fighting in Normandy, this episode takes place in '44. The only way Saunders' brother could be MIA in Okinawa is if he was shot down there, not if he took part in the landing.
• Saunders has a hole in his pants' crotch in last scene.

The Hunter (059)

Written by Edward J. Lakso
Directed by Sutton Roley
First aired 25-Feb-1964 (Episode 24 of Season 2)

CAST:
Regulars: Morrow, Hogan
Guest Star Alfred Ryder as Heismann
Ed Tierney as Brunner

Synopsis:

In an abandoned French winery, Saunders and Kirby become the prey of a fanatic German captain. He picks off Kirby with his specially made rifle. But Kirby, even wounded and captured, continues putting up a fight. With the captain's aide dead, Saunders and the captain engage in a private fight-to-the-death, until a well-timed barrage saves the day.

Review — 2 bayonets:

Guest star Alfred Ryder plays German Capt. Heisman, a former professional hunter who keeps Saunders in his sights. Much of the story centers around the two radios, and each side trying to prevent the other from getting word to their troops. Jack Hogan is superb as a Kirby that will not give up. Bleeding and in pain, he still manages to destroy the German field radio behind the back of his captor. He has some nice, in-character moments, such as when entering the winery, he immediately checks the wine supply.

By the fourth act, the battle has become personal. Saunders is unarmed, having abandoned his jammed Thompson, but he has successfully warned the Americans by radio. Morrow and Kirby are excellent in their scenes together and the revelations about Kirby's home life help round-out the character. By reading Kirby's letter from home, Captain Heisman finds out that Kirby's family calls him Bill, that he has a brother George, and a mother that lives in Chicago.

Notes, Oddities, and Bloopers:

• Kirby with M1 and B.A.R.
• Filmed at Mission Valley winery.
• Normandy has no mountains, so the magnificent views of snow-covered Mt. San Antonio rising majestically above the winery are out-of-place.
• Paul Busch is the voice on the German's field radio.
• Stuntman Earl Parker doubles both Ryder and Morrow.
• This episode has the series' smallest cast: four on-camera actors, two radio voices, and one stunt double.

Rudy Dolan, a member of a German raiding party, ties a terrified Anjanette Comer to a tree in this scene from "Weep No More."

Weep No More (060)
Written by Edward J. Lakso
Directed by Ted Post
First aired 17-Mar-1964 (Episode 27 of Season 2)

CAST:
Regulars: Jason, Hogan, Jalbert
Guest Star Anjanette Comer as Annette
Rick Traeger as German Captain
Rudy Dolan as 2nd German Soldier
Charles DeVries as 1st German Soldier
Kurt Lewin as German Corporal
John Shay as Doctor
Ted Knight as German Sergeant

Synopsis:
This rehash of the episode "Battle of the Roses" has Hanley, Kirby, and Caje encountering a mentally addled, but beautiful, young woman. She feels safe only in one place, so Hanley removes her from that place of safety. The addled girl escapes and returns to her refuge. Hanley goes back to rescue her, only to find that the Germans have moved in.

Review — 2 bayonets:
I did not care much for this premise when Rik Volaertes wrote this story for Saunders in "Battle of the Roses." I like leftovers even less, so when this cold dish is re-served for Hanley's use, as a fan of Hanley I relish the close-ups and try to ignore the story.

The direction by Ted Post serves more to confuse the action than focus it. The mood shots of the woman as she lashes out in terror are awkward, bordering on silly (especially realizing that her makeup and lashes remain perfect though her mind, hair, and clothing are in total disarray). She and Hanley roll around artfully for a bit, and, par for the course, the Germans have more than war in mind when they see that pretty face. Once again, a helpless female must be rescued from a fate-worse-than-death by a brave American G.I. Ted Knight plays the lustful German; Anjanette Comer plays the lustee.

One plot complaint: why did neither Kirby or Caje go looking for Hanley? They knew where he went. He turns up missing for hours, you would think somebody might check to see if their lieutenant is still alive.

The episode has my favorite exchange between Kirby and Lieutenant. When Hanley says "If the Krauts start moving in, you know what to do," Kirby replies, "Yes, sir. Panic."

About Filming the Episode:
Rick Jason praises actor Ted Knight, saying he was underrated, people not realizing the skill comedy requires. Jason says he was also a fine dramatic actor and a pleasure to work with, a man of simple good humor. Knight is best remembered as the news anchor on "The Mary Tyler Moore Show." In the eighties, Rick Jason guest starred on Knight's television series "Too Close for Comfort."

Notes, Oddities, and Bloopers:
• Like all addled-but-beautiful young French women in *Combat!*, this one dances and plays that popular record (also played in "War of the Roses" and "Any Second Now").
• Same farm as "Just for the Record."
• Ted Knight appeared last on *Combat!* in "The Volunteer." In real-life he was a decorated WWII soldier.

The Short Day of Private Putnam (061)
Written by Esther and Bob Mitchell
Directed by Bernard McEveety
First aired 24-Mar-1964 (Episode 28 of Season 2)

CAST:
Regulars: Jason, Morrow, Hogan, Carter, Jalbert, Peabody, Lowell
Beau Bridges as Orville Putnam
with Robert Sampson as Harvey
and with Lilyan Chauvin as Fauvette
Charles Francisco as Sgt. Darden (uncredited)
Paul Busch as Gunner (uncredited)
Richard Tretter as Ambulance Driver (uncredited)

Synopsis:
Unbeknownst to the squad, their newest replacement, Pvt. Orville Putnam (Beau Bridges), is only fifteen years old. Putting on a false front, "Putt" alienates the squad and rebuffs Billy's attempt at friendship. The squad scoffs at his bravado and his odd interest in collecting leaves. When tested under fire, Putt is unprepared emotionally and panics when his friend Harvey is killed beside him. But in the end, his keen eye and botanical hobby save him and the squad from snipers.

Review — 3 bayonets:
As in "Mail Call," this is a story highlighting the squad's cohesiveness and as in "Rear Echelon Commandos," the squad is saved by a skill they first scoffed at.

The premise, that a fifteen-year-old is not emotionally equipped for war, has little historical basis. Throughout history, teenage boys have carried arms and fought heroically. Despite the comfortable mid-life look to the *Combat!* squad, World War II was fought largely by teens. Rick Jason, Dick Peabody, and Shecky Greene were all in their teens when they served in WWII. Fifteen was young by WWII standards, (though a few "men" of that age did serve gallantly), but soldiers of that age and younger were staples of earlier armies. Some military historians think teens are better suited to war, because they have less concept of their own mortality and, unlike adults, they can be convinced that they like it.

About Filming the Episode:

Tom Lowell: "I had no idea that would be my last episode. At the time we were still in negotiations for the contract." Tom Lowell enjoyed the episode because of Beau Bridges. Actors his own age only rarely appeared on *Combat!* "Dennis Robertson, Beau Bridges, or somebody like that came along every once in a while. The irony, of course, is in WWII, they were all young kids."

Notes, Oddities, and Bloopers:

• The German snipers wear U.S. Army camouflage jackets.
• Hanley's radioman gets the call signs reversed, saying "Checkmate King Two, this is White Rook." But in the next transmission, he gets it right.

Rescue (062)

Written by Edward J. Lakso
Directed by Ted Post
First aired 31-Mar-1964 (Episode 29 of Season 2)

CAST:

Regulars: Jason
Co-starring Edward Binns as Col. Johnson
and Guy Stockwell as Jerry Bacon
Paul Busch as German Lieutenant
Ed Deemer as German Sergeant
Tom Pace as Rear Sentry
Dean Heyde as Front Sentry
Edmund Gilbert as German Private
Stephen Lander as First Soldier
David Brandon as German Soldier

Synopsis:

A shell-shocked Hanley is captured by a German, who then is shot by another "German." This soldier claims to be an American who just escaped from the Germans, leaving behind his badly wounded Colonel. Hanley and he return to the German-held farm to rescue the Colonel. When they are safely away, the Colonel pumps Hanley for troop information and the lieutenant suspects that he has been had.

Review — 3 bayonets:

"Rescue" is a strong Hanley episode with some surprising twists. Ted Post, in his last directing assignment for *Combat!*, provides tight direction and a fast pace for this clever script by Edward J. Lakso. The direction and pace are so good, viewers

may hardly notice that the story is too thin to fill an hour. A pity that the concept of B plots was not yet in vogue. It would have been nice to see what Saunders and the squad were doing. They did manage to misplace their Lieutenant an awful lot.

This episode was originally titled "The Trap," which probably gave away the plot twist too quickly. "Rescue" features some exceptional hand-to-hand fight sequences. (I believe the stunt double was Walt Davis.)

About Filming the Episode:

Rick Jason says, "I did almost all the stunts on my first series ["The Case of the Dangerous Robin"], except stair stunts." When he got to *Combat!*, he insisted on a stuntman. He thought he was getting too old for it, and he thought he was taking a job from someone else. "I wouldn't even jump over a brook without a stuntman."

Notes, Oddities, and Bloopers:

• Hanley passes out at the top of the episode and then staggers through act one. But as soon as he learns of a Colonel to rescue, he is fine.
• Opening action footage is re-used from "A Distant Drum" and "The Pillbox."
• How cliche to name the German infiltrator "Jerry." But why does the German officer continue to refer to him by his American cover name even after they've been found out?
• Good make-up job throughout. Hanley gets cold-cocked with a rifle butt about three-quarters through the show. In following scenes, the swelling gets progressively larger.
• Why did they fake having a dead German in the house? Aren't there enough real dead bodies around that they could have used? Seems like a real easy way for their plot to be revealed —Hanley should be able to recognize a dead body by this point in the war.
• Military details: Commanding Officer of the 361st is Colonel Dale, his exec is Major Barns.

Command (063)

Written by Kay Lenard and Jess Carneol
Directed by Bernard McEveety
First aired 07-Apr-1964 (Episode 30 of Season 2)

CAST:

Regulars: Morrow, Jason, Hogan, Jalbert, Peabody
Guest star Joseph Campanella as Lt. Douglas
William Arvin as Adams
Dennis Robertson as Bronson
Louis Mercier as Jean Bayard
Charles Giorgi as Anton
Danny Klega as German Lieutenant

Synopsis:

When a wounded Hanley is shipped to England for recovery, a temporary platoon commander makes life miserable for the squad. On a mission to destroy a bridge, Lt. Douglas makes sure the men go completely by-the-book, while taking all the risks for himself. His brutally strict treatment of the men covers his fears that he will lose the men under his command — just as he lost his entire platoon his last time in command.

Review — 3 bayonets:

Joseph Campanella is the hard-headed and haunted 2nd Lt. Douglas. The episode suffers slightly from slow pacing, especially in acts three and four, and loses points for shameless re-usage of previous footage. These are merely minor distractions from an over-all enjoyable patrol with our favorite squad.

I particularly enjoy watching Morrow in this episode as he walks the line between conflicting duties: obeying a superior officer and keeping his men in line and alive. Watching contemporary military shows, I always wonder where the technical advisors are as NCOs openly argue with their superiors. In the military, you obey, you don't argue. And in this episode, Morrow is excellent showing us a soldier at odds with himself as he must obey orders from a new lieutenant that he does not understand.

The show, though, suffers from being so late in the season. Because production was behind schedule, this excellent story didn't get the development it deserved. The script includes references to footage shot for other episodes, and how it will be incorporated into the current episode. This cut down on production time, allowing them to catch up, but shorted this poignant story about the high cost of duty and command.

Notes, Oddities, and Bloopers:
• Beautiful reflection shot in stream as squad marches by.
• In the battle at the farmhouse, with five vehicles in the line of fire, the squad hits no tires and no windshields.
• Filmed at Franklin Canyon, MGM, with reused footage of Mormon Rocks.
• The end of the episode is a complete lift from "Bridge at Chalons," showing Saunders blowing up the same bridge. As in "Bridge," Kirby twists his ankle and gripes about the leader.
• The by-the-book leader violates a major rule of command: he reprimands his NCO in front of the troops. A good leader does not undermine the authority of his NCO.

The Glory Among Men (064)
Written by Tom Sellers
Directed by Vic Morrow
First Aired 21-Apr-1964 (Episode 32 of Season 2)

CAST:
Regulars: Jason, Morrow, Jalbert, Peabody, Hogan, Carter
Henry Brandt as Heinecke
Jerry Douglas as Kohler
Paul Busch as Bauer
Fletcher Fist as Barnett
Richard Tretter as G.I.
Peter Helm as Laslo
Bernard Kates as Hacker
Eddie Ryder as Mason

Synopsis:
"The Glory Among Men" presents men struggling to maintain their moral center when faced with the immoral necessities of war. This particular struggle revolves around a thoroughly unlikeable squad member who becomes pinned down by a German machine gun nest. Should the squad abandon him? Should they attempt to rescue him? Is this loathsome man worth dying for? Watching the glory achieved by this small band of ordinary soldiers is great entertainment.

About Filming the Episode:
Conlan Carter: "I was having a little bit of trouble with this one scene, about what to do with it, and Vic said, don't do nothing. And it worked extremely well. It was just a simple little quick line. It was just the little things like that that he could do. He was just good."

Review — 3.5 bayonets:

In his second outing behind the camera, Vic Morrow provides superb direction for a script that is, at times, heavy-handed and overstocked with Christian symbolism. Considering the large sections of script that are devoid of action, Morrow keeps a firm hand on the pacing. But Morrow, the director, goes overboard with some ostentatious shots that do more to show off Morrow's creativity than to illuminate the story. These include showy reflection shots, half-face closeups of himself, and hand-held camera work at the beginning. He makes good use of some lovely long-lens shots with a foreground closeup of the squad and way, way in the background, Mason trapped on the tree. Kudos to the effects and technical people. The lighting is absolutely sumptuous, especially the night scenes, with flares falling, backlighting Caje, Littlejohn, and Kirby and catching a defenseless Saunders out in the open.

Despite his dual task of star and director, Morrow turns in a strong performance. Jalbert and Hogan also shine. Caje is frightening losing his cool and getting in a fistfight with Hacker. Interesting that it's a woman that gets this usually easy-going guy riled. Conlan Carter as Doc is superb, affected by the abandonment of Hacker on a more personal level than the others, not because he felt any friendship for the man, but because his duty is to save life. His restrained tears at his failure are affecting. Fletcher Fist, a semi-regular as Brockmeyer in season one, returns as an expendable.

The no-man's land where Hacker is abandoned is a sound stage set. Vic Morrow worked closely with the set crew to create the stark, surrealistic setting. The grays and blacks, trees with no foliage, and barren ground turns the surroundings into an alien landscape.

Notes, Oddities, and Bloopers:
• Blond Fletcher Fist is a brunette in this episode.
• The squad again captures Paul Busch and gets him killed.
• Why isn't Caje wearing a belt in the teaser?
• A German (shooting an authentic MG42) flips up the rear sight to get a better shot, but the front sight remains folded down the whole time.
• The no-man's land where Hacker is abandoned is a sound stage set. Vic Morrow worked closely with the set crew to create the stark, surrealistic setting. The grays and blacks, trees with no foliage, and barren ground turns the surroundings into an alien landscape.

In the hiatus after season two, those with lesser billing among the *Combat!* regulars were fearing for their jobs. Peabody was concerned that Levitt would purge everyone brought in by Altman. Even though his Littlejohn character was the favorite of Seligman's son, he decided to test the producers at the end of the season: he again went to them for a loan. Dick Peabody received the money and felt confident he would return next year.

Tom Lowell, with no contract to fall back on, was worried. At the end of the second season, Lowell voluntarily departed the show. "*Combat!* again offered me a contract, but for the same money, the money I started out with. Then, an opportunity arrived that I could not pass up," says Lowell. "I had the opportunity to join *Combat!* and could have stuck with it for the five years. I felt very badly that I didn't, because of all the friendships. But, careerwise, it was a better move to go to Disney."

Conlan Carter felt safe after receiving an Emmy nomination for Outstanding Performance in a Supporting Role by an Actor for his work in the episode "The Hostages." But the nomination caused him problems. "When Vic was nominated the first year he was in the show," says Conlan, "he held them up for a lot of money."

At the time, Conlan had been unaware of the previous negotiations, and how heated they had become. So he was surprised at the producer's reaction to a contract meeting, them saying that no matter what somebody back east thought of him, the nomination would not carry any weight with them.

"They just stepped all over me. . . And this was the highlight of my career. I couldn't believe what I was hearing. And I was working for low money relative to the rest of the cast. I just said I wanted to have my salary raised up to where they are and they said 'No! Not only are you not going to get raised to their level, you come back at your last year's salary.' ... I walked. I left the show because of it and they subsequently had like 15 scripts that I had been written into that they had already bought for the next year. So they came some couple months later and signed me at the money I wanted, but not with a contract, just on a show-to-show basis. . . . I probably did as many shows as I would have done under contract."

The walkout happened during the summer hiatus, so he missed no filming. "The upshot of it was, that they made it very clear that it was not going to get out of hand like it did with Vic. ... It was an unfortunate episode in what otherwise could have been a very pleasant experience ... I lost the Emmy to Albert Paulsen."

CHAPTER 4

SEASON THREE 1964–1965

Stuntmen Earl Parker and Ed Hice as "the bad guys" on the European street on MGM's lot 3. According to Parker, "We would go here every so often and blow up a few places and shoot and raise a lot of hell. Then we'd go out to another location and an MGM crew would patch things up until the next time we'd raid the town."

Hitting Their Stride

By season three, *Combat!* had settled into a routine of excellence, with some exceptions. The parade of new producers had ended with Gene Levitt firmly holding the producer reins. The cast list stabilized and the actors stood firmly together in their demand for quality scripts. Vic Morrow directed more episodes, earning high praise from his fellow actors for his work behind the camera.

Rick Jason was getting less time in front of the camera, but was still enjoying his contractually agreed upon equal pay and billing. He was also enjoying various hunting seasons, as he had Levitt arrange his shooting schedule around his other shooting activities. "If I'm just in the beginning of an episode, or in the end," Rick Jason says, "it was hunting season. I spent the whole five years doing that. People always ask, how come I wasn't in more shows? I went hunting and fishing. People don't understand that. If I was in the show, I got paid, if I wasn't in the show, I got paid. So what do I care?"

Location Shooting:

Franklin Canyon, Thousand Oaks, MGM, Squaw Valley

All five seasons of *Combat!* featured exterior photography shot at Franklin Canyon. "Fifth season we practically lived there," says producer/director Georg Fenady. "They're still picking up cartridges." Located above Beverly Hills, Franklin Canyon is located in a low mountain chain that separates west Los Angeles from the San Fernando Valley. The area is municipally owned and readily available to film crews. Television and movie crews have filmed Franklin Canyon scenery for more than half a century. Andy Griffith and little Ronnie Howard walked her shores in the opening of the "Andy Griffith Show" and Captain Kirk ran through the same woods where Saunders fought.

Franklin Canyon has two reservoirs: a small one about 300 yards across on the north end of the canyon, and a larger one a half mile south and 200 feet downhill from the small reservoir. A spillway from the upper reservoir flows into the lower reservoir. Culverts, which make perfect cover during a firefight, lace the grounds on the hills between the reservoirs. The reservoir area offers a variety of terrain and roads. The city permit to shoot at Franklin cost *Combat!* producers $150 per day in the sixties.

"We'd blow it up pretty good," remembers Georg Fenady, "But we always left it the way we found it. The worst you would do, we'd build our own sets and blow them up. As I said, you leave it the way you found it. The only thing is, we would make craters for bombed out areas and then bulldoze them back the way we found it."

Conlan Carter remembers the Franklin Canyon shooting as

inconvenient. "You had to leave early and usually get home late. We didn't have showers in the dressing rooms out there, so you'd come home dirty. But you just did it, you didn't think about it."

Georg Fenady said that while they were filming *Combat!*, "They were talking about filling in at least one reservoir and doing all kind of things. They put a scare into us. That was 30 years ago and still nothing's changed."

West of the San Fernando Valley, Albertson's ranch in Thousand Oaks provided locations for *Combat!* and other television shows. A freeway separated the area into two sections: the "Gunsmoke" permanent sets were on the south side of the freeway; on the north side was open land where *Combat!* shot "Hills Are for Heroes," "Gulliver," "The Hell Machine," and other episodes. The area is now Westlake Village condominiums.

The French village, with its familiar clock tower and stone bridge, was located on the MGM backlot. "At MGM we were on Lot 1 with 9,000 stages," says Georg Fenady, "And we had Lots 2 and 3 in terms of villages, French and English, and streams and rivers and lakes, any kind of terrain you needed."

The French village on Lot 2 was built for *Madame Bovary*, and the Nelson Eddy/Jeanette MacDonald musicals were filmed on Lot 2. "We destroyed it for six years every week and rebuilt it," says Pierre Jalbert. "Lot 3 was 80 acres with a lake, where they filmed *Meet Me in St. Louis* and all the MGM features. Now it's condos." Lot 3 featured Eucy Road, River Road, and the Lady L area.

The Man From U.N.C.L.E. Book: The Behind-the-Scenes Story of a Television Classic, describes how U.N.C.L.E. producer Sam Rolfe had problems sharing the MGM backlot with *Combat!* They would arrange for a location, then show up to find that *Combat!* had been there the preceding week and blown up all the streets. U.N.C.L.E. crews would repair the sets for non-wartime filming, then *Combat!* would destroy them again the following week.

Combat! also had its challenges sharing the backlot. Jack Hogan remembers, "Although you're working here, somebody else is doing a Western over here. And pretty soon you're running into their lights or into the back of their horses.'"

For the season opener, producers sent a crew to Squaw Valley to film snow sequences for *Combat!*'s only winter episode, "The Silver Service." The October 10, 1964 issue of TV Guide describes the location shooting. Local ski instructors, members of the area ski patrol, and Squaw Valley residents were hired for the background shots. The actors remained in Los Angeles, filming all their scenes on a sound stage with plastic snow. The location shooting was completed in five days at a cost of ten thousand dollars. They had enough footage left over for another snow episode: "Mountain Man."

Associate producer Richard Caffey, said in the TV Guide article that the Squaw Valley filming was grueling. They kept having to change camera positions to shoot trackless snow. Because they could not mark the snow, they had no idea how deep or safe the snow cover was. Two crew members broke ribs and one broke his hand.

Producing the Episodes

Georg Fenady started with the show in the first season. Richard Caffey, at the time the associate producer, hired him to be second assistant director.

"I did everything since then," says Fenady. "I was associated with everything except the pilot. In other words, I went in as a second assistant director, became first assistant, became associate producer, and director eventually. It was really a career show for me."

In the first season, episodes were filmed for $125,000 each. Directors came in the week before filming to prepare the script. Working with the first assistant, the director breaks down the script for production, assigning pages and locations for specific days of shooting and creates a budget. Georg Fenady remembers, "Usually the director will scream and say 'I can't make that many pages.' And I say, 'Doesn't make any difference because we're way the hell over budget and something's got to come out anyway.'"

On the set, the first assistant organizes the production end of things. "He's the one that yells 'Quiet!' all the time and the one that says 'Roll it!' and the one that takes care of the stunts and gives the adjustments." As soon as one show finished, he would get the script that night for the next episode to be filmed in two weeks. He would start breaking it down for the director, who would come in the next day, spend the week to prepare, and start the whole cycle again.

On *Combat!*, the second assistant director stayed on the set at all times. He took care of wardrobe and gave calls to the actors. "The second is running around doing the job of six people, trying to keep track of everybody on the set. He was a very busy man," says Fenady. "But that's a thing of the past. Nowadays they have a second, a second second, and a trainee. When we were doing *Combat!*, there was just the first and one second. And we were dealing with 30 and 40 people a day, and stunts, and bullet hits and effects. It was probably the most ambitious—not probably—I know it was the most ambitious television show ever undertaken. I watch 'em now and I don't know how we did them in six days."

After filming, the show would go to post-production for one to two weeks. In addition to the usual editing, *Combat!* required complex sound effects editing for the battle sequences. Musical scoring also would be added, with music by Leonard Rosenman. Episodes ran exactly 52 minutes and 46 seconds. Budgets were initially $125,000 per episode, rising to $150,000 to $183,000 in the fifth year.

The first year, all of Morrow and Jason's closeups were shot at the end of the day, after the rest of the cast went home. As

Bob Beattie of the US Olympic Ski Team and Pierre Jalbert give skiing pointers to Claudine Longet at Squaw Valley.

stars, they did not receive overtime pay, but the other cast members had to be paid extra if filming ran late. That first season, Morrow and Jason often worked sixteen hour days.

The second year, the Screen Actors Guild negotiated a new contract that required overtime pay for all actors receiving more than $1,500 per segment. The first week of filming the second season, the producers assigned the same long days for the two stars, unaware that the rules had changed. Rick Jason was pleased with that oversight: "The first week, I pulled, besides my salary, $1,800 in overtime and Vic pulled up close to the same. That was the last time we ever worked past six o'clock. We got to 5:55 and somebody would say, 'Okay, Sign 'em off.' And it didn't matter what else had to be done, they signed us off. Cause they didn't want to pay Vic and me overtime."

Water scenes and night shoots were usually reserved for Friday, so the actors would have the weekend off. Union rules limited the work day to ten hours, with the actors having at least ten hours off before being called again. If filming finished at 6:00 pm, the actors could not be called back before 4:00 am the next day. For a night shoot, the actors would often get the next day off, reporting in that night at 6:00 or 7:00 pm, depending on the time of the year. Filming for night shoots would last until 2:00 or 3:00 am. If an episode required extensive night photography, the actors would work most of the week at night.

All directors would finish filming the show in six days, with the exception of Vic Morrow. "Those were never ending," remembers Fenady. "I think the first one that he did was supposed to be a six day show. Kind of went seven and part of an eight. Then he did a two-parter and that was a monster. I don't know how many—that went over quite a bit. You know, you kind of let him have his bit. He was a helluva good director. He didn't quite have enough experience to have the discipline to do it on schedule. But he certainly was effective and a beautiful actor's director."

Costumes and Makeup

Beau Vanden Ecker and one assistant provided costumes for the cast and the armies of extras. They strove for authenticity (on a budget) and researched the uniforms of the European theater.

By second season, Beau Vanden Ecker provided special fiberglass helmets for the cast and the stunt doubles, replacing the authentic steel helmets. In the December 1983 issue of TV Collector, Rick Jason said "Our helmets were custom made because the steel pots can press your vertebrae after wearing 'em for about sixteen hours a day . . . They cost 115 bucks a copy then. I've still got mine. My boots had to be made-to-order because I wear a size 13 shoe." The fiberglass helmets, though comfortable for the actors, caused problems during shooting. When running and jumping into a foxhole, the actors would go one way and the helmet would go the other.

Beau Vanden Ecker replaced the wool uniforms with tailored cotton replicas, dyed the proper olive drab, making it easier for the actors to work in California heat. "Beau was incredible in wardrobe," says Fenady. "He could wardrobe 15 guys in 15 minutes." To entice Vanden Ecker to stay with the show, they started casting him in small roles. "It was getting boring for him," says Fenady. "We always wanted to sweeten the pot, and he said 'I wouldn't mind doing a little stunt once in a while, a few lines.' So he got plenty of them. As long as he was happy, we were happy. He was very good, too, very good." Beau later moved to Hawaii, where he acted and directed for "Hawaii 5-0" and "Magnum, P.I."

"Our makeup man was John Truey," says Pierre Jalbert. "He loved his 'boys.' He started working at MGM at age 14. He became one of the best makeup men at MGM. Worked with Elizabeth Taylor and all the great women stars. He was excellent for women. I don't know how he got Combat!, but he loved the boys, as he called us. Simple makeup, just a little base, a little dirt."

"He was a good makeup man," Conlan says of John Truey. "He did great stuff with Vic and all of us. We were dirty. He did great dirt."

Union rules require that the costumes be cleaned every night. Each morning, once the actors were in the clean uniforms, they had to be "dirtied up." Fuller's earth would be applied by hand to the costumes. "Sometimes it was faster just to roll around on the ground for awhile," remembers Dick Peabody. "About three or four quick rolls in the dirt usually did the trick."

John Truey used dog clippers on the actors' beards to keep the length of the stubble consistent. To keep that gritty look, the actors were supposed to avoid shaving. If they had to make clean-shaven personal appearances or had a special event to attend, the directors would try to work around their schedules.

At the '96 Combat! reunion, Jalbert watched the episode "Hills Are for Heroes" with the fans, and noted, "We all look so dirty and sweaty and filthy. Just terrible coming down off that hill. Then we stagger into the bunker, take off the helmets, and we all have perfect two-hundred dollar haircuts . . . My hair at the time was getting a little gray and he [Truey] had a bottle of black stuff and 'squirt, squirt' he gave me back twenty years."

Season Three Episodes

Combat! aired on Tuesday nights at 7:30 p.m. on ABC, opposite "Marshal Dillon" and "World War I" on CBS and "Mr. Novak" on NBC. ABC followed Combat! with "McHale's Navy" at 8:30 p.m.

The Silver Service (065)

Teleplay by Kay Lenard and Jess Carneol
Story by Edward J. Bonner
Directed by Sutton Roley
First aired 13-Oct-1964 (Episode 5 of Season 3)

CAST:
Regulars: Hogan, Jalbert
Guest star Mickey Rooney as Harry White
Norm Alden as Private Buford
Joe di Reda as Malloy
King Moody as Jouvet
Pat Patterson as Sergeant Hacker
Special Guest Stars:
Ramon Novarro as Charles Gireaux
Claudine Longet as Claudette

Synopsis:
Sent to the rear to recover from injuries, Kirby and Caje encounter Harry White (Mickey Rooney), a dice-cheating schemer who has been fighting the war from bar stools. During a German breakthrough, Kirby survives a barrage in the French village, fortuitously finds a B.A.R., and wanders into the home of Claudine Longet and her grandfather. To evade the Germans, all flee through the snow, dragging the ailing grandfather and Harry's mysterious package.

REVIEW — 1/2 bayonet:
In "The Silver Service," Kirby shows his leadership ability. When faced with someone more irresponsible than himself,

Claudine Longet guest stars as a French farm girl in "The Silver Service."

Kirby becomes the model of responsibility.

Former matinee idol Ramon Novarro (Ben Hur in the 1927 silent film) plays the befuddled grandfather. He later appears as the befuddled Count in the episode "Finest Hour."

Pierre says about director Sutton Roley, "He was trying to direct Mickey Rooney to play the dice. Can you imagine that? Mickey Rooney, the greatest talent that Hollywood produced. And Mickey got, excuse the expression I have to use, Mickey got so pissed that he walked off the set. He said 'I'm going to kill that son of a bitch.' I walked out and walked Mickey around the stage to cool him off so I could bring him back in and finish the scene."

About Filming the Episode:

Jack Hogan at the 1996 *Combat!* reunion said: "They sent a second unit to Squaw Valley, and the rest of us, Mickey and Claudine and myself, we worked in plastic snow. And that stuff gets in your eyes and you think you're going to croak. . . . Mickey Rooney was funny in his own way. Mickey was a compulsive talker and joke teller. Sometimes you'd do a scene and they would say cut and everybody would go to learn their next lines. But Mickey, the second they'd say

SAMPLE PRODUCTION SCHEDULE
"THE FIRST DAY"

1st Day	EXT. COUNTRYSIDE 2-1/8 pg. Squad sees half-track approaching, all take cover. Fade. PROPS: All weapons, grenades, map. VEHICLES: Half-track	R.V. Lee Ranch
	EXT. COUNTRYSIDE 1-4/8 pg. Half-track battle - Tate hit - Saunders tosses grenade to blow half-track. PROPS: All weapons **fire**, grenades, map. VEHICLES: Half-track. EFFECTS: Bullet hits on vehicle and ground, grenade hits vehicle	(Same)
	EXT. COUNTRYSIDE 1-4/8 pg. Battle over - squad discovers Tate dead. Dissolve. PROPS, VEHICLES: as above	(Same)
	EXT. COUNTRYSIDE 2-2/8 pg. Squad proceeds along road - McBride & Saunders talk - hear half-track. PROPS: as above	(Same)
	EXT. DIFFERENT COUNTRYSIDE 2/8 pg. Squad going along after battle. PROPS: as above.	(Same)
2nd day	EXT. WAR TORN ROAD 1-7/8 pg. Squad flakes out. Hears noise. PROPS: Weapons, map (no firing this day)	Lot 3 Jungle River Rd.
	EXT. WAR TORN ROAD 3 pg. Squad meets replacements - Fade. PROPS: As above, full packs, extra bandoliers, grenades, mess kits, blankets, entrenching tools, cameras, auto club maps	(same)
	EXT. ROAD 3 pg. Squad helps replacements strip packs to minimum. Exit. PROPS: as above	(same)
3rd day	EXT. DIFFERENT COUNTRY SIDE 4-6/8 pg. Tobin & McBride see Germans - Tobin shoots both - Tate freezes - Tobin is chewed out by Saunders for engaging enemy. PROPS: Weapons, map, firing. EFFECTS: Bullet hits.	Lot 3 Eucy Rd. & Jungle River Rd.
4th day	EXT. TOP OF RISE 6/8 pg. Saunders & Caje POV Ger. O.P. at junction. PROPS: Map, weapons - G.I. & Ger., (no fire)	Franklin Canyon
	EXT. TREES 7/8 pg. Squad moves from trees to viaduct. PROPS: as above.	(same)
	EXT. VIADUCT 1/8 pg. Dolly shot - squad working way down viaduct. PROPS: as above	(same)
	EXT. WALL 1 pg. Caje - Loomis - Tobin run for shed. PROPS: as above, firing EFFECTS: Bullet hits	(same)
	EXT. SHED 3/8 pg. Caje moves up. PROPS, EFFECTS: as above	(same)

	EXT. SHED 1-1/8 pg. Loomis hit saving Tobin's life PROPS, EFFECTS: as above	(same)
	EXT. NEW COVER 4/8 pg. Caje behind wagon - gets hit - dives for safety. PROPS: all firing. EFFECTS: Bullet hits	(same)
	EXT. WALL 1-2/8 pg. Squad supplies cover fire - then heads for shed - Kirby covers.	(same)
	EXT. BACK YARD 5/8 pg. Wounded German approaches shed and is shot.	(same)
	INT. SHED 2/8 pg. Tobin begins to fear. Fade.	(same)
	INT. SHED 4/8 pg. Tobin breaks down completely.	(same)
	INT. SHED 3-1/8 pg. Group makes it to shed - find Tobin - Saunders elects to go down the middle to hit Germans.	(same)
5th day	EXT. FRONT OF FARM 2 pg. Saunders heads up middle & makes it to first shell hole. Squad fires cover from all areas. PROPS: all fire, grenades EFFECTS: Bullet hits	Franklin Canyon
	EXT. FRONT OF FARM 2 pg. Saunders heads for 2nd shell hole - McBride fires cover on run. Saunders in 2nd shell hole, lobs grenade, wipes out machine gun - Kirby & McBride shoot remaining Germans. PROPS: as above. EFFECTS: Grenade, bullet hits	(Same)
	EXT. ROAD AREA 1-4/8 pg. TAG - squad says goodbye to Loomis & Tobin - new replacement arrives. PROPS: Rig jeep with stretcher, full pack, plasma bottle VEHICLES: 2 jeeps, 1 troop carrier	(Same)
	EXT. FOOT OF RISE 1-5/8 pg. Saunders briefs squad on attack on German position. PROPS: weapons - no fire, map, grenades	(Same)
6th day	EXT. OPEN ROAD 3 pg. Squad proceeds along road - McBride talks. PROPS: Map, weapons	Lot 3 Jungle River Rd. & Eucy Rd.
	EXT. COUNTRYSIDE MINE 4 pg. Squad encounters mine area and crosses it. PROPS: as above. EFFECTS: Buried mine	Lot 3 Lady L Area

Claudine Longet, Mickey Rooney, and Pierre Jalbert in "Silver Service."

cut, would grab your sleeve and keep on talking to you. And you couldn't get away to go to the john or get a drink of water because Mickey was talking."

The Long Walk (066)

Written by Peter Barry
Directed by Alan Crosland Jr.
First aired 15-Dec-1964 (Episode 13 of Season 3)

CAST:
Regulars: Morrow, Carter, Peabody
Guest star Roddy McDowall as Murfree
William Bryant as Larkin
Maurice Marsac as Armand
Peter Brocco as Lambert
Chris Howard as German

Synopsis:
The squad picks up a wounded GI, who is really the leader of a specially trained group of German infiltrators. Larkin, a boot-camp friend of Saunders, discovers the deception, but is gunned down by the infiltrator. With his dying breath, he tries to warn Saunders. The infiltrator tricks the squad into carrying him several miles to his rendezvous with his troops. But in the end, Saunders' deception proves better than the German's.

Review — 4 bayonets:
Saunders vs. an Aryan superman. Guess who wins?

Roddy McDowall as Murfree, the S.S. infiltrator, is both charming and chilling. Though spending the bulk of the episode flat on his back, he gives an energetic and engaging performance.

The first time I saw this episode, the ending took me by surprise. But even knowing the "surprise," the episode holds up well on repeat viewing. Morrow does a great job of playing the many levels that this script requires. No moralizing or intellectual introspection in this episode, just quality entertainment.

Notes, Oddities, and Bloopers:
• At end, Saunders walks off with empty weapon.
• In the last scene between Saunders and the infiltrator, the bottle of wine that Saunders' holds switches hands between shots, then just disappears.
• Littlejohn offers Murfree a drink of wine from a corked bottle. In the next cut, Littlejohn drinks from the bottle, which is suddenly uncorked.

Mountain Man (067)

Written by Edward J. Lakso
Directed by Sutton Roley
First aired 15-Sep-1964 (Episode 1 of Season 3)

CAST:
Regulars: Morrow, Hanley, Hogan, Jalbert
Theodore Bikel as Francois Perrault
Henry Brandon as German Lieutenant
Pieter Beagema as German Sergeant
Bob Beattie as German

Synopsis:
An embittered deserter is bribed into leading Saunders' squad across the mountains. They are captured by Germans and left to freeze, but manage a daring escape. Caje skis for help, and the deserter comes to realize the meaning of duty.

Review — 1/2 bayonet:
Director Sutton Roley tries to bring high art to this low tale of a man embittered by war. His symbolic opening and closing of the episode (a fragment of ice floating downstream to join civilization) is touching and silly — as silly as this episode's Germans. Their interrogation of Saunders is pathetic. A trio of interrogators surrounds Saunders, taunts him, and doesn't lay a finger on him. The Germans throwing the prisoners into an unheated bunker to chill the information out of them seems more appropriate to a "Batman" episode, than a realistic war series.

Saunders isn't himself: he lets himself be slapped around by a coward, lets himself be surprised by Germans on a mountaintop with good visibility for miles, and his PPT lacks conviction. This script by Edward J. Lakso leaves me cold. The episode is just an excuse to get world-class skier Pierre Jalbert on a pair of skis and make use of left-over footage from "Silver Service."

About Filming the Episode:

Producer Gene Levitt, wanting to take advantage of Pierre Jalbert's Olympic-class skiing ability, proudly announced that Pierre was going ski in a *Combat!* episode set in the mountains. Pierre explained, "Hey, there's no mountains in Normandy, pal." To which Levitt replied, "It's okay, Pierre. This is just TV." Of course, nobody bothered to explain how a Cajun growing up in bayou country learned how to snow ski. Pierre recalls, "The German skiing after me was Bob Beattie, the manager of the American Olympic ski team. He can still be seen as a commentator for ABC."

Notes, Oddities, and Bloopers:

•During the down-hill run, the distance shots show one of the squad members bare-headed. In the closeups, all have helmets.
•Saunders is still too lazy to get his own knife, thank goodness for lazy Germans who don't frisk prisoners well.
•In the ski chase, the hillside is covered with ski tracks.
•Snow locations were filmed in Squaw Valley, California, site of the 1960 Winter Olympic Games.

The Duel (068)

Written by Edward J. Lakso
Directed by John Peyser
First aired 06-Oct-1964 (Episode 4 of Season 3)

CAST:

Regulars: Morrow
Guest Star Bobby Rydell as Mickey Shay
Hans Difflip as German Commander
Tram Tyson as German Driver
Philip Altman as German Loader
Tom Pace as First German Infantryman
Juri Rogatkin as Second German Infantryman

Synopsis:

The Germans, caught in an Allied pincer movement, launch an all-out assault on the American lines. Saunders, weary and cut off from his platoon, meets truck driver Mickey Shay, who is delivering fuel to the front. The heavily laden truck blows a tire as a German tank approaches. Saunders attempts to hold off the tank while Shay repairs the tire.

Review — 4 bayonets:

Saunders goes one-on-one against a tank. Guess who wins? Edward J. Lakso purged himself of bad writing after "Mountain Man"; this episode never strikes a false note. His script does what *Combat!* does best: takes the mammoth, impersonal scope of the war and breaks it down to a small, personal struggle.

Saunders, the hero-in-spite-of-himself, is back in this episode. He even has that old messianic drive, as he forces a cowardly soldier to find an unsuspected strength within himself. Singing star Bobby Rydell made his TV acting debut in this episode, performing well with Morrow.

Most of the story is told in images — great images. Director John Peyser provided superb aerial shots of Saunders running

to the rescue, bounding (and later limping) up and down a hillside, and running between a German tank and a disabled American truck. One stupendous shot sweeps in on Saunders as he reaches the base of the hill and a gust of wind rips open his jacket.

About Filming the Episode:

Earl Parker, Vic's stunt double says: "I was doubling Vic where Vic finally gets up on top of a turret. And the Germans, the bad guys, sense that he was up there and were rotating the turret, trying to shed the tank of Vic, which it finally did, which of course was me."

Notes, Oddities, and Bloopers:

•This is the only *Combat!* episode to use sub-titles under German dialogue.
•The tank in the episode is not a German Tiger, but an American M41 Walker Bulldog with German markings. Saunders would have had more difficulty with a Tiger's dual machine guns and five-man crew.
•Filmed at Thousand Oaks.
•The action takes place during the battle for the Falais Pocket. This was a decisive engagement that took place on a battlefield twenty kilometers wide, involving 1,700,000 men, and 4,000 tanks. This battle happened prior to the liberation of Paris, but season two episodes indicate that Paris has already been liberated.

Bobby Rydell, popular recording, TV and film star, makes his dramatic TV debut as an in-trouble G.I. in "The Duel."

Vendetta (069)

Written by Ron Bishop and Wells Root,
Directed by John Peyser
First aired 22-Sep-1964 (Episode 2 of Season 3)

CAST:

Regulars: Jason, Hogan, Carter, Peabody
Guest Star Telly Savalas as Colonel Kapsalis
Athan Karras as Hot Dog
Peter Deuel as Szigeti
Alexis Boden as Greek #1
John Aniston as Greek #2
Peter Bravos as Greek #3
George Michaelides as Greek #4
Danny Klega as German Guard Officer

Telly Savalas leads a band of battling, dancing Greeks in "Vendetta."

Synopsis:

While roaming the countryside in *Rat Patrol*–style jeeps, Hanley is allied with a horde of dancing Greeks, commanded by Col. Kapsalis (Telly Savalas). The Colonel deceives Hanley by promising to lead them back to the American lines. Instead, Hanley and his men are coerced into joining the Greeks' battles and following the Colonel's orders, which Hanley thinks are suicidal. The Greeks dance, drink, and blast their way to a fiery conclusion where Savalas dies a hero's death.

Review — 1/2 bayonet:

Writer Wells Roots gives a tip of his hat to *Zorba the Greek* in this tale of a man obsessed with death and dancing. A few interesting moments are found between commercials. For action fans, the night battles are spectacular, with jeeps and trucks engaging in the dark, tracers lighting the night sky, and search lights blinding the drivers. Quite lovely. Director John Peyser again uses a small plane for aerial views, this time of the jeeps in action.

Unfortunately, the battle sequences have no continuity; they are flurries of action strung together for some pretty pictures, but little more.

Notes, Oddities, and Bloopers:

- Hanley wears a second pinky ring.
- Opening sequence must have been filmed many, many times: lots of tire tracks everywhere on the jeeps' first entrance.
- Captain Jampel is King Company's C.O.
- Some of the German soldiers carry U.S. Army carbines.
- When the planes attack the jeeps, Hanley identifies them as Messerschmitts. They are American P-51-C Mustangs.
- Germans standing in front of searchlights are killed by sprays of bullets that leave the lights behind the soldiers intact. Windshields and tires of the chase vehicles seem resistant to bullets.
- During much of Savalas' dance, a string from his tassel is caught in his moustache.

Dateline (070)

Written by Richard L. Newhafer
Directed by Sutton Roley
First aired 23-Feb-1965 (Episode 23 of Season 3)

CAST:

Regulars: Morrow, Hogan, Peabody, Carter
Guest Star Dan Duryea as Barton
Douglas Henderson as Reardon
Kurt Landen as Guard
Rank Kodmen as German Sergeant
Ray Baxter as German #1
Roger Gentry as German #2
Peter Hellman as German Guard
Henry Beckman as Major Mueller

Synopsis:

After losing a superior officer in the field, Saunders and squad allow themselves to be captured by the enemy to liberate a famous American correspondent (Dan Duryea) being held by the Germans. But the wounded correspondent, Robert Barton, refuses to take any risks to gain his freedom, preferring a prison cell to the dangers of an escape.

Review — 2 bayonets:

In "Dateline," Saunders teaches a war correspondent what it means to live a war, not just write about it. The script by Richard L. Newhafer is thin, requiring long marches through the woods to fill the hour. Director Sutton Roley devised innovative ways to march the squad to Rosenman's music. He creates some interesting squad-on-patrol shots: fording lakes, leaping walls, crossing rail bridges. But the shots are more interesting than exciting.

About Filming the Episode:

Dick Peabody says, "I'll give you an example of Sutton Roley. On Lot 3, up high, about ten feet off the ground, they built a section of a railroad track. And Sutton, with his wonderful sense of drama as far as camera placement was concerned, wanted a shot with the camera below, looking up through the ties at me as I'm walking along the railroad track. It was a great idea. The first take, I'm walking over there, and he says, 'Wait a minute. Cut! Dick, don't look down. That ruins the whole thing when you look down.' I said, 'If you think I'm going to walk across this thing ten feet off the ground and not look where I'm stepping, forget it.' . . . How are you going to do that. No one in their right mind is going to do that." In the sequence, all the actors who walk across the railroad tracks glance down at their feet.

Conlan Carter recalls one silly incident filming with Henry Beckman, who plays the German Major. "We were shooting the thing like at nine o'clock at night. We were bone tired, getting stupid and ridiculous. The scene was for Beckman to walk into the stable . . . and see that we had escaped. And he was to say something appropriate in German. Beckman walked in, looked at the escape tunnel, hit his leg with a riding crop and said, with a flawless Yiddish accent, 'Ho, boy!' Well, it just hit everybody and we started laughing. And we laughed for thirty minutes. We couldn't keep doing the show. We just sat down for about a half an hour, because every time we'd start to do it, we'd start laughing again. It wasn't that funny, except for that moment when we all were so goofy. And it was hysterical. The Jewish expression coming from a dyed-in-the-wool German. Nobody expected him to do it, it was a total ad lib and we obviously couldn't use it—they were rolling when he did it."

Notes, Oddities, and Bloopers:
• The cord on the hat of German major who gives Barton morphine alternates between being tucked behind the cockade and falling forward.
• In the scene where Saunders holds Barton at knife point, the knife is alternately held overhand and underhand.
• Squad wading the river is re-used footage from "Birthday Cake."
• Good job of making a few jeeps on the MGM lot look like a battalion motorpool.

Operation Fly Trap (071)
Written by Don Tait
Directed by John Peyser
First aired 27-Oct-1964 (Episode 7 of Season 3)
CAST:
Regulars: Morrow, Carter, Jalbert
Guest Star Gary Lockwood as Sgt. Meider
Leonard Bell as Major Orcutt
Bob Garrett as German Sgt.
Lee Millar as German Radio Operator
Jim Goodwin as Dispatch Rider
Mike Krempels as Half Track Passenger
Lou Robb as German #1
Herb Andreas as German #2
Frank Marth as German Captain
Paul Busch as Major's Radio Operator (uncredited)

Synopsis:

Bringing a wounded Doc to safety, Saunders, Caje, and communication sergeant Meider (Gary Lockwood) stumble upon a German patrol setting up a radio center in a French farmhouse. When Saunders overhears that the Germans are expecting a visit from an important Colonel, Saunders lays a trap. As time runs out for Doc, Saunders' plan unravels. In the end, it is a race to see who will arrive at the farmhouse first: the Colonel or a truck of German troops gunning for the Americans.

Review — 2 bayonets:

In his script for "Operation Fly Trap," Don Tait gives fans a middle-of-the-road episode that entertains, but never quite moves. This episode trods familiar ground, both in its locales and its plot. Saunders is again saddled with an uncooperative Sergeant who has special skills and an attitude. By the final act, the specialist turns out to be a softie that saves the day — been there, done that.

The story offers potential for interesting drama, but the script and John Peyser's direction gloss over the surface. Neither the plot nor the characters have any depth. Conlan Carter, as Doc, is wonderfully pathetic and helpless when appropriate. Doc is downright amiable when discussing with Saunders a decision that could mean his life. With Doc so meekly detached, how can the audience get emotionally involved?

Pierre Jalbert is particularly macho as he man-handles German prisoners and brandishes his bayonet. But Jalbert's talents are wasted — he moves around a lot, but says and accomplishes little. Even Vic Morrow takes his classic stoicism too far. The performances of all the regulars lack passion. Contrasted with a similar situation of a wounded comrade in "Glow Against the Sky," Saunders and Caje seem bored.

The best performances in "Operation Fly Trap" are from the incidental players. The script provided over a dozen speaking roles for the "enemy" actors. A steady parade of bit players enjoy their moment in front of the camera. Paul Busch is chatty as the radio operator at the Panzer camp; Lee Millar is convincing as the nervous radioman trying to function under

Saunders' Tommy gun; the beautiful Mike Krempels lingers in front of the camera as the lost half-track driver; and Jim Goodwin is deliciously befuddled as the poor dispatch driver caught in Saunders' snare. As fun as these vanity moments are, their sheer number dooms this episode to mediocrity. Too much time is spent on minor characters and not enough spent on the drama in the farmhouse.

I would have traded all the beautiful Germans in the episode for one impassioned PPT. Still, "Operation Fly Trap" is a solid two-bayonetter, an enjoyable way to spend an hour without taxing your brain or emotions.

Notes, Oddities, and Bloopers:

•Opening sequence is reused from "Anatomy of a Patrol," showing Saunders leading a much larger group than he has in this episode, with no medic, but with Kirby (who is not in the episode).

•After the opening battle, Saunders ducks under a branch, but his helmet hits the tree, knocking the helmet slightly back on his head and making an audible thunk.

•In the barn, Doc's uniform has little blood on it; but in the hayloft he drips blood on the German.

•Continuity error: Meider leaves the house with a carbine, but has no weapon when the battle begins.

•Bad location re-use. In their escape, Saunders' car pulls out past the farmhouse. A few moments later, when the car had progressed down the road, the car pulls into the same location (the only difference is that now the house isn't in the shot).

•For the conclusion, Doc recovers momentarily to walk on both feet to the truck, then immediately returns to death's-door mode.

The Impostor (072)

Written by Kay Lenard and Jess Carneol
Directed by Sutton Roley
First aired 24-Dec-1964 (Episode 10 of Season 3)

CAST:

Regulars: Jason, Hogan, Jalbert, Peabody
James Dobson as Pvt. Henderson
Edward Kemmer as Lt. Tracey
Alan Baxter as Capt. Roberts
Charles Walsh as Soldier #1
Ralph Thomas as Soldier #2
Special Guests G. V. Homeier as Sgt. Morgan
and Warren Stevens as Sgt. Walter

Synopsis:

This Hanley outing has the lieutenant on an intelligence mission he'd rather avoid, shepherding two sergeant specialists on an assignment to steal information from a German headquarters. Along the way, he discovers that an escaped German officer has infiltrated their group disguised as a sergeant. When they pick up a third "sergeant," the accusations fly and the suspicions interfere with the mission.

Review — 2 bayonets:

For those who have not seen this episode, I won't spoil the ending. Hanley, though, should have been smarter than this script. After once again losing a superior officer in the field, Hanley takes over an intelligence mission.

The entire snow-bound episode is filmed on a warm sound stage, and no breaths are seen in the winter air. Though their mission is through the snow, the squad members have no great coats, just field jacket, sweater, scarf, and gloves.

About Filming the Episode:

The most notable blooper of the series is in this episode. In the wheelhouse, Rick Jason turns to Dick Peabody and addresses him by his real name, saying "Peabody, bring up the rear." No one on the set or in post production noticed the error. But, according to Dick Peabody, his sister in Denver caught it the night the show aired and called him immediately.

Notes, Oddities, and Bloopers:

•Actor Skip Homeier, who also appears in "Entombed" is listed as G. V. Homeier.

•Hanley cites his blood type as A in this episode. It was O in "I Swear by Apollo."

•Same waterwheel from "Forgotten Front."

•Very odd overlay of map superimposed over the shot of the squad crossing a minefield.

Losers Cry Deal (073)

Written by Shirl Hendryx
Directed by Vic Morrow
First aired 19-Jan-1965 (Episode 18 of Season 3)

CAST:

Regulars: Morrow, Jason, Hogan, Carter, Peabody, Jalbert
Guest Mike Kellin as Jackson
Tom Skerritt as Hicks
George Murdock as Marcus
Fletcher Fist as Johnson
Paul Hampton as Kelly
Paul Todd as Costello
John Bedford as Burton
Dee Pollock as Thomas

Synopsis:

As members of two combined squads await orders in a battered chateau, a sarcastic, poker-playing GI creates tension. Mike Kellin guests as Jackson, the embittered veteran of too many battles. Jackson's caustic behavior bothers everyone but a young soldier named Thomas, who willingly suffers Jackson's insults and commands. When Thomas takes Jackson's place on patrol with Caje, he dies saving Caje and proving, to himself and Jackson, that he isn't a coward.

Review — 2.5 bayonets:

Vic Morrow takes another turn behind the camera in this story about an overbearing soldier with an unnatural control over a young G.I. "Losers Cry Deal" is not Morrow at his directorial best. He offers too many confusing images. The shots of Morrow in front of the swastika banner are disturbing. The swastika is too powerful a message in-and-of-itself to be used effectively for artistic statements. And why would an American squad leave a Nazi banner dominating their rest area, instead of just ripping it down (as Caje does in "Beneath the Ashes"). The episode is heavy-handed with symbolism, including the moody passover of the bombers.

Vic Morrow puts in his usual strong performance in front of the camera. Jalbert is especially powerful in this episode, portraying Caje in charge of a squad and suffering the first casualty under his command.

The cast enjoyed working on the large set, which had originally been constructed for one of the big MGM musicals. "We filmed on that huge set for nearly a week," says Conlan Carter. "Big. If you look at it, we're up at the top of the stairs and we're down at the bottom and that whole room is humongous when you look at the depth and breadth of it."

Paul Burke, guest starring as Sgt. O'Neill, brings Saunders to a near court martial with his charges of stupidity and poor judgement in "Point of View."

About Filming the Episode:

"Vic was one of the most deep, insightful actors, and as a director he was even probably more so, that I ever worked with," says Conlan Carter. "He was incredible. He had an intensity and a kind of underlying, volatility I guess is the best word for it. It was like he was going to explode at any minute and by keeping it contained he was so incredibly interesting to watch. He paid me probably the best compliment I've ever had in my career, and I say this with absolutely no humility. He said, 'You give me more with a look than most actors give me with three pages of dialogue.' We were not close friends in a personal sense, but I had tremendous respect for his talents and I will always remember him for that."

Notes, Oddities, and Bloopers:

• The squad usually travels light, but in the opening segment, they are carrying almost full field gear, looking like real soldiers.

• German soldier who charges out of the building carries an MP40, but wears K98 rifle ammo pouches on his belt.

• After several seasons of incidental parts, often uncredited, Tom Skerritt guests in a featured role.

• Caje carries the adapted Reising MP40 in one scene.

• Fletcher Fist (Brockmeyer from season one) returns in a small role.

• In opening battle, the grenade Kirby launches lands several feet to the right of the actual explosion.

• After Hicks puts on his poncho with a fellow GI's help, a later wide shot shows his again putting on his poncho with a fellow GI's help.

• After Caje makes his report, Sarge charges out to the main room and trips over Caje, who steadies him to prevent a fall.

Point of View (074)

Written by Joan Levitt
Directed by Bernard McEveety
First aired 29-Sep-1964 (Episode 3 of Season 3)

CAST:

Regulars: Morrow, Jason, Hogan, Jalbert, Peabody
Guest Star Paul Burke as Sgt. O'Neill
Gerald Trump as Howie Parker
Seymour Cassel as Doctor
Richard Schuyler as Medic
Horst Ebersberg as German Corporal
Anthony Jochim as French Farmer
H.M. Wynant as Lt. Collins

Synopsis:

Saunders is threatened with charges, being accused of incompetence that caused the death of two men. Hanley defends a Saunders reluctant to defend himself. Distracted by the fate of a wounded squad member and angry over the charges, Saunders' bitterness leads nearly to insubordination and causes him to abandon Hanley when Hanley most needs his help. In flashbacks, the squad tells the story of taking and holding a hill against a tank.

COMBAT!

Review — 3 bayonets:

The scenes in "Point of View" set in the familiar French village are moving and well enacted, especially the scene on the bridge when Saunders rebuffs Hanley. This is the best moment for showing both the professional and personal relationship between Saunders and Hanley — and how the dual relationships are sometimes at odds.

But *Combat's* takeoff on the Rashomon theme falls short during the flashbacks. The battle scenes do not match the emotional intensity of the drama in the artist's studio. Director Bernard McEveety has amply proven able to match action scenes against dialog scenes. But this time, he fails to deliver. When the audience sees Saunders through Sgt. O'Neill's eyes, Saunders looks the same as he did through Saunders' own eyes. McEveety provides no variety in the different viewpoints, just different camera angles.

Still, because of the town scenes and the great ending, this is among my favorite episodes. Paul Burke, who later starred in "Twelve O'Clock High," performs well as the sergeant-with-an-attitude du jour.

Notes, Oddities, and Bloopers:
•This episode, entitled "Point of View," has surprisingly few POV shots.
•Bad harp music going in and out of the flashbacks.
•H. M. Wynant (Lt. Collins) appears in fourth season's "Counterplay."

Brother, Brother (075)
Written by Edward J. Lakso
Directed by Sutton Roley
First aired 02-Feb-1965 (Episode 20 of Season 3)

CAST:
Regulars: Jason, Morrow, Hogan, Carter, Jalbert, Peabody
Guest Star Frankie Avalon as Eddie Cane
Charles A. Bastin as German Officer
Hans Heyde as German Soldier

Synopsis:
Eddie Cane, a cocky replacement, is anxious to join the platoon with his old friend "Wild Man" Kirby. Cane's older brother was Kirby's best pal back home. Cane thinks his brother died saving Kirby's life during a juvenile gang fight. Out of false obligation, Kirby carries his "responsibility" to the brink of disaster. When forced to choose between Eddie and Saunders, Kirby reveals the truth and a young soldier learns to stand alone.

RATING — 2 bayonets:
Kirby makes an unhappy reunion with the brother of a hometown friend, who expects "Wild Man" Kirby to give him special treatment. Frankie Avalon provides a nice performance as guest star Eddie Cane. The teen idol effectively plays this slime ball, easily switching from upbeat kid, to scheming smart-aleck, to dangerous thug, and back again.

Script writer Edward J. Lakso provides a predictable plot, having the young punk see the error of his ways and come to the rescue of our hero following an overly long, high-speed chase.

Notes, Oddities, and Bloopers:
•If the squad had a radio in this episode there would be no story, they could just radio-in the German gun positions.
•Unlike the impermeable tires of seasons one and two, these tires are susceptible to bullets.
•Bad lighting during the night-time chase; how is the front of Saunders' truck lit up, if all the lights are behind it?
•Kirby tries not to be his brother's keeper with Cane (at least his nickname in this episode is "Wildman," not Abel).

The Hard Way Back (076)
Written by Edward J. Lakso
Directed by Bernard McEveety
First aired 20-Oct-64 (Episode 6 of Season 3)

CAST:
Regulars: Morrow, Hanley, Hogan, Carter, Jalbert
Guest Star Sal Mineo as Larry Kogan
Erik Holland as 1st German Soldier
Grant Lockwood as 2nd German Soldier
Ed Gilbert as German Captain
Martin Brandt as Old Frenchman
Robert Howard as German Lieutenant
Eric Forst as German Officer

Synopsis:
During a barrage, Saunders is trapped under a beam and the only man who can rescue him is Pvt. Kogan. The scared Kogan abandons Saunders as the enemy moves into town. Kogan tells the platoon that Saunders is dead, but when they are ordered to recapture the village, Kogan returns to face Saunders and try to save him.

Review — 3.5 bayonets:
In "The Hard Way Back," teen idol Sal Mineo plays a terror-stricken young private who is transformed into a reluctant hero. This episode features fine performances by Vic Morrow and Sal Mineo.

Though their scenes are short, the squad's moments are memorable. Hanley and the regulars' reactions upon hearing of Saunders' death are subtly played — especially Pierre Jalbert, whose silent, stunned reactions speak volumes. They all are badly shaken by Saunders' death. When Hanley says, "All right. Settle down," to Kogan, he is really saying it to himself and the rest of the squad.

The script by Edward J. Lakso is very strong. Sal Mineo's dialogue as he tells the squad of Saunders' death is particularly well formed. As he stumbles through his words, making things up as he goes, Kogan conveys what he means to say as clearly as what he actually says. Desperately wanting to make sense of their loss, the squad inadvertently feeds Kogan the details he needs to make his lies plausible.

Sal Mineo and Vic Morrow in "The Hard Way Back."

Fans refer to this as a "beamer" episode: a plot device where you trap a character under a beam for dramatic effect. *Combat!* used this device in five episodes.

The Little Carousel (077)
Written by Joan Levitt
Directed by Bernard McEveety
First aired 10-Nov-1964 (Episode 8 of Season 3)

CAST:
Regulars: Morrow, Jason, Hogan, Carter, Peabody, Jalbert
Sylviane Margolle as Claudine
Warren Vanders as Henderson
Donald Journeaux as Antoine
Paul Daniel as Old Man Patient

Synopsis:
In a newly liberated French town, Saunders is reluctant to accept the ministrations of a courageous thirteen-year-old girl, whose one ambition is to serve the troops as a nurse. Despite Saunders' sometimes cruel resistance to her, Claudine grows deeply attached to him, and he to her. During a battle outside town, she risks her life to bring Saunders medical aid on the line.

Review — 4 bayonets:
"The Little Carousel" is a special episode for me. When I saw this as a child, I was devastated. I cried myself to sleep that night and remembered exact dialogue decades later. As a little girl who wanted to be a nurse, I strongly identified with the girl

in the story.

Bernard McEveety directed another superb episode in "The Little Carousel." Morrow runs the range of emotions — bitterness, anger, frustration, joy, exultation, love. Saunders fell in love with this little girl who healed not only his body, but his soul. Sylvian Margolle, as the little nurse Claudine, is a sweet breath of life amid the war. Saunders' carefully groomed, hard-bitten facade falls away when he gives in to something he had almost forgotten existed — pure joy.

At the end, the stoic Saunders openly shows his agonizing grief in a primal scream, oblivious to his men around him.

Notes, Oddities, and Bloopers:
• When Sarge is sitting on the blanket talking, after he finishes his cheese and wipes his fingers, in the next close up he is still eating the cheese.
• The length of Claudine's hair seems to change throughout the episode.
• In the scene where Claudine is killed by the land mine, Anderson's helmet keeps appearing and disappearing from his head.

Fly Away Home (078)
Written by Kay Lenard and Jess Carneol
Directed by Bernard McEveety
First aired 17-Nov-64 (Episode 9 of Season 3)

CAST:
Regulars: Jason, Morrow, Hogan, Jalbert, Peabody
Guest Star Neville Brand as Sgt. Keeley
Stephen Joyce as Polaski
Rudy Dolan as German Sgt. #1
Robert Champion as German Pvt.
Ed Deemer as German Sgt. #2
Ron Stokes as Maxwell

Synopsis:
Sgt. Keeley (Neville Brand) has lost faith in humanity and invests all his devotion to his carrier pigeons, which he has trained for military use. Under attack by the Germans, Saunders learns that Keeley would gladly sacrifice the lives of men, rather than see one of his pigeons die.

Review — 3 bayonets:
Once again, Saunders' squad escorts a Sergeant with unique technical expertise (and an attitude) on a special mission. This time it's pigeon duty. Neville Brand, a burly man with a weathered face, is a delight to watch tenderly working his pigeons. Unlike the Sergeants usually foisted on Saunders in this plot type, Brand isn't obnoxious. He is even polite — especially when he politely discourages Saunders' interest in the birds.

About Filming the Episode:
In his column in the Mountain Democrat, Dick Peabody said, "The late Neville Brand was as interesting as any guest we had. He liked to drink, but wisely held off until the last scene was shot. We invited him to the bar in Vic's dressing room, and

a couple of hours later everyone had left except Neville and myself." Dick Peabody had to drive Brand to his Malibu home, where his wife invited him in for a drink. Peabody was impressed with the floor-to-ceiling bookshelves in every room of the house. "There were literally thousands of volumes," says Peabody. "His tastes were eclectic, since almost everything interested him." Neville's wife pointed to the books and said, "He's read every one of them.'" A high-school drop-out, Neville Brand was self-educated.

Notes, Oddities, and Bloopers:
•Magnificent music sequence under the bird's escape from the coop.
•Neville Brand spent ten years in the army and is often cited as being the fourth most decorated U.S. soldier of the war. The claim is likely a press agent fabrication. Brand was highly decorated, but not a record setter. He saw action in the Ardennes, Rhineland, and Central European campaigns, and received the Silver Star for gallantry in combat while convalescing at the 21st General Hospital. His other awards and decorations are the Purple Heart, the Good Conduct Medal, the American Defense Service Ribbon, the European/African/Middle Eastern Theater Ribbon with three Battle Stars, one Overseas Service Bar, one Service Stripe, and the Combat Infantryman's Badge.

A Rare Vintage (079)
Written by Esther and Bob Mitchell
Directed by Sutton Roley
First aired 08-Dec-1964 (Episode 12 of Season 3)

CAST:
Regulars: Jason, Morrow, Carter, Jalbert
Corey Allen as Pvt. Garrett
Lyle Bettger as Capt. Brauer
Marcel Hillaire as Jean Sebelleau
Lawrence Montaigne as Sgt. Koch
Buck Holland as Lane Sentry

Synopsis:
When a wounded Hanley is held captive by Germans in a French winery, Caje disguises himself as a handicapped peasant to rescue him. But Pvt. Garrett, another GI trapped in the winery, interferes with the plans. In the end, the cowardly Garrett sees the light, and helps the squad to spirit away Hanley in a barrel of spirits.

Review — 3 bayonets
In "A Rare Vintage," Saunders and Caje go above-and-beyond to rescue a wounded Hanley from a German-occupied winery. This is a great episode for Morrow and Jalbert, not so much for Jason, who is primarily used as a prop.

Saunders goes to nearly super human effort trying to get medicine and succor to Hanley. He does not quite leap tall buildings in a single bound, but he makes a ten-foot jump across balconies. Caje again risks being shot as a spy when he dons civilian clothes to pass himself off as the crippled grandson of the vintner.

Director Sutton Roley shows what an expert, creative lensman he is. He offers some stunning dolly shots and remarkable camera zooms. A long camera shot, that zooms tightly into a closeup of Saunders hiding in the bushes, is particularly striking.

Notes, Oddities, and Bloopers:
•The German tests to see if Caje's right hand is really crippled by seeing if he can catch something in his left. Since actor Jalbert is a south-paw, this was not too difficult.
•A wimpy interrogation scene: after Hanley tells the German captain to "Get lost," the captain actually leaves, saying that he'll find some way to make him talk. This German, for some reason, did not think of slapping him around for the information.
•When Saunders and Caje come into the winery, as they lean over Hanley, a cameraman's shadow falls across the left-hand side of the shot.

The Enemy (080)
Story by Steve Fisher
Written by Edward J. Lakso
Directed by John Peyser
First aired 05-Jan-1965 (Episode 16 of Season 3)

CAST:
Regulars: Jason
Guest Star Robert Duvall as Karl
Michel Corhan as Louis Roche
Robert de Schene as Claude Roche
Kurt Landen as German #1
Gerd Rein as German #2
Anna Lee as Sister Lescaut

Synopsis:
Hanley captures a clever demolitions expert in a French spa town after the officer has booby-trapped the entire village. When Hanley is advised by a nun that the elderly citizens of the town will soon return, Hanley enlists the German's aid to remove each of the traps. The German welcomes the opportunity as a chance to escape. He turns the tables on Hanley, catching him in one of his traps.

Review — 3 bayonets:
Robert Duvall is convincing as a confident super-man playing a dangerous game with explosives. A strong script keeps Duvall and Jason on each other's nerves throughout the episode. Great tension throughout: you know Duvall will try something at every turn, and, along with Hanley, you try to figure out ahead of time what it will be.

About Filming the Episode:
Robert Duvall is a quiet man and an actor who takes acting very seriously. He kept to himself during his three guest stints on *Combat!* He spent his off-camera time running lines behind the sets.

Notes, Oddities, and Bloopers:
•Hanley wears two rings in this episode.
•Another instance of non-bulletproof tires.

A Gift of Hope (081)
Written by Anthony Wilson
Directed by Bernard McEveety
First aired 01-Dec-1964 (Episode 11 of Season 3)

CAST:
Regulars: Morrow, Hogan, Carter, Peabody
Guest Star Rip Torn as Avery
Malcolm Brodrick as Jimmy
Joe Allen Price as Larkin
Robert Yuro as Vitelli
Anthony Eisley as Lt. Gates

Synopsis:
Saunders learns that his hero and role-model has feet of clay. Sergeant Avery, thought killed in action at St. Lo, shows up alive and well, and must clear himself of suspicion of desertion. With Saunders at his side, Avery makes a journey of discovery about himself and about what it takes to be a frontline soldier.

Review — 3.5 bayonets
In "A Gift of Hope," Saunders will not listen to Kirby's accusation that Avery had deserted under fire. Just not possible. Not the man that Saunders' infused with his trust. But when Avery appears, alive and well, the stern moralizer Saunders goes cold, announcing that he wished his friend — his hero — had died, rather than be revealed as a coward.

Though the story takes awhile to get revving, once up to speed it is incredibly strong. Rip Torn offers a fine performance as Avery. "A Gift of Hope" is one of Morrow's best performances. The difficult scene where Avery walks a wounded Saunders back to the aid station is moving. The bulk of that act is Torn's monologue. Morrow says nothing, but viewers know exactly what he is thinking about Avery's pained confessions.

Jack Hogan gives a strong performance as a Kirby out for revenge, and Rick Jason's Hanley walks the tightrope between duty and friendship. Bernard McEveety provides excellent direction plus some great night-time battle scenes.

Anthony Wilson's script reveals the psyche of a frontline soldier. Avery's undoing was not the fear of battle, or the terror of dying, it was the most terrible gift the hard-core veteran could imagine: hope.

Notes, Oddities, and Bloopers:
• Saunders again without his own knife, he must borrow Avery's.
• R.H.I.P. — Saunders is the only one in the cellar quarters with a real bed.

A Walk with an Eagle (082)
Written by Rod Peterson
Directed by John Peyser
First aired 02-Mar-1965 (Episode 24 of Season 3)

CAST:
Regulars: Jason, Carter
Lee Philips as Major Robert Caldwell
William Cort as Private Harmon
Pat Colby as Private Palmer

Synopsis:
Hanley takes three men into enemy territory to rescue a U.S. flying ace, Major Caldwell, who has parachuted to safety. The ground-pounders resent the arrogance of the flyer. The Major is ungrateful and willful, showing little understanding of a war he has seen only from thousands of feet above the ground.

Review — 2 bayonets:
The most enjoyment I have in this episode is smiling at Hanley talking about the Air Corps. Knowing that Rick Jason served in the Army Air Corps in WWII, adds a zip to this dialog, especially as he deals with an arrogant ace who must be taught the difference between fighting a war in the air and a war on the ground.

Notes, Oddities, and Bloopers:
• Filmed at Korbel winery.
• Long motorcycle chase up Korbel's hills, but no tension or drama in the chase.
• Major Caldwell is credited with 22 kills, but his P-47s get easily jumped by a flight of Stukas.
• Moments after Major Crandall's plane is shot down, a corporal in a jeep finds Hanley and relays orders to rescue the flyer. How did they know exactly where Hanley was and how did the word get to the corporal so quickly?
• The closeup of the dead German's face during the vineyard firefight shows that his machine gun belts have crimped blank cartridges.

Birthday Cake (083)
Written by Ed Adamson
Directed by John Peyser
First aired 29-Dec-1964 (Episode 15 of Season 3)

CAST:
Regulars: Morrow, Hogan, Jalbert, Peabody
Co-Starring Phillip Pine as Pvt. Steve Cantrell
Jean del Val as French Farmer
Beau Vanden Ecker as GI Driver

Synopsis:
Littlejohn receives a birthday cake from his mother, with the explicit instruction to not open until the 21st. He carries it on a dangerous patrol into enemy territory. Along on the mission is Cantrell, a man waiting for orders to go home. Littlejohn's adherence to his mother's request brings the squad into harm's way and leads Cantrell to doubt he'll live to see home.

Review — 1.5 bayonets:
Littlejohn receives a cake on the 20th, with instructions not to open it until the 21st (which 21st? It doesn't say). The audience endures a day of this cake causing complications for Littlejohn and for an obnoxious translator forced to go along with the squad and the cake.

The script makes Littlejohn come off as a slow-witted bumpkin — something that he is not in most episodes. But in this episode he really takes the cake.

COMBAT!

This story could not quite decide if it was truly a comedy. There's a bit too much bloodshed, angst, and abandonment of wounded soldiers to really make it amusing. The episode originally aired Christmas week, just before the new year.

Notes, Oddities, and Bloopers:
- Filmed at Korbel Winery.
- This episode is first time Dick Peabody is credited on his own title card, but still listed after Hogan and Jalbert.
- First on-screen credit for wardrobe man Beau Vanden Ecker
- On the walk back, the squad stops and Saunders looks through binoculars. He says that nothing is there, but people are moving in the shot.
- After the squad makes a stretcher for Cantrell they are seen all wearing their jackets (usually a field stretched is made by threading the arms of jackets through poles); if they didn't use their field jackets, where did the fabric from the stretcher come from?
- When Littlejohn moves into the river, the outline of the camera platform, a cameraman, and another person is reflected in the water.

The Cassock (084)

Story by James L. Wixted
Written by Esther and Bob Mitchell
Directed by Bernard McEveety
First aired 12-Jan-1965 (Episode 17 of Season 3)

CAST:
Regulars: Morrow, Hogan, Carter, Jalbert, Peabody
Guest Star James Whitmore as Hertzbrun
Glen Stensel as Weaver
Ross Sturlin as Stevens
Mart Hulswit as Ryan

Synopsis:

A German captain, Hertzbrun, is ordered to blow up a bridge that the Americans will use to enter a French town, but Saunders' squad moves in before he can complete his mission. He poses as the local priest while awaiting the chance to finish his mission. He offers spiritual guidance to the men, but former altar boy Private Ryan discovers his deceit and dies for it.

Review — 3 bayonets:

"The Cassock" is a taut thriller about a German officer posing as a priest. The episode boasts strong acting, good direction, and a well-designed script. But, in an abandoned French village, who keeps lighting all those candles in the empty church?

James Whitmore, who starred in Robert Pirosh's *Battleground,* plays Hertzbrun superbly. Mart Hulswit is the sensitive soldier who seeks the comfort of the church from a heartless saboteur.

Notes, Oddities, and Bloopers:
- Mart Hulswit appears again in "The Ringer" in season four.

- The teaser re-uses footage from season one, showing Kirby carrying an M1 rifle. After the battle, he again has his B.A.R.

The Town that Went Away (085)

Written by George F. Slavin
Directed by Sutton Roley
First aired 22-Dec-1964 (Episode 14 of Season 3)

CAST:
Regulars: Jason, Hogan, Carter, Peabody, Jalbert
Guest Star Jay Novello as Paul Lejeune
Billy Beck as Rafe
Danielle Beausejour as Yvette
Danielle Aubrey as Marie
Gerald Michenaud as French Boy
Susan Silo as Annice

Synopsis:

Hanley and men are sent to evacuate the town of Bonnaire, which has been targeted for German attack. But the mayor, his three beautiful daughters, and the townspeople thwart Hanley's every effort. They switch road signs to send the weary soldiers in the wrong direction and invent a fake monastery to hide their real efforts: to save the town's cognac supply from destruction.

Review — 1 bayonet:

In the conclusion to "The Town that Went Away," Hanley says, "I guess the war can wait for one short hour." That line sums up this light diversion from the usual grim *Combat!* episode. "The Town that Went Away," is done strictly for laughs, appropriate for the holiday season, when the show originally aired.

The squad regulars are thoroughly charming as they allow themselves to be wined, dined, and duped by the mayor. Jack Hogan's Kirby is his usual skirt-chasing self, and winds up a prisoner of love. Dick Peabody and Conlan Carter make the most of their on-screen time with the ladies and Hanley provides an outstanding example of a patented pep talk designed to inspire civilians.

About Filming the Episode:

"It was always special on the set when there were ladies around," says Georg Fenady. "But actually it was a little difficult to get the crew to act any different in terms of language and, well, boys will be boys." Many of the regulars engaged in pranks and games to amuse themselves between takes. They would sometimes abscond with jeeps and have races around the MGM backlot and engage in rowdy competitions. Fenady recalls one director who refused to come back unless the regulars promised to avoid playing one particular game. The director had gotten caught in the crossfire.

Notes, Oddities, and Bloopers:
- Danielle Aubrey, one of the mayor's daughters, appeared in second season's Christmas week episode, "The Party."

The Convict (086)

Written by Kay Lenard and Jess Carneol
Directed by Bernard McEveety
First aired 16-Feb-65 (Episode 22 of Season 3)

CAST:

Regulars: Jason, Morrow, Hogan, Jalbert
Guest star Gilbert Roland as Boulanger
Clive Clerk as Pierre
Peter Camlin as French Engineer
Benito Prezia as Andre
Sheldon Jacobs as German Major
Chris Anders as German
Robert Carricart as Lambrelle

Synopsis:

A German bombardment strikes a prison, releasing convicted criminals into the countryside. One unscrupulous convict, Boulanger, assumes the identity of a French resistance fighter and teams up with Hanley's squad. Boulanger uses the squad to travel safely to a rendezvous with his son. The son believes in the father, thinking him guiltless of any crime.

Review — 1/2 bayonet:

This light-weight story benefits from the presence of veteran screen actor Gilbert Roland. He instills passion and energy in this slight story of a hard-bitten convict and his devoted son.

Hanley starts out with the squad, but after a convenient wounding, hitches a ride to the rear on a steam locomotive. In reality, Rick Jason had received an invitation to go hunting on the Korbel winery property and wanted out of that episode. His exit provided some magnificent shots of the Lieutenant riding MGM's grand old steam engine. Director McEveety shoots some entertaining sequences at the mine and provides a well-choreographed battle. The predictable plot, though, is uncompelling.

About Filming the Episode:

Jack Hogan remembers working with Gilbert Roland, that he was not "the warmest guy in the world" but a fine actor. "He had been around since silents. He was a legend and was supposed to be a health-food addict. He was getting on and he looked better than we did."

Notes, Oddities, and Bloopers:

•Action of the plot takes place near Avignon.
•The trainman uses an American Colt .45 revolver to shoot Hanley.

The Steeple (087)

Written by Don Tait
Directed by John Peyser
First aired 09-Feb-1965 (Episode 21 of Season 3)

CAST:

Regulars: Morrow, Hogan, Jalbert
Robert Cornthwaite as Captain Priller
Jean del Val as Father Bomar
Steve Landers as Hans
Horst Ebersberg as Sgt. Dekker
Patrick Michenaud as Boy
David Sheiner as Captain Ridell

Synopsis:

Saunders, Caje, and Kirby try to rescue a paratrooper captain before he is spotted by the Germans. The captain dangles from a church steeple, his chute caught on the spire. With the aid of the town priest, Saunders pulls the captain off the spire right before the eyes of the Germans below.

Review — 3 bayonets:

This episode has so many flaws in the action and the plot that it should be laughable, but, somehow it all works. A guilty pleasure, I enjoy this story more with each viewing, even as I notice more problems.

"The Steeple" has Saunders to the rescue once again, trying to save an injured paratrooper hanging from a steeple in a German-occupied town. Saunders does all the cliche hero-things that fans have come to expect, and he does them brilliantly. Yes, another patented "let's berate the superior officer for his own good to knock him back to his senses" speech, plus the usual "let's put on a German uniform and fool the bad guys" scenario, and another German with bad footwear that makes him come to a bad end. Somehow it fits together and entertains.

About Filming the Episode:

Pierre Jalbert was impressed with the technical skills of regular *Combat!* director John Peyser. "As he shoots [an] episode, he was cutting it in the camera. Directors who don't know what they're doing, they roll a lot of film and let the editor put it together. It's like reconstructing a house. But Peyser, he knew the business backwards and sideways. So we'd come in the morning, do ten pages—doesn't matter if it's tanks, explosions—and we'd go home at 3:00. He wouldn't watch as we rolled. He didn't have to. He'd play frisbee."

Notes, Oddities, and Bloopers:

•Saunders has remarkably good hearing. From thirty feet above, he hears quiet conversations on the ground.
•In the belfry as the church bells peel, Kirby and Caje cover both ears to protect their hearing. Saunders only covers one, to no ill effect.
•Immediately after being deafened by church bells, Caje hears the whispered voice of the priest on the ground floor.
•Why doesn't the bell ring when four soldiers climb down the bell rope?
•Again, the plot features one-size-fits-all German uniforms. When Saunders puts on the German uniform jacket after knifing the German, the jacket has no hole or blood, and neither is there any sign of a wound on the dead German.
•Saunders leaves his camoflauge helmet behind in the belfry but has it back again in the next scene.
•Jean del Val, who plays the priest, appeared in "Birthday Cake" and "The Mockingbird."

More Than a Soldier (088)

Written by Shirl Hendryx
Directed by Bernard McEveety
First aired 26-Jan-1965 (Episode 19 of Season 3)

CAST:

Regulars: Morrow
Guest Star Tommy Sands as Carey
Ron Soble as German Sergeant

Synopsis:

Saunders and a young soldier, Private Carey, are in a fight for their lives against the Germans. But Carey has never killed anything or anybody, and will not defend himself. Saunders and he become trapped in a mine with a wounded German who is pinned beneath the rubble. When the Americans escape and Saunders is wounded, Carey considers abandoning the German to a ghastly death in the darkness.

Review — 3.5 bayonets:

This story deals with the integral *Combat!* theme: the search for how to remain true to your own moral integrity while still being a soldier. In "More Than a Soldier," Carey (played by Tommy Sands) first learns the high price to be paid for failing as a soldier, and then questions the difference between being a murderer and being a soldier. This episode employs the oft-used device of trapping a soldier under a beam (a plot used five times in *Combat!*)

Director Bernard McEveety provides great action scenes: beautifully choreographed and emotionally riveting. His camera lingers tenderly on the weapons of war and on the men handling them. But he also brings a light touch to the intimate scenes in the cave as Saunders and Carey deal with life, death, and morality.

Notes, Oddities, and Bloopers:

• As Saunders is digging, he scrapes his knuckles and seems to whisper "damn." His knuckles in other scenes are scraped.
• This episode has the shortest credit list in the series, though the cast is fairly large (the opening battle sequence uses many extras and stuntmen).

The Long Wait (089)

Written by Edward J. Lakso
Directed by John Peyser
First aired 09-Mar-1965 (Episode 25 of Season 3)

CAST:

Regulars: Jason, Morrow, Hogan, Carter, Jalbert, Peabody
Guest Star Terry Carter as Archie
William Wellman as Sgt. Brice
Edward Tierney as Klaus
William Splawn as Coates
David Adams as Peter
Fletcher Fist as Carson

Terry Carter fights to save four wounded soldiers in "The Long Wait."

Synopsis:

In "The Long Wait," a German machine gun pins down Saunders and company, along with four seriously wounded GIs, a truckful of desperately needed munitions, and a truck driver more interested in saving lives than playing soldier. The driver, Archie Masters, cannot bear the suffering of the wounded soldiers in his care. He wants to fight. But Saunders insists on waiting until an American tank can move in and destroy the German guns.

Review — 2 bayonets:

This story by Edward J. Lakso lets the audience inside the psyche of Saunders the soldier. His view of war — as bloody mathematics — is at odds with the needs of the truck driver, and at odds with Saunders' own emotions.

In "The Long Wait," director John Peyser does his best to stretch out this story that really cannot fill the hour. He pads it with stock footage, with shots of the tank moving in and moving out, and with close-ups of tank treads. But the premise is established early in the episode — that nothing much is going to happen until the tank comes — and all the padding of pretty shots cannot hide the fact that nothing really does happen until the tank arrives. This episode is a long wait, not just for the soldiers, but also for the viewers.

Notes, Oddities, and Bloopers:
- Fletcher Fist (Brockmeyer in season one) appears in this episode, hidden behind face-covering bandages and flat on his back.
- The heavyweight German up in the rocks keeps switching position from shot-to-shot, even though in all closeups he is on the right.
- The opening sequence re-uses shots from "Bridgehead."
- The long shots of the truck on the road are lifted from "The Duel."
- Early in the episode, one of the wounded soldiers dies in the truck. The body is not shown again, with no explanation of what happened to it.
- In five seasons, this is the only episode to feature a black actor.
- William Wellman (Sgt. Brice) appeared in "Anatomy of a Patrol."

The Tree of Moray (090)

Teleplay by Anthony Spinner and Don Tait
Story by Anthony Spinner
Directed by Bernard McEveety
First aired 16-Mar-1965 (Episode 26 of Season 3)

CAST:
Regulars: Jason, Hogan, Peabody, Jalbert
Robert Loggia as Etienne
Emile Genest as Duval
P.L. Renoudet as Louis
Charles Giongi as Maquis
Norbert Seigfried as German M.P.
Tom Pace as German Lt.
Mike Krempels as German Sgt.
Robert Ellenstein as Rene

Synopsis:
Hanley's efforts to bring to London a Frenchman with information valuable to the Allies is hampered by a lynching party that wants him for themselves. A hanging tree awaits Duval, whose collaboration with the Germans meant death for the innocent citizens of Moray.

Review — 2 bayonets:
In "The Tree of Moray," Robert Loggia is excellent as an underground fighter determined to exact justice. But none of the *Combat!* regulars (Jason, Hogan, Jalbert, and Peabody) or director McEveety seem comfortable with this script or with the actions of their characters. McEveety and *Combat!* are on more sure ground with clear moral issues.

The action scene between the Germans and the squad is

exciting, almost a relief. But the later "action" sequences between Americans and French, who are reluctant to engage each other, are stilted and uncomfortable.

The story is an interesting one, with some intriguing moral questions that never get developed. The script is talky, with the squad describing the action as it happens.

About Filming the Episode:
Dick Peabody recalls that Robert Loggia joined easily into the pranks and games of the cast regulars, especially the "disgusting sounds symphony." "You couldn't invite just anyone to these concerts, which took place in our clubhouse—Vic Morrow's motorhome. The object was to make the most disgusting sounds, vocally, that you could think of. At the end of each session we would vote on which of us was the most sickening. Loggia won twice; not bad for a novice."

Notes, Oddities, and Bloopers:
- Filmed at Franklin Canyon and MGM.
- Great set dressing, making the usually bomb-destroyed French village look even more desolate.
- The branches of the Moray tree are blackened, but the trunk is not.
- Emile Genest (the traitor Duval) was in "Any Second Now" and "Anniversary."

Cry in the Ruins (091)

Written by Edward J. Lakso
Story by A. M. Zweiback,
Directed by Vic Morrow
First aired 23-Mar-1965 (Episode 27 of Season 3)

CAST:
Regulars: Jason, Hogan, Carter, Jalbert
Guest Star William Smithers as Lt. Markes
Glenn Cannon as Pvt. Cane
John Crawford as Capt. Werner
Henry Horman-Cattani as Kranz
Ben-Ari as Le Page
Bob Kanter as Pvt. Hunstell
Larry Gelbmann as Gunnar
Frank Oberschall as Bruck
Gerd Rein as Heismann
Lisa Pera as Madame DuBois

Synopsis:
A desperate woman searches for her missing baby as American and German soldiers watch helplessly from opposite ends of the street. The woman begs for help to rescue her infant son, whom she believes to be trapped in a wine cellar beneath the street. In an uneasy truce, the enemy soldiers agree to work together to help the woman. The enemy squads cease being soldiers for a time, until a wounded German officer crashes into their artificial peace.

Review — 4 bayonets:
Directed by Vic Morrow, "Cry in the Ruins" shows his remarkable strengths as a director. Though he occasionally falls into "art" shots that are more showy than revealing, he delivers a brilliant episode. This story of enemies uniting in

the name of common decency is riveting. The conclusion is surprising and haunting.

Morrow knew how to get the best out of Rick Jason. His Hanley is superb as he arranges a wary truce with a German patrol and struggles to find a way to do the right thing. Lisa Pera is exceptional as the distraught Frenchwoman who serves as the catalyst for this story. As a mother desperate to save the life of her child, she temporarily halts a war and reminds two warring groups that they are more than just members of an army, but members of humanity. By the end of the episode, her tragedy shows these soldiers, in heart-breaking clarity, the real cost of the war and who pays the price.

About Filming the Episode:

Dick Peabody about Vic as a director: "Vic had everything Burt [Kennedy] had and everything [Robert] Altman had. Vic could have been an absolute superstar motion picture director . . . The talent was there, and so obvious to everyone."

Heritage (092)

Written by Barry Trivers
Directed by John Peyser
First aired 04-13-65, Episode 30 of Season 3

CAST:

Regulars: Jason, Morrow, Hogan, Carter, Peabody
Guest Star Charles Bronson as Velasquez
Robert Fortier as Captain Jampel
Kort Falkenberg as German Sergeant
Michael Stroka as Scope Man
Gunther Weishoff as 1st German Soldier
Alf George as 2nd German Soldier

Synopsis:

An artistic stone mason, Corporal Velasquez, is assigned to Hanley's outfit with orders to destroy a German observation post. Velasquez was a sculptor of cemetery monuments as a civilian who longed for the skills to be a great sculptor. When he discovers world-class art treasures sequestered in the vault that he must destroy, he cannot bring himself to deprive the world of such beauty — even at the cost of American lives.

Review — 2 bayonets:

Charles Bronson guest stars as a specialist who must choose between saving American lives and preserving a priceless heritage for future generations. It's a great opportunity for real conflict and moral dilemmas: the present vs. the future; the temporal vs. the eternal; the physical vs. the ephemeral. Since the episode wastes the first three acts getting to the central conflict, little of this is examined. But Bronson delivers the goods as an earthy, everyman type who longs to be something more.

Action fans will be disappointed by this episode. It is almost completely devoid of fighting, with even the standard action opening foregone. The episode opens after a battle, with the squad injured and exhausted.

In *Combat!*, Saunders seems to get the obnoxious specialists and Hanley the ethereal ones. Velasquez's biggest problem

in the field is keeping his mind on soldiering and away from rock formations, sculpture, and classical art. Jason is fine as Hanley, in what little he has to do in this episode. Hogan, as Kirby, is just along for the ride. But this great actor makes the ride a fun trip, even though the script hampers him with asking the stupid questions that progress the plot. This episode is all Bronson's, and he is very watchable making the big sacrifice: giving up more than his life in the name of the greater good.

About Filming the Episode:

Rick Jason says, "Jack Hogan, I think, is the finest actor of all the bunch of us. Absolutely superb. Better than Vic, better than me, better than anybody who ever visited the show. Very underrated."

Notes, Oddities, and Bloopers:

•Charles Bronson's publicity information used to state that he flew as a bomber gunner in WWII. Actually, he drove a delivery truck in Kingman, Arizona, for the 760th Mess Squadron.

•For once, the commanding officer, Jampel, journeys to the front to check on his troops.

•Beautiful lighting on the sound stage, giving a glow in the fog.

•Sculptor Jacob Epstein, who Bronson's character refers to, was a controversial American-born sculptor who worked directly in hard stone.

The Hell Machine (093)

Written by Edward J. Lakso
Directed by John Peyser
First aired 30-Mar-1965 (Episode 28 of Season 3)

CAST:

Regulars: Morrow
Guest Star Frank Gorshin as Pvt. Gavin
Lou Robb as Lt. Bruner
James Arthur as German Colonel
Gene Benton as Tank Commander
Dick Raymond as German Infantryman
Heinz Sadler as Sgt. Peter
Chris Anders as Lt. Krause
Than Wyenn as Captain Beggs

Synopsis:

When their jeep hits a land mine, Saunders, a tank captain, and Private Gavin attempt to maneuver an abandoned German tank through enemy territory.

Review — 3 bayonets:

The budget saved by deleting action sequences from "Heritage," was spent on "The Hell Machine." Vehicles, tanks, and extras abound in this high-action episode starring Frank Gorshin as a washed-out, claustrophobic driver who must bring Saunders and his wounded CO to safety in a hijacked German tank. The story is completely ridiculous and completely entertaining. Strong script, well-paced episode, good acting, and even one of Saunders' patented pep talks.

The heavy equipment and extras cover the hills at Thousand

Than Wyenn, Frank Gorshin and Vic Morrow in "Hell Machine."

Oaks where the episode was filmed. This provides wide-open vistas to contrast with the claustrophobic interior of the tank.

About Filming the Episode:

When *Combat!* needed a tank, they contacted the California National Guard. They paid only the costs of the sergeant and major who supervised and operated the tank,

along with gasoline and other expenses. The tanks were shipped to location on a flatbed truck.

A cold snap hit Los Angeles during filming of this episode. The crew dressed warm to work behind the cameras and the actors bundled themselves in blankets between shots.

Billy the Kid (094)

Teleplay by Esther & Bob Mitchell
Story by Bivings F. Wallace
Directed by Bernard McEveety
First aired 06-Apr-1965 (Episode 29 of Season 3)

CAST:
Regulars: Jason, Morrow, Hogan, Carter, Jalbert, Peabody
Guest Star Andrew Prine as Lt. Benton
Mike Masters as Burns
Ron Mills as Garn
Norbert Seigfried as German Leader
Ed Deemer as German #1
Jim de Closs as American Sentry
John Milford as Sgt. Stone

Synopsis:

Lieutenant William Benton, the son of celebrated General Bull Benton, leads a mission to locate a big artillery piece that is cutting up the American lines. He is accompanied by a surly sergeant. The inexperienced lieutenant's seemingly irrational behavior worries the squad. When battalion pulls back, stranding the squad on the ridge, his Sergeant tries to abandon the mission. "Billy the Kid" finally shares his plan with the squad, destroys the gun, and returns a hero with a now converted, faithful sergeant at his side.

Review — 3 bayonets:

Andrew Prine is splendid as an artillery lieutenant out to prove himself in "Billy the Kid." Saunders is saddled with this untried officer, unsure whether this son of a famous general knows what he's doing. Spurning the advice of Saunders, "Billy the Kid" makes some odd decisions in the field as he leads the squad on a dangerous mission to destroy a massive German gun.

As usual, Saunders is on an expedition with a sergeant-with-an-attitude. Saunders deals with him by delivering a patented pep talk, non-comm variant. All ends well in this clever script that ties the loose ends neatly together without seeming contrived.

Rick Jason's stunt double, Walt Davis, stands in for Andrew Prine in the scene where Billy the Kid is blinded.

Beneath the Ashes (095)

Teleplay by George F. Slavin and Richard P. McDonagh
Story by Richard P. McDonagh
Directed by John Peyser
First aired 27-Apr-1965 (Episode 32 of Season 3)

CAST:
Regulars: Jason, Morrow, Hogan, Carter, Peabody, Jalbert
Guest Star Chad Everett as Steve Kovac
Noam Pitlik as Mac
Robert Fortier as Capt. Jampel
Robert Champion as German Capt.
Gregory Mullavy as German Sgt.
Heber Jentzsch as German Lt.
John Gilgreen as Ambulance Driver
Robert Glenn as Lt. Coates

Synopsis:

Hanley receives a scrawled letter saying that the wife of one of his men, Kovac, is dying. To spare the soldier unnecessary anxiety, Hanley withholds the letter pending verification. But Kovac and the squad are missing in action by the time the Red Cross confirms that Mrs. Kovac is dying. When the squad finally returns, it is too late, and Kovac vows to make Hanley pay.

Review — 3.5 bayonets:

"Beneath the Ashes" has Saunders-to-the-rescue again in a slightly schizophrenic episode that is fun to watch. The weakly structured script presents two disjointed story lines that bump up against each other. But they are two marvelous stories, allowing special acting moments and character development.

In story one, Saunders and squad are trapped in a German-held town with a wounded Littlejohn. In story two, Hanley comes to terms with guilt over an MIA squad and a murderous GI bent on avenging himself on Hanley.

The ending of the show suffers from use of stock-footage from previous episodes. The fight in the woods has no original footage until Hanley is shown pinned in the crater. Prior to that, it is all reused shots from six (possibly more) previous episodes. Even the Germans that pin down Hanley are from another episode. When the wounded Kirby explains about the battle he was just in, his description does not match the scenes.

Too much talking, not enough "real" action. Saunders comes over the hill in the end to save a wounded Hanley after giving the patented pep talk (PFC version) to Chad Everett. Great performances from Jason, Morrow, Peabody, and guest star Chad Everett.

Notes, Oddities, and Bloopers:
• Second appearance this season of Robert Fortier as Captain Jampel. Episode shows that Hanley's platoon is actually part of a company that includes other lieutenants and a C.O.
• Saunders has a great line after being MIA three days: "I guess we're late."
• Jason again wears two pinky rings.
• The closeup of Saunders running and throwing the second grenade at the end of the episode is actually Earl Parker. Parker could stand in for Vic just a few feet away from the camera without anyone knowing it was him.
• Only story credit for Richard P. McDonagh, who was the *Combat!* story consultant for seasons two through five.

Odyssey (096)

Written by Anthony Wilson
Directed by Alan Crosland, Jr.
Produced by Andy White
First aired 20-Apr-1965 (Episode 31 of Season 3)

CAST:

Regulars: Morrow, Hanley, Carter, Peabody, Jalbert
Special Guests Bert Freed as Sgt. Weber and
Teno Pollack as Pfc. Loring
Peter Coe as Orderly
Sasha Hardin as S.S. Lieutenant
Maurice Marsac as French Peasant
Ivan Triesault as Doctor
Paul Werner as German Teenage Soldier
Bing Russel as Gaines
Larry Billman as Reiter
Marika Monti as French Peasant
Robert Donner as 1st American GI
Otto Reichow as German Guard #2
Vince Barbi as German Guard #1
Eric Forst as German Lineman

Synopsis:

Saunders, trapped behind enemy lines, passes himself off as a shell-shocked German corporal. In his odyssey back to his own lines, Saunders encounters a suspicious Nazi doctor, an inexperienced G.I. with writing aspirations, and a compassionate German sergeant who takes Saunders under his wing.

Review — 4 bayonets:

Vic Morrow performs brilliantly as Saunders in "Odyssey." A beautiful script by Anthony Wilson takes viewers on a gentle ride through the countryside, slowly picking up pace until the story, by the fouth act, is accelerating on a breakneck roller-coaster ride. A true tragedy in the classic sense, "Odyssey" shows the hero who wins a bitter victory, and the warrior with the fatal flaw that leads to his death.

Tino Pollack is excellent as the tanker who dreams of being a writer and Bert Freed is touching as the German sergeant killed by Saunders.

Notes, Oddities, and Bloopers:

• The German jeep is really American, painted with German markings.
• Sasha Hardin, a regular German who was featured in five episodes, plays the evil German lieutenant who suspects Saunders and shoots his own men for cowardice.
• Toward end, Morrow throws himself into a bomb crater and bonks his nose.
• Saunders spends episode in a one-size-fits-all German uniform removed from a dead German. But it has no bullet holes or blood. It looks not only tailored for Saunders, but freshly pressed.

The tank that becomes Saunders' personal nemesis in "The Duel." Filmed on location at Thousand Oaks.

Vic Morrow's "Hear No Evil" gallery: All these photos are from the original proof sheet from the "Hear No Evil" episode. Note Vic Morrow's right index finger, which was malformed at birth and which you never saw on air. Vic uses his right middle finger to pull the trigger on his Thompson. Official publicity pictures never show either the shortened finger or that he shoots with the "incorrect" trigger finger.

As the fourth season began, the cast was celebrating their success of the previous season. They had finished in tenth place in the ratings. Prior to that, many individual episodes had been ratings successes, but third season was the first (and last) time the series as a whole scored well.

Vic Morrow used the success to launch another bid for salary increase. He was successful, raising his (and Rick Jason's) salary to $6,000 per episode, making him one of the highest paid actors in series television. It also prompted Selmur to start looking for alternatives to their high-paid stars. They produced a pilot for another television series. It was not picked up, but they hoped the pilot would help show Vic Morrow that he could be replaced.

The continued clashes wore on producer Gene Levitt. Rick Jason recalls, "It got to the point where Gene Levitt just hated him [Vic Morrow]. I was in the office one day with Gene, and Gene said to me 'I hate him.' We were at the end of the third year and Gene had one more year to go. At the end of four years, Gene quit." Gene quit toward the end of the fourth season. He could not take the stress any longer. He was worn out and exhausted.

After a full season of working without a contract, Conlan Carter decided that enough was enough. He walked into the front office and said that he wanted a contract or he was quitting. They agreed. "It changed nothing really, except the security of a contract," says Conlan Carter. He appeared in as many shows with or without a yearly contract.

Combat! began to show its age in the fourth season. Plots started to be recycled and some new, inexperienced directors helmed the cameras. Michael Caffey and Georg Fenady, who had been assistant directors for *Combat!* since the first season, became directors in the fourth season. Their familiarity with the locations and the actors served them well.

This season produced what is arguably the finest episode of the entire series: "Hills Are for Heroes," directed by Vic Morrow. The show, which ran over schedule and over budget, became a source of contention between the producers and Vic Morrow. But the cast enjoyed the 21-day shoot, many giving their best performances in the two-part episode.

"A great part of my performance was due to Vic," says Rick Jason. "I was able to do it, because Vic gave me the time to do it. And I'd never been given the time before, none of us were given the time. . . I tried never to repeat myself, but it was almost impossible. But [in 'Hills'] he gave me an opportunity to think. He [Vic] gave me time. This is why feature films will always be better than television, because television doesn't give you time. You have to settle into a character, and just play the character straight down the line without thinking."

CHAPTER 5

SEASON FOUR 1965–1966

Location Shooting (Europe, Korbel Winery, Hop Kiln)

During the hiatus between seasons three and four, Gene Levitt took a production crew to Europe for location shooting. Rick Jason remembers, "They came to Vic and me and they said they wanted to shoot six weeks in Europe to get some background stuff for stories next year. They'd already started buying stories, so they knew what they had to shoot footage for. Vic and I said that's nice. They said they'd pay all our expenses. No salary. Vic and I said no."

Stuntman Earl Parker went with the crew to Europe and did all the stunts. "They asked me to go and double Vic whenever needed," says Earl Parker. "From a distance of course, but they could photograph me pretty close." Local actors stood in for the other actors. The segments with Earl look like Morrow is in the shots, but the other doubles fall short, with an ungraceful man walking stolidly as Caje and a Littlejohn much slighter than Dick Peabody.

The crew filmed at several chateaus in Loire, France and in the French countryside. The shots are expertly cut into the episodes "The Linesman," "The Main Event," "Hear No Evil," and "Evasion."

A favorite location shoot for the cast was the Korbel Winery in Guerneville, California. The sprawling winery on the Russian river provided a change of scene for the *Combat!* episodes. The actors loved the two times they went to Korbel. The crew would stay at Korbel for several weeks, filming a couple episodes at a time. The cast first went to Korbel in the third season and returned in the fifth season.

The owners of the winery enjoyed hosting the cast. During

the season, they invited hunter Rick Jason for deer hunting on their property. Jack Hogan fondly remembers filming at Korbel. "It was run by the Heck brothers. Every morning they would mix us champagne and orange juice before we went to work. We were drunk for two weeks. They have a picture of us that's still in the winery and we're so bleary-eyed you can't believe it."

Korbel offered diverse scenery, including acres of vineyards, bridges, and steep hills along the Russian river. A range of hills and small canyons are to the north of the Korbel building complex that stretches back several miles.

In the fifth season the crew again went to Northern California, this time to Hop Kiln Winery, to film the episode "Ollie Joe." This historic California landmark is located in the heart of the fine wine growing region of the Russian River area of Sonoma County. The winery provided 60 acres of vineyards for filming and the then-deteriorated hop kilns.

The third season episode "The Hunter" was shot in Cucamonga at Mission Vineyard winery.

Prop Warfare

"When we started the series," says Rick Jason, "our property master, Tommie Thompson, handed me the machine gun. I said, 'Are you crazy? Do you think I'm going to haul sixteen pounds of steel around for three years? What's the lightest weapon you've got?' So I was given the .30 caliber carbine (which would have a hard time dropping a sick mouse) and Vic inherited the .45 Thompson. After two weeks, he was so tired from carrying all that metal, they had to make a wooden mock-up for him and the only time he ever used the real one (which was choked down at the barrel tip to create enough back pressure to throw out the empty shells) was in fire fight shots for the show. It jammed constantly, causing him to use some four letter expletives even I had never heard. The carbine was also choked down for back pressure, but though it's a weapon of very little power, its manners were much more in keeping with what I needed; hardly ever jammed."

Later in the show, the props were taken over by Bob Henderson. "We had a prop man and one assistant for all those weapons," says Fenady. "Today there'd be ten people for the same job. We had a helluva job keeping a prop man. Every year I had to wine him and dine him. He'd say 'I don't want the money. I want to live.' Bob Henderson, helluva prop guy."

Jack Hogan often carried a fake B.A.R. "They figured I could make more noise with a B.A.R.," says Jack. "I had a prop B.A.R., because the B.A.R. was rented and it was hard to operate, and they didn't want me getting the real one dirty. So, if I had a scene where I didn't have to shoot it, I would use the phony. And also it was lighter. They brought an armed guard every night to pick up the weapons and bring them back."

Though American accessories were available in abundance from a variety of sources, the German equipment often had to be manufactured. Many of the bayonets worn by the Germans and Americans were made in the prop shop by pouring hot lead into metal molds and then painted. Real bayonets were used only when a scene required pulling one out of the scabbard. Often the German gun belts and canteens were wooden mockups.

The MGM shop manufactured many of the non-firing arms for the show or parts from various weapons were cobbled together to simulate actual weapons. A Reising machine gun was adapted with MP40 parts and is used frequently in the show by the German extras.

Camaraderie

The cast and crew of *Combat!* were a congenial bunch. Though not all the actors were close friends who socialized after hours together, they all were friendly and have developed lifelong friendships. That feeling of camaraderie they tried to extend to the guest stars.

At the 1996 *Combat!* reunion, the actors reminisced about the feeling of family on the set. Jack Hogan said, "There was something macho about the show, everyone would love to do it."

Pierre Jalbert recalls, "One of our great pleasures was, on Friday night, we'd say to the Assistant Director, 'Who's coming next week?' meaning, who's the guest star. We were installed, we didn't have any anxiety. Our game was to make the guest star as comfortable as we could. Invite him in our trailer and put him on — put 'em in a barrel. As Peabody would say, we'd throw a bone on the table to see if they would go with it."

"We'd all have our director's chair," said Jack Hogan. "We'd sit around between shots and role play. One of us would be the psychiatrist and we'd have different roles and discuss world situations, but you couldn't keep a straight face."

"That's how we'd entertain ourselves, while the guests would entertain us," said Pierre. "You must understand we respected these guys, these guys had reputations, they were stars."

"But we were the show to be on," added Rick Jason. "And they were happy to be there."

Part of what made the set so pleasant was a fabulous caterer. "Millie catered the food," says Tom Lowell. "I started the show at 165 pounds, I weighed 187 when I left the show two years later." Conlan gained about thirty pounds. Millie was wife to a grip and started cooking for Gene Autry's films. Rick met her at ZIV catering out of the back of a station wagon for the "Bat Masterson" series. Rick got Millie to cater the *Combat!* show.

Georg Fenady also enjoyed the cooking. "May and Millie, who were our caterers, were unbelievable. They'd lay out a banquet every day. Ours was the only show that during the hiatus they'd lose weight. During the season they'd gain fifteen pounds."

All the actors were happy to be associated with the series, and with Vic Morrow. "As we relaxed into our parts and the show took off," says Rick Jason, "I discovered his sense of

humor. It was quite dry. Quite often, while shooting a scene, he'd throw an ad lib at me to see if I was listening. The first time he did it, I just stared at him and the director yelled, 'Cut!' After that, realizing what he was doing, I'd throw an ad lib back at him, and we'd do this for six or seven lines (all in character). Sometimes we could hear crew members stifling laughs. Our script supervisor was going crazy, riffling through the script for pages he thought he might be missing. Eventually, he'd whisper to the director that what we were saying wasn't in the script. 'CUT!' he'd shout. 'C'mon fellas, we have a lot of stuff to shoot today,' or something to that effect. I understand a lot of those were printed as out-takes and saved on a special reel by our head editor. I have no idea where they are, or if they still exist.

"You know Vic hated firearms," continues Rick. "Guns of any kind. He could also break me up any time he chose; a very funny man, he was. One rare afternoon we were wrapping early, perhaps about 4:00 pm. I had a couple of shotguns in back of my station wagon so I said to him, 'Hey, wanna go shoot some skeet?' He said, 'Nah, I can't stand to kill clay.' He made me laugh."

In an issue of TV Collector, Dick Peabody said, "Vic was an extremely generous guy and he shared everything he had. His motor home (was) the best dressing room, so that was our clubhouse. And he got ABC to keep each of us stocked with our favorite brand of liquor for five years . . . Vic was the most misunderstood person in the world, very shy guy, he wasn't good around large groups. He appeared one way to people who knew him only casually, and he was an entirely different person to those who knew him well. He had, probably, the wildest sense of humor of anyone I've ever known."

Tom Lowell says, "Nobody ever threw a temper tantrum, as far as the players were concerned, the actors on the set. There were little things that went on regarding dressing rooms and this and that, and little snit fits every once in awhile. It was never one actor against another, it was usually the actors against the front office."

Friendly rivalry developed for screen time. With six actors vying for the attention of the camera, each would develop tricks to be noticed in their scenes. They would all try to personalize their costumes to make them distinctive or hold their weapons differently.

"Bernard McEveety caught me," says Tom Lowell. "He was a wonderful director. He was given those kind of scripts that were always very action-filled and we all had one lines and you know, you pop in there, and come down on one knee and everybody would be sitting around saying 'Where are the Krauts?' 'They're over there' 'Okay, let's go.' And that's it. . . . Everyone is looking for camera time, you know, everybody's always doing little schticks to try to get themselves noticed. One day we came into this little clearing and it was a close shot on all five of us sitting there and I turned and took off my helmet—all the other guys are doing schtick looking around, you know, I took my helmet off and turned right toward the camera and Bernie stopped, said, 'Cut! Tom, the Krauts are that way!'"

Dick Peabody used his height to good effect. "I used to bump into things. Any opportunity to bump my head on a low doorway, I would do it—a kind of a schtick that would be useful to gain attention. Though I was probably the most schtick-free actor on the show. Mostly because I didn't know if I could handle the schtick very well. I remember in *Support Your Local Sheriff,* Walter Brennan and Gene Evans and I are sitting at a table in a bar and all three of us have drinks in front of us. And Brennan and Gene Evans are, from time to time, taking a sip out of their shot. And I didn't touch my glass because I didn't know if I could remember exactly at what point that I picked up the glass and took a sip of it, you know. So, I decided I'm gonna play it safe and not touch that glass. You know, most actors, give 'em a prop and they'll go crazy with it. But I had this strange kind of ego that—I think Vic was the only person who understood this, I don't think any of the production people at *Combat!* knew—they thought that I was just too insecure to do anything. Only Vic knew that the reason I didn't feel any compulsion to play with props or move around or scratch my nose, as actors will do, or any of those attention-getting things, because my ego told me that I didn't have to. That my presence there was enough.

"[Littlejohn's] character sort of evolved. Part of it just came out of my natural awkwardness. I think all of our characters evolved. I don't think they were set to begin with. Saunders was not the same Sgt. Saunders he was at the beginning. There was a tremendous evolution. And in all of us, I think."

Season Four Episodes

Combat! aired at 7:30 p.m. on Tuesday nights, opposite CBS's "Rawhide" and NBC's "My Mother the Car" and "Please Don't Eat the Daisies." *Combat!* was among eight military shows, both comedies and dramas, airing on the major networks.

The Linesman (097)
Teleplay by Edward J. Lakso
Story by Gene Levitt
Directed by Tom Gries
First aired 05-Oct-1965 (Episode 4 of Season 4)

CAST:
Regulars: Morrow, Jason, Hogan, Peabody, Jalbert
Guest Star Jack Lord as Barney McKlosky
Peter Duryea as Pvt. O'Connor
Heinz Brinkman as German Lieutenant
Horst Ebersberg as German Sergeant
Gerd Rein as German
Tom J. Stears as Pvt. Locke
Peter Hellman as German Soldier
Chris Anders as German Sergeant

Synopsis:
A hostile signal corps sergeant, McClosky, balks at having Saunders as escort on a mission to lay wire. He holds Saunders responsible for the death of one of his men. The mission is nearly botched by McClotsky's attitude and Littlejohn's loss of a reel of phone wire.

Review — 2 bayonets:
Viewers of the episode "Bridge at Chalons" will have *deja vu* watching "The Linesman," right down to Littlejohn bumbling the wire. Jack Lord's specialist-with-an-attitude does not trust the lives of his men to Saunders' care. By fourth season, Saunders is less willing to take abuse from an arrogant specialist, but otherwise, the story is much the same as "Bridge at Chalons" — except this time no medal recommendation for

Saunders, just the satisfaction of knowing his patented pep talk (NCO variant) still works its magic.

European footage opens up this episode, and surrounds the squad with non-tropical foliage. The story drags, possibly because of too many scenic shots. The long shots inserted to justify Gene Levitt's European vacation are lovely, especially when using the distinctive architecture of the area. But the extreme long shots in the farmland might as well have been shot at Thousand Oaks. From that distance, grass looks the same the world over.

Notes, Oddities, and Bloopers:
• Vic Morrow and Jack Lord were antagonistic on- and off-screen. They had clashed in the past, coming to blows during the filming of *God's Little Acre*.
• The exteriors of bridges, chateaus, and farmlands are shot in Loire, France. The editor interspersed these with the MGM backlot and Franklin Canyon. Note how shots of Earl Parker in a tree, with authentic French village in the background, intercut to a closeup of Jack Lord in the tree.

About Filming the Episode:
Jack Hogan says, "Actors love to be loved. But sometimes you'll come on and you're supposed to be the bad guy. Vic was supposed to be the good guy in that show and Jack was supposed to be the bad guy ... Jack didn't want to be ugly. So, he wasn't really doing his job. He was trying to be more wonderful than our fearless leader, Vic Morrow. That happened a lot of times. Rip Torn, who was a nice guy and a terribly good actor. Same thing."

Main Event (098)
Written by William Fay
Directed by Tom Gries
First aired 14-Sep-1965 (Episode 1 of Season 4)

CAST:
Regulars: Morrow, Jason, Hogan, Jalbert, Peabody
Guest Star Jack Carter as Murphy
Vic Werber as Ferguson
Hans Difflip as German Sergeant
Todd Lasswell as Driver
Ben Cooper as Willy Kleve

Synopsis:
Saunders' latest green replacements are a boxer and his cocky fight manager, Murphy, who wants to run both the war and Saunders. Murphy fights a losing battle to keep himself and his boxer out of action when the squad is sent on a mission.

Review — 2.5 bayonets:
"Main Event" provides nice action sequences and fine performances in a predictable story about a boxer and his manager. Ben Cooper (who played the appropriately named Corporal Cross in "Next In Command") portrays a likable, all-American contender for the middleweight championship. Jack Carter, who plays his contrary manager, is perfectly grating in his efforts to keep his boy out of harm's way.

The best scene shows Cooper engaging the enemy for the

first time; his reactions are beautifully handled. Kirby trades great lines with comic Jack Carter and winds up with the best punchlines.

Notes, Oddities, and Bloopers:
• In the final battle, one of the dead Germans either has a ripped crotch or his fly is open.
• When Saunders halts the half-track, he is wearing a helmet. In the next shot, he is bare-headed and is reaching down to pick up his helmet.
• Uses footage from location shooting in Loire France, including the shots of "Saunders" searching in the French farmyard and the long shot of the squad walking down the road past a French church.

Hear No Evil (099)
Written by Tim Considine and John Considine
Directed by Sutton Roley
First aired 26-Oct-1965 (Episode 7 of Season 4)

CAST:
Regulars: Morrow
Richard Tretter as Johnson
Gene Otis Shane as Medic
Gary Lasdun as German Squad Leader
Edgar Winston as German Soldier
Roger Gentry as German Soldier
Chris Anders as German Motorcyclist
Tom Pace as German Motorcyclist
Ernst Winters as German in Jeep
Bruce Hayes as German in Jeep
William Harlow as G.I.
Peter Haskell as German Hostage

Synopsis:
A grenade leaves Saunders deaf and helpless to defend against unheard dangers. Seeking safety in a deserted abbey, Saunders befriends a stray dog. With the dog acting as his ears, Saunders strikes out toward his lines. En route, the dog is killed, Saunders bags a prisoner, and regains his hearing.

Review — 2.5 bayonets:
Morrow suffers through hearing deprivation and fifty pages of weak script in "Hear No Evil." Morrow is great to watch as his Saunders struggles back to the American lines after a near encounter with a grenade. But when the script resorts to a cute dog exhibiting Lassie-like intelligence so that our hero can escape, the story fails.

The story is little improved when Saunders replaces his hearing-ear dog with a German soldier (played by Peter Haskell, who will return to guest in two fifth-season episodes). The script is by the writing team of Tim and John Considine. John played Temple in two first-season episodes; his brother/co-writer was a child actor at Disney.

Director Sutton Roley helps bring out the best from both Morrow and this weak script. Roley's strong visuals add interest to a contrived story that tries to be as grand as "Survival," but falls short. In first draft, the script had more dialogue, with Saunders often talking to himself and even naming the dog.

About Filming the Episode:
Earl Parker doubles for Morrow in all the French chateau shots. The film used under the opening credits shows Earl's remarkable ability to mimic Morrow and to perform with his same sense of timing and drama. "Earl Parker became Vic Morrow," says Georg Fenady. "I mean, we could shoot over the shoulder with him. Get him three feet in front of the camera and you'd never know it wasn't Vic. He had his mannerisms, his everything. It was unbelievable."

Vic Morrow in "Hear No Evil."

9 Place Vendee (100)
Written by Kay Lenard and Jess Carneol
Directed by Alan Crosland, Jr.
First aired 11-Nov-1965 (Episode 9 of Season 4)

CAST:
Regulars: Jason
Introducing Patrick Michenaud as Jacques
William Leslie as Captain Clinton
Mike Ragan as Pvt. Walsh
Mike Stroka as German Drunk #1
Chris Howard as German Drunk #2
Max Kleven as German Lt.
Paul Busch as German Soldier
Dick Raymond as German Soldier
Philip de Firmian as German Sgt. #1
Mark Russi as German Sgt. #2
Alf George as German at Chow Wagon
Geoffrey Norman as German in Truck
Lee Patterson as Captain Howard
Christopher Dark as German Agent

Synopsis:
After (again) losing a superior officer in the field, Hanley goes alone to locate a wounded intelligence officer in German-

held territory. He is impeded by a French boy who has returned to town for a missing dog. He then mistakes an incapacitated German for his OSS contact.

Review — 1/2 bayonet:

The episode title provides the first hint that the writers were lacking a theme for their story — the best they could come up with was a street address. Usually a title sets a mood, or gives the audience some idea of what the story is about.

Director Alan Crosland, Jr., when given strong scripts such as "Odyssey," knows how to pace an episode. In "9 Place Vendee," he failed to rise above the script limitations. The stunt choreography on the rooftops is inventive and dramatically filmed, but quite implausible considering that the German racing across the French village's skyline had not the strength to leave his room earlier in the episode.

Notes, Oddities, and Bloopers:

•Uses footage shot in France for long shot of "Hanley" entering the town.
•Same dog from "The Walking Wounded."
•The street where Hanley climbs over the metal fence is the same set used for the orphanage in "The Furlough."
•The German trucks used are American, but the German command car is real.
•When the drinking Germans leave the shop, one puts his helmet on backwards.
•A great switch in the roof stunt: in a single shot, Rick Jason is on a ledge crawling around a corner, just as he gets off camera, but still in the same shot, his stunt double leaps across to another roof. The same trick is used moments later in reverse, as in a single shot, stunt double Walt Davis hangs from a ledge, pulls himself up, then crawls into a corner that Rick crawls out of.
•The credits say "Introducing Patrick Michenaud as Jacques" but he first appeared in *Combat!* in third season's "The Steeple."

A Sudden Terror (101)

Written by Edward J. Lakso
Directed by Michael Caffey
First aired 29-Mar-1966 (Episode 29 of Season 4)

CAST:

Regulars: Jason
Guest Star Brandon De Wilde as Wilder
Hank Brandt as Martin
David Moss as Fire Director
Earl Parker as Cooper
Mark Russi as Radioman
Paul Busch as German Officer
Jan Malmsjo as Bruener

Synopsis:

On his first night mission, a young G.I. is up to his neck in trouble. After an attack on a German fuel dump, Pvt. Wilder (Brandon DeWilde) becomes trapped in quicksand, and a wounded Hanley's attempts to rescue him fail. When a burned

Vic Morrow between scenes on the MGM back lot.

and dying German decides to take Wilder with him, he shoots the G.I.'s only support out from under him. A well-timed barrage in the closing act is the vehicle for Wilder's rescue.

Review — 2 bayonets:

Brandon DeWilde stars in "A Sudden Terror." This intelligent script by Edward J. Lakso is just a bit thin for an hour. Still, it offers strong performances by Jason and DeWilde, and a fair directing job from rookie Michael Caffey in his first time behind the camera for *Combat!*

Michael Caffey started with the show as first assistant director. His brother Richard Caffey became producer of *Combat!* in the middle of fourth season. Their father, Frank Caffey, was head of production at Paramount for many years.

About Filming the Episode:

Earl Parker, who doubled Vic and was one of the show's two stunt coordinators, plays Cooper. This episode and "The Masquers" are the only times Earl Parker is listed in the credits in his five years with the series. Earl says about his acting. "I'd rather do what we would call 'gags,' and not get involved in this serious one-foot-in-front-of-the-lens stuff. That's spooky. I'd rather be doing stunts."

Notes, Oddities, and Bloopers:

•When the demolition man dies, he tumbles into a puddle several yards away from Hanley. In the next shot, the body is next to Hanley.
•When Hanley is wounded, he falls down with his carbine in his hands, but in his reaction shot he has no carbine. When he rolls over, the carbine is again in his hands.
•Jan Malmsjo, who plays the burnt German, is featured in the fifth season episode "Chapel at Able-Five."
•Quicksand in Normandy?

Evasion (102)

Written by Esther and Bob Mitchell
Directed by John Peyser
First aired 19-Oct-1965 (Episode 6 of Season 4)

CAST:

Regulars: Jason
Guest Star Lloyd Bochner as Major Thorne
Monique le Maire as Julie
John Lodge as Major Ramsey
Anthony Rogers as Lt. Maples
John Levingston as Capt. Todd
Phil Bonnell as Frost
Herb Andreas as German Lieutenant
Willy Kaufman as German Ticket Agent
Peter Marks as Max
Ralph Josephs as Hans
Normand Houle as French Waiter
Socrates Ballis as Albanian Soldier
Karl Sadler as German Lieutenant
Robert Chapman as German Guard
Jacques Aubuchon as Kopke

Synopsis:

Hanley escapes from a Nazi prison camp and dons a perfectly tailored Albanian uniform. He is thwarted by a sharp-eyed Hitler youth with a passion for arcane military uniforms. Fortunately, Hanley is turned over to a better disguised Allied officer, Major Thorne, who is escaping in an authentic German uniform. In their adventures in France, Thorne and Hanley encounter a real Albanian officer, get captured by the Gestapo, and are rescued by an attractive woman.

Review — 2.5 bayonets:

Lloyd Bochner plays Thorne, a stiff-upper-lip, unflappable British intelligence agent who aids Hanley. I find this character type annoying (as does Hanley). But if a story must have an annoying British twit, he might as well be played by a great actor. Bochner does everything but chew the scenery, but does it so "British" that I applaud his tenacity and verve.

Earl Parker performs a great stunt, climbing out a second-story window, crawling down a long rope, and dropping into a river. He also went over a small waterfall doubling for Rick. The stunt work was filmed in Loire, France.

About Filming the Episode:

Rick Jason says, "I tell you, where I'm in the water and you see the back of my head wearing a wool cap, I would swear it looked like me. They intercut that at the studio and you cannot tell the difference . . . I remember the intercuts. It stuck in my mind, I thought, 'My God, they're good the way they did this stuff.' And you see me going down through the waterfalls but you never see my face, you only see me wearing a wool cap." He didn't know why they wanted him to wear the cap until he saw the episode.

Finest Hour (103)

Written by Don Tait • Directed by Sutton Roley
First aired 21-Dec-1965 (Episode 15 of Season 4)

CAST:

Regulars: Jason, Jalbert
Guest Star: Luise Rainer as Countess De Roy
Guest Star: Ramon Novarro as Count De Roy
James Dobson as Lt. Schaefer
John Mylong as General Kroehler
Lou Robb as Capt. Roswald
Karl Sadler as German #1
Norbert Meisel as German #2
Larry Gelbman as Sentry
Kurt Kreuger as Major Werner
Maurice Marsac as Claude

Synopsis:

Caje forces a Frenchman to aid him and a wounded Hanley. The Frenchman takes them to a German-occupied chateau, where the Countess must tend to his wounds while keeping his presence a secret from the German soldiers garrisoned in her home. The Countess saves Hanley's life, but he refuses to leave her household in peace, coercing the countess into spying for him. She discovers information that leads to the destruction of her home and all her husband's dreams.

Review — 3.5 bayonets:

"Finest Hour," by Don Tait, is a vibrant story, capturing the essence of a *Combat!* morality tale, of people sacrificing more than their lives for the greater good. Count de Roy, played by veteran Hollywood actor Ramon Novarro, is a feeble, befuddled man, but when tested, he rises to achieve his "Finest Hour," putting his life and his heritage on the line.

Luise Rainer, a two-time Academy Award–winner for best actress, was coaxed out of retirement for this episode. Novarro was a silent-screen star, the original Ben Hur.

Rainer performs with great power, dignity, and grace, though her style is at odds with the regular cast. She acts with a style of the thirties in a sixties television show. Both she and Novarro had been away from the cameras so long that they had trouble with many of their scenes, requiring numerous re-takes.

Rick Jason has an edge to his performance that adds spice, not just to this story, but to his character.

About Filming the Episode:

Jack Hogan says of Luise Ranier, "She was into some kind of yoga. So, you'd be on the set and look over in a corner, and she'd be in some sort of headstand with her skirt over her head doing her yoga exercises to get ready for her scene."

Sutton Roley set up a tall shot of Rick Jason on the ledge of the chateau, but Rick would not work from that height. "No, that's a stunt," he told Roley. "I don't do stunts." The shot had to be restaged to shoot Jason closer to the ground.

Notes, Oddities, and Bloopers:

• In the scene where the Countess first tends Hanley, after Caje hands the blood-stained cloth to the Countess, he switches his bayonet to his other hand and pokes himself in the eye.
• Toward the end, when our heroes are hiding behind the truck waiting to escape, when the Countess says, "It's Claude" and Caje answers "Yeah," neither of their lips move.

COMBAT!

Breakout (104)

Written by Edward J. Lakso
Directed by John Peyser
First aired 14-Dec-65 (Episode 14 of Season 4)

CAST:

Regulars: Jason, Morrow, hogan, Peabody, Jalbert, Carter
Guest Star Fernando Lamas as Vertrain
Peter Hellman as Sgt. Hunte
Mark Tobin as Hans
Ross Sturlin as Rankin

Synopsis:

Facing a German advance, Saunders and squad are ordered to destroy a valley full of construction equipment, to keep it out of the hands of the Germans. Fernando Lamas stars as the Frenchman enraged over the destruction of his property. Lamas' sniper shots at Saunders' men fail to inflict injuries, but attract a German patrol that traps the squad in the quarry. To escape, Saunders assembles an armored vehicle out of the broken equipment on the construction site.

Review — 1 bayonet:

Reminiscent of the film *Flight of the Phoenix,* which premiered the same year, "Breakout" has Saunders assembling a makeshift tank out of a bulldozer, with the Germans watching. Pretty silly stuff made watchable by Saunders' scenes stating his philosophy of war. Fernando Lamas makes his first guest appearance in "Breakout." Both he and his wife, Esther Williams, loved *Combat!*

Rick Jason was delighted to meet Fernando Lamas, since he says he owes his career to Lamas. His first year in Hollywood, under contract to Columbia, Rick Jason made no films. His first film break came because MGM needed someone to replace the hastily departed Fernando Lamas in the film *Sombrero.* That film launched Jason's Hollywood career.

About Filming the Episode:

Jack Hogan says about Fernando Lamas: "You couldn't keep a straight conversation for five minutes with that guy, he would turn it into something humorous. Very funny."

Notes, Oddities, and Bloopers:

• Opening sequence is a direct lift from "Odyssey," including Rick Jason's dialogue.
• Lamas fires an M1 rifle at squad in long shot, but later, Lamas has a Mauser.
• Somebody in civilian clothes, wearing a vest, is in background of one shot. As Saunders is crouched next to Kirby, who is on the bulldozer, asking him what he needs to make repairs, a man passes behind Saunders in his close-up.
• When Saunders passes his Thompson to Caje, Caje grabs it by the hot barrel. He quickly drops the Thompson, and re-takes it by its wooden stock.

The Farmer (105)

Written by Andy White
Directed by John Peyser
First aired 10-12-65 (Episode 5 of Season 4)

CAST:

Regulars: Jason, Morrow, Hogan, Jalbert, Peabody, Carter
Guest Star Dennis Weaver as Noah
Felix Locher as Old French Farmer
Belle Mitchell as Old French Woman
Dina Harmsen as French Girl
Anthony Aiello as G.I.

Synopsis:

Waiting for the battle, Noah (guest star Dennis Weaver) plants the crops of an evacuated French farmer. His love for the land and farming overshadow his obligations as a soldier. Absorbed in a way of life he understands, the farmer-soldier endangers the squad when he disobeys orders so he can care for a new-born calf.

Review — 1 bayonet:

Dennis Weaver stars as "The Farmer" who cannot comprehend that he is now a soldier. The embattled farmer may have stood at Lexington and Concord and fired the shot heard round the world, but if they had been represented there by farmers the like of Dennis Weaver, they would have been too busy chasing cows and planting crops to have been bothered with starting the fight for American independence. From the first scene, this character is bayonet-bait.

The scenes of Weaver dragging Doc, Littlejohn, and Caje into his silliness are charming and Morrow is engaging as a Saunders fighting against the emotions engendered by this farmer's love of the land. Weaver jumps in with both feet and plays the role with utter conviction, but he fights a losing battle with the silly plot.

Notes, Oddities, and Bloopers:

• While resting at the farmhouse, during the conversation between Caje and Saunders, the camoflauge helmet alternates between hanging in the background and perching on Morrow's head.
• Hanley's driver is Walt Davis, who he addresses as "Davis."
• Filmed at Thousand Oaks.
• Dennis Weaver did not join in any of the cast antics, avoiding any overtures to come play.

The Raider (106)

Written by Kay Lenard and Jess Carneol
Directed by John Peyser
First aired 28-Dec-1965 (Episode 16 of Season 4)

CAST:

Regulars: Jason, Morrow, Hogan, Jalbert, Carter
Guest Star Martin Brooks as Corporal MacGowan
Raymond McGrath as Tim
Don Knight as German Sgt.
George Sawaya as G.I. #1
Gerald Carter as Wounded German
Edgar Winston as German #1
William Mahoney as German #2
Gil Peterson as German #4
Roger Gentry as German #5
Wally Berns as German #6
Peter Church as German Corporal
Raymond Mayo as G.I. Officer #2
John Tarangelo as G.I. Officer #1
Leonard Nimoy as Pvt. Baum
George Backman as Capt. Reichhardt

Synopsis:

Hanley is captured by the infamous S.S. Captain Reichhardt. Saunders captures Reichhardt's men but does not learn the location of Hanley. Corporal MacGowan, anxious to even a score with the Germans, wants to use sterner interrogation methods. He disagrees with Saunders' plan to flush out the captain and the information.

Review — 3.5 bayonets:

It's Saunders to the rescue in "The Raider," going above-and-beyond to rescue his Lieutenant from the clutches of a Nazi super-man who specializes in collecting American officers. Scriptwriters Kay Lenard and Jess Carneol get the silliness out of the way up front: the crack SS unit surrenders to a small force of Americans and an SS officer submits to posing as an enlisted man. Accepting the initial premise, viewers are now set

Vic Morrow and Pierre Jalbert relaxing between takes of "The Farmer." Dick Peabody and the crew are in the background.

for a great episode where Saunders must out-think and out-wit the Nazi superman. And, he does it brilliantly! No patented pep talks in this episode, just cool thinking, good planning, and an indication of just how far Saunders will go to save Hanley.

Notes, Oddities, and Bloopers:

• The scene where the German soldiers are looking to their leader, some of the shots are printed backwards to make the profiles point in the correct direction. The give-away is that the insignia and helmet buckles are on the wrong side.

• When Hanley's jeep crashes, it is upright. When the platoon members arrive, the jeep is on its side.

• Caje is wearing a wedding band and a pinky ring in one scene.

• Opening jeep sequence is lifted from "Vendetta." The jeep wheels in those sequences are striped, the wheels in the jeeps used in "The Raider" are not.

• German uniforms are one-size-fits-all when Germans swap them, just as when Americans swap them.

Crossfire (107)

Written by Edward J. Lakso
Directed by Alan Crosland, Jr.
First aired 02-Nov-1965 (Episode 8 of Season 4)

CAST:

Regulars: Jason, Morrow, Hogan, Jalbert, Peabody, Carter
Guest Star Don Gordon as Pvt. Stevens
Burt Douglas as Pvt. Clark
Ron Foster as Pvt. Marshall
Rand Brooks as G.I. Lieutenant
Walter Gregg as Pvt. Coates
Robert Hoy as G.I. on Radio
Paul Busch as German Captain
Bob Turnbull as G.I. Corporal
Robert Champion as German Sergeant
Angelo De Meo as Doan

Synopsis:

Saunders returns from patrol with one of his squad, a decorated veteran of Omaha Beach, under arrest. Stevens disobeyed a direct order, causing the squad to be trapped by a German machine gun and two men to be killed. This Frankenstein-style story shows the making and unmaking of a frontline soldier.

Review — 1/2 bayonet:

Through flashbacks, "Crossfire" shows the making and unmaking of a combat soldier. In this Frankenstein-type story, Stevens is Saunders' creation who he cannot control. As Hanley delves into the situation, Saunders relates how the two met on D–Day. Saunders took Gordon, a frightened private, and molded him into a soldier who would keep moving and kill Krauts. But the lesson was learned too well. By the time he is assigned to Saunders' squad, Stevens has developed a hair trigger and is trouble.

The third flashback merges into the same scene that opened the show (and repeats all the footage the audience has already seen). Eventually, the script meanders back to the present and resolves itself.

In a television series that made some rather intrusive use of incidental music, this episode is the nadir. Normally, I am fond of the high-volume, often overpowering score. My tolerance was severely tested in the teaser of this episode. By second act, I laugh at the music instead of paying attention to the story. Low-tension scenes of men scurrying across fields have high-tension music, heavy on woodwinds and tympani. Every dramatic sentence is punctuated with a heavy downbeat and an occasional *da-dum!*

The D–Day flashback does not match "A Day in June." Saunders was not separated from Hanley and squad long enough to have had this encounter with Stevens. In this episode, all fighting on Omaha Beach ceases when Saunders wipes out the single machine gun nest — however, in "A Day in June" he fights his way off the beach with his own squad while under continuing German machine gun fire.

The scenes between Saunders and Gordon are biting and believable as Saunders has to deal with this monster that he has created. But the odd twists and turns of flashbacks and the exact duplication of the teaser is annoying.

Notes, Oddities, and Bloopers:

• Don Gordon accurately throws a grenade after being shot in his pitching arm, then fires 11 rounds from an 8-round M1.

• Saunders' shirt is alternately buttoned down to nearly his navel then down to only the first button.

• Filmed at Thousands Oaks, MGM, Tranca's Beach, and long shot of jeep at opening is from Korbel.

• Angelo De Meo, one of the show's stunt coordinators, gets screen credit in this episode. His only other credit is in "Gulliver."

• With the re-use of "A Day in June" footage, plus the complete re-use of the teaser segment and other lifted scenes, this episode probably has less than a half-hour of original footage.

Soldier of Fortune (108)

Written by George F. Slavin
Directed by Sutton Roley
First aired 23-Nov-1965 (Episode 11 of Season 4)

CAST:

Regulars: Morrow
Guest Star Burt Brinckerhoff as Pvt. Andy Marsh
Ed Deemer as German Lt.
John Gentri as Karl
Buck Holland as Rudi
Ernst Winters as German Soldier
Nikolaus Kopp as German
William Campbell as Pvt. Ed Wallace
Wesley Lau as Meyer

Synopsis:

An explosion destroys the cellar of a German communication center where Saunders, Marsh, and Wallace were tapping lines. Trapped beneath a beam and fearing he will be left behind, Marsh uses information he has overhead as insurance for a safe return to American lines. Saunders forces a captured

German to free the trapped soldier and carry him to safety. But the German, who had been in charge of communications, claims no critical information came over the phones and that Marsh is duping them.

Review — 2 bayonets:

"Soldier of Fortune" provides the fourth "beamer" episode in the *Combat!* cannon. This time, an obnoxious private is trapped beneath a beam in the rubble. The script cleverly toys with the audience, making them wonder whether or not he really has any vital info.

Some striking performances are provided by Burt Brinckerhoff as the slimy G.I. and William Campbell as the staunch soldier who distrusts Marsh. William Campbell will appear again in the fifth season episode "Nightmare on the Red Ball Run."

"Soldier of Fortune" is a fun entertainment. Slow at the beginning, but once it picks up, it is quite enjoyable.

The First Day (109)

Written by Esther and Bob Mitchell
Directed by Georg Fenady
First aired 21-Sep-1965 (Episode 2 of Season 4)

CAST:

Regulars: Morrow, Hogan, Carter, Jalbert
Dee Pollack as McBride
Buck Taylor as Tobin
Kevin Coughlin as Loomis
Robert Biheller as Tate
John Nealson as Anderson
Rick Weber as German

Synopsis:

The squad, worn-out and exhausted, receives four green replacements. The story follows these four teenagers as they attempt to survive their first day on the front line. Among the newbies are: a high-school football star, a street-smart kid, a sweet country boy, and the clean-faced boy next door. Who will survive?

Review — 3 bayonets:

This fat-free script by Esther and Bob Mitchell shows green recruits making the squad's mission difficult. Georg J. Fenady (listed incorrectly as "George" Fenady in some episode credits), a regular associate producer of *Combat!*, debuts behind the camera as director of this episode. He makes sure the pacing of camera and actors matches the pace of this first-rate script. Later in the season, this same combination of writers, Esther and Bob Mitchell, and the director show the flip side of this story, as three old men become the squad's replacements in the episode "The Old Men."

About Filming the Episode:

"Coincidentally and ironically," says Georg Fenady, "my first

Vic Morrow as Sgt. Saunders in "The First Day."

episode directing for *Combat!* was called 'The First Day.'" Tom Gries was to have directed, but he received word that his own TV show, "The Rat Patrol," would go immediately into production and had to fly to Spain. He recommended Fenady take over for him.

Georg Fenady was pleased with his first directing work for the series. "Vic insisted on doing a couple of his own stunts. He got a big gash on his leg jumping on a moving half-track, throwing a grenade in it, and jumping off it again. The whole crew, I tell you, you know you hear it all the time, that it was a labor of love and a family, but it really and truly was. We truly enjoyed each other."

Notes, Oddities, and Bloopers:

• Kevin Coughlin appeared as an MP in "Off Limits." In that episode, shot three seasons earlier, no one thought he was too young to be a soldier.

S.I.W. (110)

Written by Shirl Hendryx
Directed by John Peyser
First aired 28-Sep-1965 (Episode 3 of Season 4)

CAST:

Regulars: Morrow, Hogan, Jalbert, Peabody, Carter
John Cassavetes as Kalb
William Stevens as Fleming
Paul Sherif as Sawyer
Mike Krempels as German

Synopsis:

Kirby rejoins the squad in the field, bringing with him a new replacement, Kalb. But Kalb is already known to Fleming. Fleming believes Kalb is a coward who ran at Omaha Beach and has been running ever since. After a firefight, Kalb turns up wounded, but the powder burns on his legs lead the squad to think that it was a self-inflicted wound (S.I.W.).

Review — 4 bayonets:

This story by Shirl Hendryx skillfully keeps Kalb's guilt or innocense in constant question. The script makes a stinging point about the cancer of gossip and innuendo. John Peyser, in his best directorial work for *Combat!*, creates a dark, oppressive atmosphere as Kalb's fear and fate are dissected and discussed. Peyser is in firm command of the action and the camera, creating some great visuals: long gunfighter-like shots down the main street and brooding close-ups in the church.

Morrow and Carter are standouts in this episode as they deal with the possibility of a soldier with a self-inflicted wound. Guests Cassavetes and Stevens are excellent.

About Filming the Episode:

Conlan Carter about John Cassavetes: "John and I hit it off immediately. John didn't have an agent. He did all of his own stuff that way. We talked about that for hours, because I was fascinated with that process. It was tough to get jobs *with* an agent. John was a different breed, he was a different cat. I would have liked to have known him better. We talked a lot about stuff, not all of it Hollyweird. He was a good guy. Very bright. Very real. One of the nicest, down-to-earth good guys in Hollywood."

Notes, Oddities, and Bloopers:

•As the squad enters the village in their shirts (no jackets), closeups of Saunders show the collar of the jacket he is wearing.

Korbel was a favorite location shoot for the cast. The Heck brothers made sure the cast and crew were never thirsty while they were their guests. The "civilians" pictured with the cast are, from top to bottom: Ben Heck, (Vice President, Marketing), Paul Heck (Vice President, Ranch Operations), and Adolf Heck (President, Champagnemaster). This photo hangs in the Korbel visitors gallery in Guerneville, California. Six Combat! *episodes were filmed there.*

Luck With Rainbows (111)

Written by Wells Root and Ron Bishop
Directed by Alan Crosland, Jr.
First aired 07-Dec-1965 (Episode 13 of Season 4)

CAST:

Regulars: Jason, Hogan, Peabody
Guest Star Michael Evans as Major Cole-Hughes
Roy Dean as Wilson
Peter Hellman as German Truck Driver
Dirk Hansen as German Convoy Officer
Stephen Ferry as Paulsen
Paul Busch as German Fuel Tanker
David Adams as German #1
Kurt Landen as German #2
Bill Glover as Sgt. Leighton

Synopsis:

Hanley, Littlejohn, and Kirby attempt to salvage film from a crashed reconnaissance plane. They are interrupted by a British Major who commandeers the film and abandons the squad as Germans approach. Through daring and luck, the outmanned and outgunned squad destroys the attacking German half-track. This so impresses the British Major that he requests Hanley and Kirby to go with him on a sabotage mission to destroy V-2 rockets.

Review — 1.5 bayonets:

Michael Evans, as the British Major, shows typical English pluck in his "pip-pip, cheerio" scenes. He is almost haunting talking about his hero, Bertie, who was once a great soldier and tactician, but his "light had gone out." After sending too many men to their deaths, Bertie was left only with a death wish for himself.

This device was hackneyed when Alexander Dumas used it in *The Three Musketeers,* so it should surprise no one when the

Crew sets up a shot for "The Flying Machine" on location at Thousand Oaks.

Major turns out to be the tragic Bertie. Through a series of pep sentences and general derring-do, Hanley re-establishes Bertie's will to live, saves the Major's life, and completes the mission by finding a map showing the location of the V-2s.

The teaser, the first act, and the second act are fun, as Hanley and the Major are civilly at odds with each other. Kirby is delightful enjoying his drinks and interacting with the British sergeant. Acts three and four go downhill in script, pacing, and general goofiness. In the end, the Major does not go out in a blaze of glory as he had wished, and neither does this episode.

The Flying Machine (112)

Written by Edward J. Lakso
Directed by Alan Crosland, Jr.
First aired 22-Feb-1966 (Episode 24 of Season 4)

CAST:
Regulars: Jason
Guest Star Keenan Wynn as Lt. Brannagan
Peter Brocco as Claude
Peter Coe as Captain Zweiger
Ross Elliott as Lt. Colonel
Bard Stevens as Kruger
Norbert Meisel as Lt. Croftsen
Dick Raymond as 1st German
Horst Ebersberg as Brucke
Larry Gelbman as 1st German Soldier

Synopsis:

Hanley flies in a rickety observation plane with a wise-cracking pilot (Keenan Wynn). Returning from their mission, they see a German convoy and fly in for a closer look—far too close. They are shot down twenty-five miles behind enemy lines. To get his information back in time, Hanley must repair the downed plane and fly it himself.

Review — 1.5 bayonets:

The script for "The Flying Machine" tweaks the show's Air Corps veteran, Rick Jason. Several *Combat!* scripts put his character in uncomfortable flying situations, showing him to be a nervous flyer.

In "The Flying Machine," the bulk of the action follows

Hanley as he makes a grounded plane air-worthy. To do this he: makes a hardware fix, repairs the torn wing, obtains gasoline, and removes a stone wall blocking the runway — all this without attracting the attention of the German soldiers camped at the base of the hill. These amazing feats would have impressed MacGyver, but when Hanley also has to fly the plane out (and, presumably, land it) willing-suspension-of-disbelief collapses.

Keenan Wynn, in his second guest role on *Combat!*, creates a fascinating character who is unimpressed by Hanley or his orders. The two are delightfully at odds. Peter Brocco, who plays the Frenchman Claude, was last seen in the episode "The Long Walk."

The Old Men (113)

Written by Esther and Bob Mitchell
Directed by Georg Fenady
First aired 16-Nov-1965 (Episode 10 of Season 4)

CAST:
Regulars: Morrow, Hogan, Jalbert
Guest Star Simon Oakland as Clawson
Arnold Merritt as Private Fisher
Paul Busch as German Corporal
Norbert Siegfried as German #1
William Harlow as GI Jeep Driver
Tom Drake as Private Todd
William Phipps as Private Barnhill

Synopsis:

The squad is saddled with three over-aged replacements: an injured vet of the Italian campaign who refuses to accept that he is incapable of fighting as he did in his youth, a homesick family man, and a politician with senatorial ambitions.

Review — 2 bayonets:

"The Old Men" is the flip side of the episode "The First Day," showing old recruits, not young ones. It seems no matter what their age, new recruits always cause problems for Saunders and his men.

Nice direction by Georg J. Fenady in his second turn behind the *Combat!* camera and an entertaining script by Esther and

Bob Mitchell. Nothing spectacular here, but an interesting hour's entertainment.

Some familiar faces from first season are in this episode: Arnold Merritt is Fisher. He appeared as Crown in "Rear Echelon Commandos," "I Swear by Apollo," and "Off Limits," and died as a different character in "The Long Way Home." William Harlow played Davis in seasons one and two. And Paul Busch appears as the ever-present German who again is captured by the squad.

About Filming the Episode:

Director Georg Fenady remembers, ". . . the squad rounds the bend, the enemy comes over the hill, and a battle ensues. One-eighth page in the script and it takes you a day to shoot the sucker. The sets were enormous. Everybody's firing and you're firing blanks and the automatic weapons particularly would jam like crazy. They didn't have enough thrust to kick these shells out. Poor Vic was going crazy with his Thompson."

The Casket (114)

Written by Ed Waters and Paul David Moessinger
Directed by Bernard McEveety
First aired 30-Nov-1965 (Episode 12 of Season 4)

CAST:
Regulars: Morrow, Hogan, Jalbert
Guest Star Nina Foch as Madame Carmaux
Raymond Cavaleri as Michel
Henry Brandt as German NCO

Synopsis:

In "The Casket," an irresistible force meets an immovable object: Saunders (the irresistible force), trying to get a wounded Kirby to a hospital crosses an elderly mother (the immovable object) determined to give her son proper burial. She has the truck that Saunders and Caje need to transport Kirby. But the widow has no love for Americans. Saunders confiscates the truck, with the casket, and forces her and her surviving son to come with him.

Review — 2 bayonets:

Though not a sterling episode, "The Casket" provides an interesting diversion. Nina Foch, as the old French woman driven to extremes by grief, is a joy to watch, especially when she gets the upper hand with Saunders. The script by Ed Waters and Paul David Moessinger has her going over-the-top a little too often, but Foch and director McEveety do their best to rein in the cliches. But where does an old woman in a war-torn France get a truck, gasoline, and a semi-automatic pistol? Vehicles were routinely confiscated and gas was rationed.

This episode has my favorite Kirby line: when Saunders helps the wounded Kirby into the back of the truck, and he nearly falls into the open (empty) casket, Kirby says "Gee, Sarge, you think of everything."

Notes, Oddities, and Bloopers:
• Saunders effortlessly lifts a five-gallon can of gasoline.

• Flashlights used by the Germans are not Wehrmacht issue.
• The actor playing the son, Raymond Cavaleri, also plays the young boy in "A Silent Cry."

The Good Samaritan (115)

Written by Shirl Hendryx
Directed by Bernard McEveety
First aired 11-Jan-1966 (Episode 18 of Season 4)

CAST:
Regulars: Morrow, Jason, Hogan, Jalbert, Carter
Guest Star Tom Simcox as Marsini
Henry Brandt as German NCO
Paul Busch as German Radio Man

Synopsis:

Tom Simcox plays Marsini, the sole survivor of an ill-fated patrol. He blames Saunders for the death of his fellows, since Saunders had orders to keep his position and could not render aid. On recon, Saunders and Marsini destroy a German observation post. When Saunders is pinned under a heavy pipe, he orders Marsini to leave him and get the valuable information to Hanley. But Marsini will not abandon Saunders, refusing to do to Saunders what Saunders had done to Marsini's men.

Review — 3 bayonets:

A gut-wrenching script by Shirl Hendryx, "The Good Samaritan" explores the moral issues of sacrificing a single life to save many lives — and the consequences of living with that decision. The protagonists strive to do what is right, but each acts from a different moral base: for Saunders, the mission comes first, but in Marsini's view, if he is to remain human, the man must come before the mission.

Great performances by Simcox and Morrow, and the usual crisp, clean direction from Bernard McEveety. The episode climaxes with a superb hillside battle sequence, where McEveety does a credible job of making ten men look like an entire platoon. As a rarity, a German prisoner speaks no English, but since Marsini also speaks German, communication is no problem.

This episode is a startling contrast to the other Saunders-trapped-under-a-beam episode, "The Hard Way Back." Though similar, these excellent episodes tell very different stories. "The Hard Way Back" is the story of the transformation of a scared boy into a soldier. "The Good Samaritan" is about a veteran soldier's struggle to remain human while following his duty as a soldier. In one, Saunders has to force Kogan to stay and help him; in the other, he must convince Marsini to leave him behind.

Notes, Oddities, and Bloopers:
• Marsini's stunt double throws himself backward into a stranglehold in the fight on the hill.
• Filmed at Franklin Canyon.
• "Good Samaritan" is the fifth *Combat!* "beamer" episode—a story involving a character pinned under a beam (or, in this case, a pipe).

Retribution (116)

Written by Edward J. Lakso • Directed by Bernard McEveety
First aired 18-Jan-1966 (Episode 19 of Season 4)

CAST:

Regulars: Morrow, Jason, Hogan, Jalbert, Peabody, Carter
Guest Star Albert Paulsen as Col. Bruener
King Moody as Andre
Rachel Rosenthal as Micheline
Frank Koomen as Capt. Klaus
Ulf Balk Moller as German Sergeant
Paul Huston as G.I. #1
William Harlow as G.I. #2

Synopsis:

Hanley sends Saunders' squad after a wounded intelligence officer. Kirby is excited about this mission when he learns the intelligence officer is Eddie Kopachek, a childhood friend and his sister's fiancé. But when Kirby finds Eddie beaten to death, he launches a personal vendetta against the S.S. Colonel he holds responsible.

REVIEW: — 3 bayonets

This episode starts with a light scene of Hanley and Saunders needling Kirby. It gives little hint of the grimness to follow. Jack Hogan provides an outstanding performance in "Retribution." It is his best work in the series after "Hills Are for Heroes." The moment where Kirby decides to exact his own vengeance on the German is thoroughly chilling.

Argentinean-born Albert Paulsen returns to *Combat!* in his fourth guest appearance. Paulsen played a wide variety of Germans for *Combat!*: the endearing deserter in "Forgotten Front," the manipulative prisoner in "The Pillbox," the tragically noble officer in "Escape to Nowhere," and now the cold, sadistic killer. In "Retribution," for the third time he is a prisoner whose life is in the hands of a squad member.

The script by Edward J. Lakso drags slightly after Kirby's escape from the German Colonel, but director McEveety moves the action along. He provides some wonderful foreground/background action sequences in the French village as Saunders searches among a battling American platoon for one German trying to sneak out in an American uniform.

About Filming the Episode:

The opening sequence has a rare shot of Hanley arriving in jeep and getting out. Rick Jason says they avoided shots of him climbing into/out of a jeep, usually cutting as one foot was about to make the move. It took too long for him to fold his long legs into the tiny vehicle.

Notes, Oddities, and Bloopers:

• As Paulsen escapes, in the background several Germans are slaughtered by river. In the next cut the same slaughter repeats, just in a closer view.
• Paulsen pilfers a rifle and helmet from an American corpse, then he pilfers the same helmet a second time.
• American uniforms are one-size-fits-all.
• Script action takes place around Avignon. Filming was at Franklin Canyon and MGM backlot.

The Mockingbird (117)

Teleplay by Esther and Bob Mitchell
Story by by Rev. Thomas A. Conway CPPS
Directed by John Peyser
First aired 04-Jan-1966 (Episode 17 of Season 4)

CAST:

Regulars: Jason, Hogan, Jalbert
Guest Star Jeremy Slate as Lt. Asher
Jacques Roux as Gautier
George Brenlin as Pvt. Banning
Nelson Welch as Abbot
Hans Difflip as Col. Richter
Felix Locher as Brother Jasper
Ben-Ari as Monk
Jean del Val as Brother Edmundo
Kurt Landen as Sgt. Mueller
Mark Russi as German Soldier
George Michaelides as Marcel
Max Kleven as Patrol Leader #1
Walter Alzmann as Patrol Leader #2
Dusty Cadis as German Pilot
John Agar as Capt. Thorpe

Synopsis:

Three days before a German advance, a spy posing as a downed American flyer is sent to secure information on the French resistance. The staged plane crash, though, attracts Hanley instead of the resistance. The spy changes plans when he learns the intelligence officer that Hanley is escorting has valuable information about the German attack plan.

Review — 2.5 bayonets:

Jeremy Slate, in his second *Combat!* appearance, plays Lt. Asher, a German posing as an American aviator. As Asher, Slate plots, charms, and murders his way through this suspenseful story.

Pierre Jalbert and Jeremy Slate have a nice chemistry. On paper, their scenes in the monastery would seem ordinary, but in front of the camera, these two sizzle. A shame they had no further interaction. Their brief exchange has the same resonance and charisma as Morrow and Coburn's verbal duel in "Masquerade."

The story drags in the third and fourth acts, with too much filler of walking through the woods and sloshing through the rain.

Notes, Oddities, and Bloopers:

• Caje wears pinky ring on his right hand in some scenes.
• In the scene by the stream, the "guest victim" is already soaked before he enters the stream.
• When moving the wounded within the monastery, the barrel of Caje's M1 strikes one of the monks in the head, causing him to rub it.
• Another partisan clergy who does not blink or show charity to three Germans killed in front of him.
• The monastery entrance is the same used for the convent entrance in "One More for the Road."
• Action of story takes place eight miles behind the enemy lines near Boussac.

127

Hills Are for Heroes (118 and 119)

Written by Gene L. Coon
Directed by Vic Morrow
Part 1: Aired 01-Mar-1966 (Episode 25 of Season 4)
Part 2: Aired 08-Mar-1966 (Episode 26 of Season 4)

CAST:
Regulars: Jason, Morrow, Hogan, Jalbert, Peabody, Carter
Paul Carr as Kleinschmidt
Joseph Walsh as Einstein
Anthony Call as Morgan
Michael Forest as Company Commander
Earl Parker as Machine Gunner (uncredited)
Steve Marlo as Radio Operator (uncredited)
Walt Davis as Tank Driver (uncredited)

Synopsis:

Hanley must secure, at any cost, a strategic road guarded by two bunkers. Machine gun fire from the bunkers decimates the platoon and wounds Saunders. With no artillery support, Hanley is ordered again and again to try to take the hill. The suicide runs take a heavy toll in lives and morale, especially Hanley's. With help from a tank, the bunkers fall, but half the platoon lies dead on the hill. Before Kirby and the others can climb to the top to claim their prize, the platoon receives orders to fall back and abandon their hard-fought position.

Review — 4 bayonets:

The squad's doomed attempt to take a hill provides a searing anti-war commentary. "Hills Are for Heroes" is Vic Morrow's greatest gift to *Combat!* fans. His direction is remarkable, especially the exquisite composition in his shots and the evocative performances he elicits from the actors. Peabody and Jalbert turn in standout performances. Both Jack Hogan and Rick Jason do some of their best *Combat!* work in "Hills."

This episode has a great team feel. Morrow peoples the scenes with full-platoon strength. Earl Parker, Vic's stunt double, has a featured, but uncredited, role in Part 1 as Chester, the machine gunner who questions Kirby about Hanley.

Gene L. Coon (of *Star Trek* fame) wrote the screenplay. Morrow helped craft some of the dialogue, but took no script credit. The story gives viewers several great Saunders moments: his refusal of the morphine, his gentle reassurance of Littlejohn, and his spectacular PPT to Hanley.

"Vic did not direct me in one scene, until the last one, when I sit down and I fall apart," says Rick Jason. "I had gone over the hill in the first rehearsal. And Vic says, 'Okay, cut. Let's take five minutes. Rick come on, let's go in the dressing room. Frank come on.' Frank [Kowalski] was on the book, so he had to be there. And Vic talks to me for five minutes. And then he says 'All right, let's do it.' I did the first three lines and suddenly Frank got up and ran out of my dressing room. Ran. I mean, he didn't walk out, he ran out. After we shot the scene — and we did it in one take, by the way, and we printed the first take — I went over to Frank and asked why he ran out of the dressing room. And he said, 'You absolutely freaked me out. The difference between what you had done in the rehearsal and

Series star Vic Morrow behind the camera as he directs "Hills Are for Heroes."

what you did in the dressing room — I was so freaked out I had to get away. You got to me. You got right to my gut and I couldn't stay there.'

"It's among the best work I've ever done in my career," says Rick Jason. "And I thank Vic Morrow for that. I've watched 'Hills' several times, and every time I do, I think about his direction, not my performance."

About Filming the Episode:

Morrow filmed "Hills" at Albertson's ranch because MGM

Paul Carr, Jack Hogan, Joey Walsh, and Vic Morrow (seated) directing "Hills Are for Heroes."

In next shot as Hanley enters bunker, Caje is already inside.
•"Hills Are for Heroes" shows how a few well-prepared and well-equipped men (the Germans) can stand off a superior force.
•Selig Seligman was so pleased with the episode, that he threw a wrap party after filming. At the party, Frank Kowalski gave the episode its current title.
•Among the regular cast, this two-parter tops the list as personal favorite *Combat!* episode, even Tom Lowell, who does not appear in it. Dick Peabody rated it as possibly the best war film ever made.

Counterplay (120)

Written by Edward J. Lakso
Directed by Alan Crosland, Jr.
First aired 25-Jan-1966 (Episode 20 of Season 4)

CAST:
Regulars: Morrow, Jason, Hogan, Jalbert, Peabody
Guest Star Mark Richman as Marchand/German Lt.
Robert Crawford as Pierre DuBois
Louis Mercier as Paul DuBois
Gary Lasdun as Marchand/French
Paul Busch as German Officer
Walter Davis as German #1
Gerd Rein as German #2
Chris Anders as German #3
H.M. Wynant as Sgt. Rawlings
Robert Ellenstein as DuBois

Synopsis:
An impostor masquerades as a French resistance fighter to lead Saunders' squad on a mission. They are escorting a radar expert to evaluate and destroy a German radar installation. The impostor leads them through an elaborate ruse, including a staged raid on a fake radar setup. When two resistance fighters stumble into the German's lair, the plot is revealed.

Review — 1/2 bayonet:
Mark Richman stars in "Counterplay," his second guest appearance on *Combat!* He leads the squad through an intricate plot in a sloppy suspense story. The episode is padded with footage of B52s and planes in flight, making the show look more like an episode of "Twelve O'Clock High" than *Combat!*

Both the script and direction are weak. The Germans have devised a detailed ruse and constantly watch the squad throughout their mission — but they foolishly establish their base in a room formerly occupied by the resistance and do not take the precaution of keeping strangers from entering.

Elements of a coming-of-age story are tossed in, along with a Frenchman making the noble sacrifice. The story is a hodgepodge of plot elements and stock footage.

Notes, Oddities, and Bloopers:
•As the squad is in the sniper's sights, they are already wet before they enter the stream.
•The town is part of the MGM backlot that *Combat!* never blew up. The same streets were used for Annette's home in

did not have the terrain the story needed. Two German bunkers and the American bunker were built on location. A replica of the American bunker was built on an MGM sound stage for filming the interiors of the bunker. Vic dragged out his twelve-day filming schedule to 21 days, more than doubling the budget. ABC regularly sent notes to Vic about the overrun — Vic used the notes to light his cigarettes. By finish, Vic Morrow spent a half million of ABC's dollars.

Notes, Oddities, and Bloopers:
•Caje wears a pinky ring in several shots
•Part 1: Hanley enters bunker wearing a pack; when he gets inside, he has no pack.
•Part 1: Kirby has a bandage on his left index finger in some firefights.
•Part 1: In the last firefight of part 1, when platoon starts up the hill, the machine gun is picked up, then next shot it is picked up again.
•Part 2: The squad never checks the tank to see if any of the crew is alive.
•Part 2: In credits, Jack Hogan is listed on separate card in Part 2 only.
•After Caje charges down the hill unable to get close enough to toss a couple of grenades, he stands outside the bunker catching his breath and Hanley walks past him into the bunker.

"Just for the Record" and Anne's orphanage in "The Furlough," among others.

• An oddly bullet-free episode: Caje and Kirby kill Germans by striking their faces with rifle butts. Saunders dispatches one by breaking his back on a rock.

• The squad avoids gunfire to silently kill the radar technicians, then they set off noisy grenades and Saunders uses the Thompson on the equipment. Why take the trouble to be quiet in the beginning?

Nothing to Lose (121)
Written by Richard Wendley
Directed by Georg Fenady
Produced by Richard Caffey
First aired 01-Feb-1966 (Episode 21 of Season 4)

CAST:
Regulars: Jason, Hogan, Peabody, Jalbert
Guest Star Sal Mineo as Vinnick
Tom Skerritt as Burke

Synopsis:
Vinnick, a tough G.I. with no regard for danger, clashes with Burke, a soldier who covers his own cowardice with big talk. Vinnick risks his life to save Kirby, garnering him a Bronze Star recommendation from Hanley and hatred from Burke. Burke's anger erupts into blows and gunfire. Hanley arrests Vinnick when he receives word that Vinnick is wanted for murder. Vinnick escapes and the squad is ordered to bring him back, dead or alive.

Review — 3 bayonets:
Sal Mineo plays street kid Private Vinnick opposite Tom Skerritt as Burke. The two put in crisp performances. The script by Richard Wendley explores the nature of killing: the difference between taking life on the battlefield and taking life on the street. For the one, Vinnick was to receive a medal, for the other, the electric chair.

Jack Hogan is excellent playing a Kirby who sees some of himself in this troubled tough guy — and is frightened by what he sees. If life had dealt him a different hand, Kirby might have wound up like Vinnick. Hogan and Mineo's scenes work far better than Skerritt's, due more to a script that gives the Burke character little depth. Dick Peabody has a striking scene as a Littlejohn troubled to be hunting down someone wearing the same uniform as he.

About Filming the Episode:
Jack Hogan remembers working with director Georg Fenady and the pranks they would play on set. "They used to bring the tour busses by on the back lot and people would get off the bus. Georg was so funny, but he'd treat us like absolute dogs. And he'd come storming over to the trailer yelling 'Come on you guys, come out of there! I told you!' And we'd come out throwing helmets, throwing belts down, saying we'll never work on this damn show again, and stalk off and the tour people would just look around in amazement."

Filming the fourth season episode "The Ringer" on MGM's Lot 3 in Culver City. From left to right: director Mike Caffey, Vic Morrow, cinematographer Emmett Bergholz, and camera crew.

Notes, Oddities, and Bloopers:
• Mineo and Skerritt fight in a dark room that is suddenly bright after commercial break. A lit candle appears in the background later in the scene.

Ask Me No Questions (122)
Written by Edward J. Lakso
Directed by Alan Crosland, Jr.
First aired 08-Feb-1966 (Episode 22 of Season 4)

CAST:
Regulars: Morrow
Guest Star Claude Akins as Mastin
Ed Peck as Pvt. Coker
Carl Reindel as Pvt. Murray
Craig Curtis as Pvt. Beecher
Curt Lowens as Capt. Haus
Charles Maxwell as Corp. Giles
Vic Dana as Pvt. James
Featuring Henry Evens as Corp. Rogers
Ted Jordan as Pvt. Brand
Barry Ford as First German Sentry
John Siegfried as 2nd German Sentry
Mark Tobin as 1st German Soldier
Ivan Henry Fairbanks as 2nd German Soldier

Synopsis:
A German Lieutenant posing as an American sergeant (Sgt. Mastin) is placed among arriving American prisoners, including Saunders. Mastin learns locations of key American units. As Saunders is transported away, the deception is revealed by a prisoner who served with the real Sgt. Mastin. Saunders engineers his escape and his re-capture to make sure the infiltrator makes no use of the information.

Review — 2.5 bayonets:
In "Ask Me No Questions," Saunders is again a prisoner. He was captured after (again) losing a superior officer in the field. In the POW camp, Saunders (again) encounters a German mas-

querading perfectly as a G.I.

Though the elements in this episode are familiar to *Combat!* fans, the cliches are packaged nicely. The fun in the episode is waiting for Saunders to catch on that he has been feeding information to a German spy, and then to watch our hero as he tries to set everything right. Morrow's look at the end of act one, when he realizes he has been duped, is pure Saunders — the Saunders you don't want to meet in a dark alley.

Notes, Oddities, and Bloopers:
• Morrow takes on Claude Akins in a fist-fight and wins? Akins has at least thirty pounds on him and his character is well-fed and rested. My money would be on Akins.
• During the final barrage, the fleeing American POWs battle across a raised wooden bridge. But after they safely cross it, a different bridge (the one from a "Bridge At Chalons") is shown blowing up.
• Claude Akins appears twice in the fifth season: in "Ollie Joe" and "Nightmare on the Red Ball Run."
• Again, a well-timed artillery barrage is the device that resolves this episode.

The Ringer (123)

Teleplay by Gene L. Coon
Story by Gene L. Coon and Del Carnes
Directed by Michael Caffey
First aired 15-Feb-1966 (Episode 23 of Season 4)

CAST:
Regulars: Morrow, Jason, Hogan, Jalbert, Peabody
Guest Star Mart Hulswit as Arthur Adams
Peter Colton as Johnson
Tom Pace as German #1
Mike Krempels as German #2

Synopsis:
In "The Ringer," a suspicious straggler joins the squad and behaves erratically, endangering the lives of Saunders and company. Who is he? Where did he come from? Is he even an American? He convinces Saunders he has seen enough action to warrant his accompanying the squad on a mission, where he disobeys orders and raises everyone's suspicions.

Review — 3 bayonets:
Mart Hulswit is Arthur Adams, the mysterious straggler with something to hide and something to prove. Some good action sequences at the end of the episode surround an ultimately unsatisfying conclusion, but, what-the-heck, getting there is fun.

Morrow does his usual excellent job, especially chewing out Adams. Hogan, as Kirby, again shows his gentler side in this episode. This is a trend that I hated to see develop. By fifth season, Kirby has been so "niced-up" that he has become nearly a caricature: the curmudgeon with the heart of gold.

The exterior sets and devastation at the bombed out house look cartoonish and contrived. The craters, fence, and buildings look hastily assembled and fresh. The interior sets do not quite match the exteriors.

Notes, Oddities, and Bloopers:
• Much of the opening fight is reused footage from first season episodes.
• Caje is wearing a pinky ring and a wedding ring. When did he have time to sneak in a furlough and a wedding?
• In the first battle, the wooden barrel Morrow hides behind is shot through, but the bullets exit the side (making fountains of water) instead of passing straight through to hit Saunders.
• Pierre Jalbert's pant leg catches fire as he tries to put out the fire in the farmhouse. After Caje puts out the fire, it is still burning in a later clip.
• Filmed at Franklin Canyon and MGM.
• Littlejohn is shot in the shoulder, but the blood and treatment are on the arm.

Vic Morrow and Pierre Jalbert in "The Ringer"

One at a Time (124)
Written by Esther and Bob Mitchell
Directed by Bernard McEveety
First aired 22-Mar-1966 (Episode 28 of Season 4)

CAST:
Regulars: Vic Morrow, Peabody
Jan Merlin as Sgt. Erich
Larry Kert as Fry
Ronnie Welsh as Peal
Robert Yuro as Tanner
Rod Lauren as Guerney
Jerry Ayres as Sims
Walt Davis as Kerrigan
Hagen Smith as Daniels

Synopsis:

After the slaughter of his untried troops, a German sergeant vows vengeance against Saunders and his squad. The sergeant stalks the squad, always one step ahead of them, and picks off Saunders' men one by one. Saunders outwits him in the end, and the German dies clutching his stolen weapon and calling the names of his fallen men.

Review — 1.5 bayonets:

"One at a Time" opens with a great battle. I love these shots everytime I see them (they're re-used from "Anatomy of a Patrol"). These clips are edited seamlessly into the new footage, since "Anatomy" and this episode were both directed by Bernard McEveety. McEveety's strength as an action director is evident in this episode, especially as he shows the horror of battle through the eyes of the inexperienced German soldiers.

The action scenes are the best part of this episode about a German sergeant seeking a convoluted revenge on Saunders and his squad. The script by Esther and Bob Mitchell stretches credulity too far as the German, by happy coincidence, overhears the intended route of Saunders' squad, escapes with weaponry appropriate to allay certain suspicions, and other contrivances. The fourth act is very talky, with Saunders successfully deducing all the sniper's plans and motivations from the barest of hints.

The scene with Littlejohn, Saunders, and Fry near the end of the episode is unintentionally amusing. They discuss Saunders' odd plan to ferret out the German, talking about Littlejohn as if he were not there. Littlejohn listens dumbly as they discuss his abilities and actions, never throwing in his two cents or even just piping up with a "Hey! I'm here!"

Notes, Oddities, and Bloopers:
• The railroad set in this episode is the same used in the two-parter "What Are the Bugles Blowin' For?" The Bee Gees disco classic "Staying Alive" was also shot there.
• Dick Peabody's billing is very low in the cast list, after minor guests.
• Rick's stunt double, Walt Davis, has a featured role as Kerrigan.

Gitty (125)
Written by Judith Barrows
Directed by Georg Fenady
First aired 15-Mar-1966 (Episode 27 of Season 4)

CAST:
Regulars: Morrow, Jason, Peabody, Carter, Jalbert
Andrea Darvi as Gitty
Richard Bakalyan as Sgt. Piper
Tom Nolan as Pvt. Hamilton
John Himes as Gitty's Father
Bill Harlow as Captain's Aide

Synopsis:

While clearing a town to set up an observation post, Saunders kills a German straggler. Meanwhile, a young girl anxiously waits for her soldier father to come claim her, not knowing Saunders just killed him. She learns the truth, hates Saunders, but forgives him for making her an orphan at the first sight of Saunders' blood.

Review — 1 bayonet:

Andrea Darvi is adorable as "Gitty," an unlikely young girl with perfect tri-lingual abilities. The first act drags waiting for the inevitable moment when Saunders discovers the little girl.

The direction of this silly plot is uninspired and the acting predictable. The best acting comes from Andrea Darvi as Gitty. *Combat!* viewers saw Andrea Darvi grow up over the first four seasons of *Combat!* "Gitty" is the third time she plays an orphan that tugs at the heart of a squad member.

Notes, Oddities, and Bloopers:
• Saunders has killed hundreds of Germans. Why would he remember the face of this particular one? Also, what is so deadly about his rifle butt that one smack kills Paul Busch?
• The German shoots at the fleeing backs of Saunders and Gitty, but only hits Saunders.
• The machine-gunned Saunders lands with his back across the curb; but in the next shots, his unconscious head rests comfortably on the curb.
• Richard Bakalyan (Sgt. Piper) appeared in season one's "The Prisoner."
• Jack Hogan does not appear, but is listed in the credits.
• Today, Andrea Darvi is a writer. She used her own acting career as the starting point for her 1983 book *Pretty Babies, an Insider's Look at the World of the Hollywood Child Star.*

Run, Sheep, Run (126)

Written by Esther and Bob Mitchell
Directed by Bernard McEveety
First aired 05-Apr-1966 (Episode 30 of Season 4)

CAST:

Regulars: Morrow, Hogan, Jalbert, Peabody
Guest Star Dwayne Hickman as Corey
Walter Maslow as Booker
Chris Howard as German Corporal
Frank Marth as Lt. Vogler

Synopsis:

In his first battle, Pvt. Corey freezes. Afterward, the squad commends him for his actions, believing he destroyed a machine gun nest and captured a German officer. He is terrified that the squad will brand him a coward if they discover his moment of panic was the reason his squad mate died. His fear of discovery is heightened when he learns that the prisoner he guards speaks English and could reveal what really happened.

Review — 2 bayonets:

In this re-tread of "The Medal," Dwayne Hickman plays a G.I. with a secret that can be exposed by the German prisoner he is tasked with guarding. Nothing spectacular here, just solid directing, writing, and acting. This story delves into the meaning of cowardice, whether one moment of weakness can define a man's whole life.

Dwayne Hickman (who starred in the TV series "The Many Loves of Dobie Gillis") as Private Corey is excellent, as each effort to cover his deceit gets him deeper into trouble, until finally he must decide if protecting his reputation is worth another man's life. Frank Marth plays the German prisoner, unsure whether his secret will set him free or get him killed. His death scene is poetic in its simplicity. This is one of Esther and Bob Mitchell's strongest scripts.

Notes, Oddities, and Bloopers:

• The "Run, Sheep, Run" title card is styled after the "Run, Dick, Run" readers.
• Pierre Jalbert wears his wedding ring in some scenes.
• Kirby drinks from Caje's canteen.
• Toward the end of the episode, when the squad chases the three remaining Germans, Saunders fires his Thompson and a B.A.R. sound is heard, immediately after Kirby fires his B.A.R., which makes Thompson noises.
• Filmed at Franklin Canyon.

The Leader (127)

Written by Esther and Bob Mitchell
Directed by Georg Fenady
First aired 12-Apr-1966 (Episode 31 of Season 4)

CAST:

Regulars: Jason, Morrow, Hogan, Jalbert, Peabody, Carter
William Bryant as Maynard
Michael Vandever as Scott
Steven Marlo as Austin
Tim Felix as Stice
Andre Phillippe as Grover
Richard Chambers as Lloyd
Richard Tretter as Wills
Michael Barrier as Dean
Beau Vanden Ecker as German
Larry Gelbman as German Sergeant
David Ross as Wounded Soldier
Bill Harlow as Sgt. Meade
Mike Masters as Runner
Louie Elias as Johnson

Synopsis:

PFC William G. Kirby, the squad goldbrick, is left in uneasy command of the squad during a German advance. As Kirby holds the fate of eleven men in his hand, he finds that the soldier most uncertain about Kirby's ability to lead, is Kirby. Not helping matters, Kirby has his own "Kirby" to deal with — Maynard: a wise-cracking, smart-mouthed B.A.R. man, who is always belly-aching and questioning orders.

Review — 4 bayonets:

"The Leader" shows Kirby going through a spectrum of emotions. In a nearly flawless script by Esther and Bob Mitchell, he matures before our eyes, until (with the sage advice of Doc) he comes to trust his own instincts and becomes a true leader among men.

The script is packed with action, moving quickly through both a complex, shifting tactical situation and the constantly flowing emotional state of the characters. The first act contains more plot than in some entire episodes. The growth and forced maturity of Kirby under fire is believable, thanks to this intensely literate and thoughtful script and a strong performance by Jack Hogan. Littlejohn, in a nice twist on their usual relationship, becomes Kirby's staunch and vocal supporter.

About Filming the Episode:

Costumer Beau Vanden Ecker appears as a German. "He wanted to be an actor so badly, he wanted to be an actor more than any of us," said Jack Hogan at the 1996 cast reunion. Beau did stunts on the show in addition to his wardrobe work. "You didn't want to cross Beau. He was about five feet tall and the toughest guy you'd ever met . . . He could do karate kicks fifteen feet in the air."

Notes, Oddities, and Bloopers:

• In the opening sequence, some sort of metal is dangling from Caje's right trouser pocket (possibly keys).
• At end of episode, footage of the ambulance from "Off Limits" is re-used.
• Saunders is on death's door for half the episode, yet at the end all he seems to be suffering from is a crease on the temple.
• Lovely night-time barrage effects.
• William Bryant, Maynard in this episode, became squad regular McCall in the final season of *Combat!*

CHAPTER 6

Season Five (in color) 1966–1967

The actors received word that they would be renewed for a fifth season while shooting the last episode of season four. To everyone's delight, the show would go to color. Conlan Carter says, "We all sort of wanted it for a long time before it happened. We thought that might save the show. The color episodes were, we thought, much better received. Everybody said they liked it a lot better in color. As far as the work itself, there was no appreciable difference. A little bit in some of the wardrobe. Some of the color stuff had to be color coordinated with the wardrobe stuff so it wouldn't jump. But as a general rule, all of our stuff was olive drab anyway . . . There was a little question about whether it [*Combat!*]would be back. It was never a lead pipe cinch. And you live in that kind of awful insecurity all the time. There were rumors, little stuff would start to fly, everybody would pick up on it or hang on it."

Rick Jason says, "ABC killed us. They didn't realize what they had on their hands. At end of the fourth year, Emmett Bergholz convinced ABC to go to color. He did some night shots to show them that it could be done. ABC was scared that they wouldn't be able to get their money back in syndication with four years of black-and-white shows."

Pierre Jalbert, in a 1966 interview for the Social Security Administration, said about the transition to color, "Some people say the grimness of war works only in black and white. Plus, the library stock film we use is black and white. The conception of most people is that the war in color is inconceivable, except in the Pacific."

The technicians overcame the problem of using stock war footage. They tinted archival footage and were able to use it with the new color photography. More difficult to overcome was the loss of the MGM lot.

Fifth season, MGM doubled the rent for the sound-stages. So production moved to CBS. "MGM kicked us out," says Georg Fenady. "They just got so busy over there. They were loaded over there and we were just renting space, it wasn't an MGM show, it was an ABC show. So they were crowded for space, so we went to CBS. Now at MGM . . . we very rarely had to leave the lot for any length of time. At CBS, if you wanted to shoot a tree you had to leave the lot, there was nothing there."

Most of the season five episodes were shot at Franklin Canyon, this forced a different look to the show. Besides going to color, the primarily outdoor look of season five makes the show bright. The look of the backlot and war-torn devastation of the villages, and the rarity of night shooting, creates a very different mood to season five episodes.

Seasons one through four used the MGM French village extensively, but only a few episodes in season five feature the familiar standing sets.

Dick Peabody and Rick Jason.

In the fifth season, Richard Caffey replaced Gene Levitt as producer. Caffey had been production executive for the pilot, and associate producer for seasons one through four. Under his leadership, he took the show from black-and-white *film noir* to red-white-and-blue carnage.

In the fifth season, the concept of the "squad" story completely disappeared. Only four episodes in the fifth season feature all the regular cast members. Also, many shows seem written by committee, with several people credited with story and with teleplay on a single episode.

Though the scripts under Caffey lost their edge and their immediacy, the acting in season five continued strong. Some of the show's finest episodes appear in this last season: among them "Conflict," "The Furlough," and "The Chapel at Able-Five."

Selmur's Pilot Show

Another change happened going into season five: Selmur Productions made another pilot for a war series. The episode featured Lieutenant Hanley introducing a group of guerrilla soldiers with appearances by Caje and Kirby. Morrow was nowhere to be seen in the pilot. It turned out to be the pilot for Selmur's next war series, "Garrison's Gorillas."

Rick Jason talks of the episode that featured the Garrison characters. "They filmed it in November, going to have a chance to cut the thing together in April. If it didn't sell, they would have used it as a *Combat!* segment and there would have been 153 segments."

Rick Jason says of the first day of filming, "I said to Cesare Danova, who played the character named Actor, 'What are you guys doing, shooting a pilot spin-off?' He said 'Shhhhhhhhhh.' I said 'I know, nobody's supposed to know, right?' He says 'Shhhhhhhhh.' He had been signed for a six-month hold. They

were going to jettison us. I was the only one who knew. Vic didn't even know. He just knew he wasn't working that week, but there were some weeks he didn't work. And I am pissed. I am so pissed I can't see straight. I mean, they are using us. They have used us for five years. They've done everything they could to short-circuit us every time we turn around . . . They bring in Joe Sargent, I think, to direct. And Joe Sargent, I know, only directs pilots. He doesn't direct segments because he gets big money. I did my work. Period. I did my work, and walked away and went into my dressing room. And when they needed me, they called me, I came out, and I did my work and went back in the dressing room. I was friendly with the other actors on the set and that was about it . . They sold the show, but they cut my footage out. It was a ninety-minute version, I remember, because I got an extra paycheck. What they did is, they did it in such a way—cause they did two versions of some cuts where they couldn't cut me out of the long shot. They'd shoot it twice. And somebody would say, 'Okay, Rick, you can sit down.' And he says, 'All right, let's have the other guys cross without Rick.' And I knew what they were doing."

For *Combat!,* the expensive transition to color failed to give the show a bump in the ratings. Plus, it made it difficult to include the stock action footage that they had filmed during the four black-and-white years. Fans had come to expect an opening battle sequence in each episode, which was proving costly in color.

The ratings were still respectable, making *Combat!* one of ABC's more popular shows. So what happened next, came as a surprise.

The Final Patrol

In the end, it was not Germans that halted Saunders' advance to Berlin, or the network, or poor ratings. It was federal regulations. With the mass conversion of TV viewership to color, the industry feared that the backlog of black-and-white prime time shows would have no market in a few years. If Selmur wanted to see any return on their investment, they would have to start syndicating their old shows, before people stopped watching black-and-white shows altogether. At that time, the FCC would not allow a show that was currently in prime time to also be in syndication. So, to free up the black-and-white *Combat!* shows for the syndication market, *Combat!* had to leave the air. Selmur Productions did not have to worry. They had another World War II series ready: "Garrison's Gorillas."

Georg Fenady recalls, "We were going to a *Combat!* party, the wrap on the end of the fifth year at CBS. And Dick [Caffey] said 'Hang in there with me for a minute and we'll go over together.' And so we walked over to the party together and he says 'Don't tell the guys, but I just got the word that *Combat!* is canceled and they picked up Garrison's.' They didn't want to go with two war shows. And they thought that *Combat!* had maybe run its course. If it wasn't for the Garrison's pilot we would have gotten another year for sure. They made a choice and made a bad choice . . . Of course, we didn't break it at the party and spoil everybody's enjoyment."

The last episode filmed for the show was "Jonah." This episode about a man convinced he's a curse to his friends, ends oddly. The Jonah gets shot (non-lethally) and believes that his curse is finally over, or perhaps it never existed. But the episode doesn't show the squad returning safely to camp; so the question of whether his curse is over is still open as the final credits roll. As *Combat!*'s last filmed episode, "Jonah" leaves the fate of not just the recruit-of-the-week in question, but also that of Hanley's entire squad. Their five-year battle across France ended not in triumph or tragedy, just a question mark.

Waging War Safely

The special effects artists at MGM were experts at waging war safely. *Combat!* had a great safety record for its five seasons of filming. Effects men who worked on the show included Academy Award-winner A.D. Flowers, Bill Ferrier, Bill Pearson, and Virgil Beck.

In a 1963 interview for the Social Security Administration, Vic Morrow says, "MGM, where we shoot the show, has, I think, probably the greatest technicians in the world. Sometimes they have to plant like 25 charges. And these are explosives that are buried in the ground. And on top of that, they put fuller's earth. But this earth has to be strained to get all pebbles and little rocks out of it. Then you have a group of actors, maybe twenty, running over it. And you have to make sure an actor isn't standing over it. At the same time you have tanks moving, you have blanks going off. It can be dangerous. But so far, luckily, nothing."

Morrow went on to describe the only incident they had up until that point. They were filming a scene where a tank had to run over a truck. The army tank driver had to have the hatch open to see where he was going. The lid of the tank, which weighed several hundred pounds, came crashing down on his head. Luckily, he was wearing his helmet, but it knocked him out. The tank continued forward, heading toward an extra, about forty yards ahead, that was sprawled in the road playing dead. The tank just missed him by two feet.

Though no major accidents happened, almost everyone got hit with squibs. "Squibs are little charges planted in a wall," said Vic Morrow in that same Social Security interview. "They use these for tight-in shots. Now they would go off in a series, and it's very fast, and they try to get as close as possible. There's no way of knowing for sure which way this blast is going to take, and it does blast off particles. I got hit a couple of times in the face and the hand. Pierre, who plays Caje on the show, got hit in the mouth. Joe Mantel got raked across here [his eyebrow, in the episode 'Far from the Brave']."

Tom Lowell says, "I think we all wound up with M1 thumb. And everyone got hit with a squib and with shell casings. All the guys who were left-handed, there was no adaptation for a left-handed person. So, the shells would eject to the right, so any left-handers always got hit in the arm. Pierre's got burns on his arms and I'm sure Jack has burns on his arms. A right-hander, no problem. But, you're standing there on the set, you're waiting to do your thing, you're rehearsing, you've got this stupid helmet on, you're standing there, so you just naturally start playing with that rifle. I remember one day we were just standing there, and I was just doing this, clicking it off, and I got my thumb caught!"

Rick Jason once had a hot casing ricochet off a beam and fall down the back of his shirt during filming. It left a burn on his back the size of a quarter.

Dick Peabody was injured during "Gulliver" — the only major accident to happen on the show. A reflector left in his path ripped cartilage in his leg. He did the rest of the episode on crutches. And he stayed on crutches for three months. According to Dick, "ABC insisted that I be propped up in at least the opening sequence or anywhere they could fit me in."

Georg Fenady says of on-set accidents, "The closest we ever came was Johnny Penner. He was on a boom, and he sits on his big steel chair with a cushion on it. He was the assistant camera guy, the one on focus. And what happened, his chair swung out, unbeknownst to him, as the boom was moving. And it ended up right smack over a pot. The explosion went off under him. All it did was scare the hell out of him. It scared the hell out of all of us. It went up directly under him and hit that steel plate. He was covered with soot and everything . . . Angie [DeMeo] got hit one time. He got a bruised kidney taking a flop off a roof. He did a beautiful fall, landed just about where he wanted to. It was just one of those things, he kind of landed a little flatter than he wanted to. He was only out for a couple of days."

Striving for safety can cause some inconveniences. "Our form of communicating from one hill to another," says Fenady, "was to scream, 'Are you ready?' Or, since we'd become half deaf, we'd signal with gun shots. One shot was come ahead, two shots was cut, and that sort of prearranged signal." Walkie-talkies could not be used around explosives, since there was a slight possibility that they could be triggered by the walkie-talkie. "So we didn't even take a gamble. But, as I said, they really didn't work that well in those days and they were also expensive and we didn't have them budgeted. So we did a lot of yelling. We put the money on the screen."

During firefights, the actors and crew would often have cotton in their ears to protect their hearing.

The special effects team also had fun with the pyrotechnics. Leonard Goldenson, president of ABC, once brought execs from New York to see filming of an episode. As they came on to lot three in a string of black limos, A.D. Flowers and the special effects crew rigged explosions to blow up all around them as they came down Eucy Road.

A.D. loved playing tricks with his explosives. At the Combat! cast reunion in Simi Valley in 1998, he told of a special gift he arranged for Vic. It was Vic's birthday and they brought in a big, special cake, with candles and pink icing. Of course, A.D. rigged it to explode and cover Vic with pink goo.

COMBAT!

Earl Parker in 1997, temporarily sidelined by a free "stunt" he performed while getting the mail. Decades in the business without a major accident, Earl broke his leg slipping on ice at a mailbox. Earl passed away in February of 2002.

Stunts

Georg Fenady says, "We had a real good nucleus of stunt guys and extras. When they'd leave at the end of the day we'd say 'Okay, tomorrow wear the German and bring the American.' These guys would end up shooting each other all the time. They'd line up as the Germans and fire, fire, fire. Then knock off the Americans and vice-versa. Our stunt guys probably killed each other more than anything in the history of television." The stunt men could be counted on to be killed at least once per week.

Earl Parker and Angelo De Meo were the show's stunt co-ordinators. Parker explains how the stunts were set up: "The stunt co-ordinator usually was present on the show. Usually the two of us, Angelo DeMeo and myself, were there as kind of key stunt people." Extra stuntmen were hired as needed, often from the extras who worked the series. Earl or Angelo would work with the director, going over the script for stunts. "We'd just sort of lay out what has to be done, and some figuring into it and cinematography . . . It has to be choreographed in time for a camera and special effects, and then you just improvise and take over from that point. . . . And you'd set up your routine like a dance routine, sometimes a little more violent. Maybe like the deep dip doing the tango or something like that. You might have to bend this way, bend that way and take an explosion."

Other stuntmen who worked on the show were Eddie Heis, Walt Davis, Phil Altman, and Ken DeLong.

Earl Parker became so good at doubling Vic that it became

WOUND TALLY

In the 152 episodes:

- Vic Morrow appeared in 121, was wounded in 41, and captured in 16.
- Rick Jason appeared in 111, was wounded in 16, and captured in 10.
- Conlan Carter appeared in 63, was wounded in 8, and captured in 3.
- Shecky Greene appeared in 8, was wounded in 2, and captured in 2.
- Jack Hogan appeared in 120, was wounded in 37, and captured in 10.
- Pierre Jalbert appeared in 114, was wounded in 18, and captured in 10.
- Tom Lowell appeared in 27, was wounded in 7, and captured in 4.
- Dick Peabody appeared in 103, was wounded in 15, and captured in 6.
- Steven Rogers appeared in 21, was wounded in 0, and captured in 1.

---

a career for him. Whenever Vic was filming and needed a double, he would request Earl Parker. Conlan Carter says of Earl, "He was his double, yeah. And they were fairly good friends. And he was good. He was so good, he could walk by the camera within three feet and you couldn't tell it was him. I could tell it, because I knew him, but you would never pick him up. He even had — Vic had a slightly deformed index finger on his hand, and Earl used to imitate that when he was walking. And he had his walk down to a fare-thee-well."

The Sound of Combat

Robert Blees says that *Combat!* had "tremendous sound effects editing, music was unusual. Leonard Rosenman had already been signed from the pilot. He had a scholarship in Rome while this was going on. I talked to him once before he left. I said 'Look, it's a war series. Here's what's going on, it's a war series, you know that, it's just going to be a lot more honest than the pilot. We're going to have exteriors and some interiors under tension.' We couldn't send the film to him to score, because he was in Rome. He wrote eight to ten hours of cues, some cues would be thirty seconds of dum-de-dum stuff. And then he'd write a minute cue, and a two-minute cue, and a three-minute cue and a soft cue, and all these kind of basic cues, and his editors had to adapt this stuff, music that had already been written. Nothing was scored for our series. And it turned out very well."

Leonard Rosenman gave descriptive titles to his various compositions. Some of the hit tunes were "Tortured Crawling," "More Tortured Crawling," "Confused #1," "Man Drowns," "Soldiers Searching," and "Saunders' Theme." In the book *TV's Biggest Hits,* by Jon Burlingame, Leonard Rosenman compares the style of his *Combat!* compositions to avant-garde composer Gyorgy Ligeti (brought to prominence for his music to Stanley Kubrick's *2001: A Space Odyssey*).

Season Five Episodes

In its final season, *Combat!* kept its Tuesday night, 7:30 p.m. time slot on ABC. Its competition was "Daktari" on CBS (which finished seventh in the ratings) and "The Girl from U.N.C.L.E." on NBC. ABC showed *Combat!* reruns from March 28 through August 28, ending the season with "Gadjo."

The Gun (128)

Written by Esther and Bob Mitchell
Directed by Michael Caffey
First aired 13-Sep-1966 (Episode 1 of Season 5)

CAST:

Regulars: Morrow, Hogan, Peabody, Jalbert
Guest Star Warren Stevens as Sgt. Hagen
Wayne Rogers as Reiser
Tim Felix as Weed

Synopsis:

The squad, backed by a half-track and a tank, must destroy a German field artillery piece before the company moves forward. But the Germans destroy the tank and half-track. They appropriate a German artillery piece that Saunders wants to use in place of the lost tank to destroy their initial target. But Hagen wants to destroy the gun that killed his crew and his tank. Saunders cajoles his despairing men into the backbreaking effort of hauling the gun miles overland to position.

Review — 3 bayonets:

Three bayonets for this simple Man vs. Technology tale embroidered with some stunning location photography and big-budget special effects. In this episode, the cast and crew escape the familiar backlots and travel to Korbel winery. Though the subject of the story is fairly intimate, the location shooting is broad and expansive. Long shots of vineyards make the squad's struggle with the gun seem insignificant against the vast landscape.

The episode works best when the focus is narrow, looking at the grim battle of the squad against this gun. The gun develops a personality of its own as the squad is forced to drag it up hills and through the rough French terrain. It claims the life of Private Weed, almost as though demanding a sacrifice beneath its wheels. Even the easy-going Littlejohn wants this weapon destroyed. But Saunders is determined to make this gun do his bidding, even if it breaks the squad.

The final battle provides some impressive pyrotechnics. The multiple explosions by the lake spew flame, smoke, and oil drums over 100 feet in the air. The fiery display is truly lovely, a pyromaniac's delight, but it seems contrary to the spirit of the early *Combat!* episodes where the drama was character-based rather than special effects–based. This fiery episode started *Combat's* only color season off with a bang!

About Filming the Episode:

"The Gun" and several other episodes were shot at Korbel Winery, run by the Heck brothers. The brothers entertained the cast well when they were on location, giving all of the cast complimentary cases of champagne. Also, they would come with bottles of Seven-Up filled with champagne for the cast in the morning. So, unbeknownst to the crew, the actors had their 10:00 am and 3:00 pm champagne breaks during filming. "It's a war show," says Dick Peabody, "soldiers are supposed to look a little unsteady." A photo of the cast and the Heck brothers hangs in the tourist center. Dick Peabody never liked that photo, afraid that the early morning picture showed too many signs of the late-night partying.

Notes, Oddities, and Bloopers:

• Why is a fuel depot located by the side of a lake, in soft sand that would swallow any truck or tank that tried to get near?
• Saunders calls Wayne Rogers' character by his real name, "Rogers," not by the character name of Reiser.
• The gun is a light-weight mockup of a 57mm anti-tank gun.

The Losers (129)

Written by Edward J. Lakso
Directed by Michael Caffey
First aired 20-Sep-1966 (Episode 2 of Season 5)

CAST:

Regulars: Morrow, Jason, Peabody
Guest Star Bill Bixby as Kline
Harry Landers as Ash
John Considine as Lennon
Bill Gray as Candell
Ed Deemer as American Lieutenant
Mark Russi as German Officer

Synopsis:

Saunders and Littlejohn arrive at a command post to pick up six men for a mission as the town is under attack and everyone evacuating. They find four G.I.s in jail who had been left behind. They conscript them into duty to blow up a bridge. When this ragtag lot encounters Germans, the worst of each of the men comes out.

Review — 2 bayonets:

In five seasons of picking up raw recruits and bad apples, Saunders scrapes the bottom of the barrel with his conscripts in "The Losers." This story of second chances has remarkable opening footage showing the devastation of war. Rubble and corpses are everywhere and medics rush desperately to save lives in a world exploding around them.

John Considine, who plays Lennon, appeared twice in season one as Private Templeton. In "The Losers," he plays a delicate soldier arrested for desertion under fire. Ash (played by Harry Landers) is a busted sergeant who wants to take charge . His sidekick Candel (Bill Gray) was arrested for drunk and disorderly. Klein (Bill Bixby) is a gum-chewing black marketeer.

Writer Edward Lakso captured Littlejohn well in this

"The Losers" with Bill Bixby, Harry Landers, Dick Peabody and Vic Morrow

episode. Lakso has the essence of this gentle giant. In fifth season, most writers give Dick Peabody little to work with as Littlejohn, relegating him to a bumbling hayseed. But when he is given something to sink his teeth into, as in "The Losers," Dick Peabody rises to the challenge. This script shows both sides of Littlejohn's nature and his intense loyalty to Saunders. Littlejohn is gentle and sympathetic with Lennon, but with Klein, who doesn't even fire a shot during the battle, he is threatening and dangerous.

About Filming the Episode:

The opening sequence of the rubble, "that was shot in downtown L.A. in a building that had just been demolished," says Dick Peabody. "Our producer, when he read about the demolition in the paper, wisely said, hey, lets do it down there."

Bill Gray and Dick Peabody spent some nights over drinks and Bill talked extensively about his career as a child actor. Dick said how surprised he was at the pain and anger that he expressed, having never considered how inside Hollywood would through the eyes of a child.

Notes, Oddities, and Bloopers:
•Shot at Korbel Winery, Franklin Canyon, and downtown L.A.
•Bill Bixby chews gum throughout the episode, even while in the river, setting charges.

The Chapel at Able-Five (130)
Written by Phillip W. Hoffman
Directed by Michael Caffey
First aired 11-Oct-1966 (Episode 5 of Season 5)
CAST:
Regulars: Morrow, Jason, Hogan, Jalbert, Peabody, Carter
Guest star Fritz Weaver as Major Chaplain Ernest Miller
John Hudson as Captain Jampel
George Sawaya as German Sergeant
Paul Busch as German Sergeant (uncredited)
Louis Elias as Pvt. David Cochran
David Armstrong as American Corporal
Jan Malmsjo as Captain Krauss

Synopsis:
Saunders is blinded and a companion killed by a land mine explosion as they attempt to get vital information back to their lines. The blinded Saunders is rescued by a German chaplain who pretends to be English to get Saunders' help in carrying a wounded German captain to safety. When he learns the identity of his rescuer, Saunders is held prisoner by the chaplain. The appearance of both Hanley and a German patrol put the decision of who lives and dies in other hands.

Review — 3.5 bayonets:
"The Chapel at Able-Five" provides a thought-provoking moral dilemma in the best tradition of the series. At first, the viewer may question whether the Chaplain is using Saunders, with no concern for his well-being. As the story progresses, the Chaplain's dilemma is how to save both charges that God has placed in his hands.

The interplay of the three characters is well written. It shows that all three characters (Saunders, Krauss, and Miller) are behaving in a moral manner, by their own standards of battlefield morality. All are willing to sacrifice their lives in the pursuit of a higher purpose. The two soldiers operate under the principle that it is better to sacrifice one or two soldiers so that the greater number can survive. Kraus is willing to commit murder to save his people, even to attack a priest; Saunders is willing to let a man bleed to death for the same purpose.

The chaplain thinks the soldiers are fools, so dedicated to destruction that they cannot see the waste. Fritz Weaver instills his chaplain with tenderness and understated power.

Notes, Oddities, and Bloopers:
•On radio, the captain says that he's King Two. Actually, he's King Six.
•Filmed at Franklin Canyon.
•Saunders conveniently loses his .45 when the script calls for it.
•The two Germans speak English among themselves.
•When Caje is moving through a ditch, his beret is alternately falling off, strapped securely, and falling off again.
•For throwing himself on top of a live grenade, the Chaplain's body was amazingly in one piece.

Vic Morrow in "The Chapel at Able-Five."

The Letter (131)
Written by Shirl Hendryx
Directed by Georg Fenady
First aired 25-Oct-1966 (Episode 7 of Season 5)

CAST:
Regulars: Jason, Morrow, Hogan, Carter, Jalbert
Guest Star Randy Boone as Jim Hummel
Barry Russon as Johnson
John Nealson as Pvt. Fisher
Mark Bailey as German Soldier
Peter Hellmann as German Soldier
Mike Masters as Mail Caller
Mark Tobin as German Lieutenant
Walter Davis as 1st German
Mike Krempels as 2nd German
Howard Gray as G.I.
Carl Carlsson as German Storyteller

Synopsis:
A replacement arrives who reminds Saunders of his kid brother, who he just found out has dropped out of high school and enlisted. Saunders coddles the kid, keeping him out of harm's way. In the second battle, the kid moves up against orders, saving Kirby's life, but earning Saunders' ire. At the supply depot, Saunders again leaves the kid safely behind. But when both Saunders and Kirby are wounded, their lives are in the hands of the boy soldier.

Review — 2 bayonets:
In "The Letter," Saunders says that for his men to stay alive "I'll do your thinking for you." But he is not thinking straight in this story by writer Shirl Hendryx. As with many of her *Combat!* stories, this deals with familial relations. Her scripts are usually strong, though in a Hendryx script, the men spend more time sharing their feelings than in a typical *Combat!* episode.

Contrast this episode with "Mail Call," where the squad is also concerned about Saunders. Nobody will take the direct approach with him there. But in "The Letter," Doc is willing to butt into his personal problems — not just once, but twice.

Doc knows details about Saunders' family life. But in "Mail Call," no one knew a thing about his background. Three seasons later, out of the blue, Doc is Sarge's confidant.

Notes, Oddities, and Bloopers:
• The kid brother sends a color photograph of himself. Extremely unusual for 1944, it should be a black-and-white photo.
• Caje is wearing a wedding ring and pinky ring that appear and disappear on the march to their mission objective.
• During mail call, there's a letter for Nelson.
• Why are the wounded soldiers out in the hot sun and under wool blankets, on a day that the script describes as "hotter than August in Texas." A perfectly good tent is in the scene, why aren't the wounded men in there?
• Earl Parker, as an American soldier, does a great back flip death in the teaser. As a German soldier, he is killed by Saunders at the checkpoint. He is killed again outside the bunker.
• The bunker from "Chapel at Able-Five" is the supply depot in this episode.
• Nobody checks Kirby's wound in the episode, but Doc treats Saunders' and tells him to treat the kid's.

Conflict (132)
Written by Esther and Bob Mitchell
Directed by Georg Fenady
First aired 29-Nov-1966 (Episode 11 of Season 5)

CAST:
Regulars: Morrow, Carter, Peabody, Jalbert
Karl Sadler as Machine Gunner
Tom Pace as German Corporal
Bill Harlow as G.I. Sergeant
Horst Ebersberg as 2nd Sentry
Gerd Rein as 1st Sentry
Buddy Pantsari as G.I. Medic
William Bryant as McCall

Synopsis:
Exhaustion and lack of sleep cause a breakdown of morale in Saunders' squad. After two days of continuous patrol in bad weather, Caje and Littlejohn are at each other's throats. Saunders looks scared as he follows his squad out into the rain. For once, he is unsure of the core group of men he has always counted on. The animosity between Caje and Littlejohn threatens to get everyone killed. But when Saunders and McCall are wounded, the squabbling duo comes through.

Review — 4 bayonets:
This gritty story presents the members of the squad at their worst and their best — and, therefore, at their most human. In "Conflict," the unending rain is as oppressive as the squad's humor. These conditions and privations affect the closest of comrades-in-arms and the audience watches helplessly as characters they have come to love begin to tear each other apart. For the first time in the series, the greatest danger to the squad's survival is the squad itself.

Kirby's absence from the episode works well. The audience expects conflict from Kirby. But trouble coming from the gentle Littlejohn and easy-going Caje is jarring. Pierre Jalbert is particularly frightening when he lets Caje lose his temper; in the dark, brooding shots, he looks positively satanic.

The scene between Saunders and McCall is weak. McCall asks questions when he and Saunders scope out the farmhouse, great dialogue such as "Sure looks quiet," "What do you think?" and "How much further, Sarge?" Such dialogue would have been excised in earlier seasons. The better written *Combat!* scripts don't require supporting actors to ask stupid questions.

Earl Parker is the German smoking a cigarette in the corner of the farmhouse. He later dies rolling down a tree log — managing to lose his helmet to reveal his blond hair. He is killed again later when a grenade explodes in his face.

Notes, Oddities, and Bloopers:
• During the final firefight, after McCall has left and Saunders is alone behind the tree trunk, the tip of a B.A.R. is in the corner of the picture.
• Opening sequence is "colorized" war footage. Even the lightning is reused from "Second in Command" and colorized.
• Almost all the episode was filmed on the green set at CBS.
• At MGM, the walls were really falling apart. At CBS, they had to paint the walls to look that way. Very apparent as "painted" decay in the final scenes when Littlejohn leans against the two-color textured cracks in wall and in back of Saunders and McCall in hospital.
• Only seven Germans are at the farmhouse, but the squad kills eighteen and takes one prisoner. Germans killed in this episode: 25. Americans: none.

A Child's Game (133)
Teleplay by Gilbert Ralston
Story by Sidney Elliss
Directed by Bernard McEveety
First aired 18-Oct-1966 (Episode 6 of Season 5)

CAST:
Regulars: Morrow, Peabody, Carter
Peter Haskell as Carl Muller
Henry Brandon as Hans
John Maurer as Kurt
John Walker as Heinrich
Jim Henaghan as Gunther
David Loring as Karl
Eric Vaughn as Wilhelm
Mark de Vries as Ernest
Dennis Olivieri as Dieter

Synopsis:
The squad tries to set up an OP in a French farmhouse occupied by teenaged German soldiers. Saunders is given one hour to take the house, by any means. They try to scare the kids out with a blaze of bullets and with grenades, but the kids hold. None of the squad want to needlessly sacrifice these young lives. But when their young leader is captured and refuses to

yield, Saunders must change tactics.

Review — 1.5 bayonets:
This episode, directed by Bernard McEveety, has much to like — unfortunately, the script and the casting are not among them. "A Child's Game" has lots of exciting battles and nice performances from the usual suspects. But the script is weak and features the premise that sixteen-year-olds make lousy soldiers. Historically, teens have made excellent soldiers.

The casting of the soldiers could have been better. These boys look no younger than the actor who played the young American soldier Danny in "Cry For Help." To really feel for the plight of these kids, real kids should have been cast. Toward the end of the war, the Germans were putting thirteen-year-olds in uniform. These actors are young men who have attained their full growth.

This script has many missed opportunities. This was the only script to deal with the terror of the Hitler Youth, but glossed over it. Also, the dilemma of Dieter, the reluctant orphan soldier who finds himself in command of a doomed squad, is explored only superficially.

Notes, Oddities, and Bloopers:
• Saunders looks as if he is shot by the German Sergeant, but in the next scene he is unharmed.
• The same dog from "Hear No Evil."
• McEveety has a couple trademark shots: a series of crisp pans and stops on faces (all in one camera shot, with appropriate martial music), soldiers firing almost directly into the camera, and filming through the sights of a rifle. Several instances are found in this McEveety episode. His opening—moving from German face to German face in the windows—is almost identical to his opening in "Bridgehead."

The Brothers (134)
Written by Irve Tunick
Directed by Bernard McEveety
First aired 04-Oct-1966 (Episode 4 of Season 5)

CAST:
Regulars: Jason, Hogan, Peabody, Jalbert
Guest Star Fernando Lamas as Leon Paulon
Special Guest Sal Mineo as Marcel Paulon
Kurt Landen as 1st German Sergeant
Paul Busch as 2nd German Sergeant
Ted Knight as Lt. Herlmoch

Synopsis:
Marcel, the younger brother of a French partisan, freezes when confronted with danger. His older brother, Leo, refuses to acknowledge those fears, forcing his brother on a mission. Marcel comes because he does not want his brother to be ashamed of him. Marcel kills a German on patrol but cannot deal with it, saying he can go no further. They are captured by

Sal Mineo and Fernando Lamas return to Combat! *in the episode "The Brothers." This is Mineo's third appearance and Lamas' second as guest warriors on the show.* Combat! *was known around Hollywood as a happy set. Many rising and established stars of the day returned again and again to "play soldier" with the cast.*

Germans and tortured. All are afraid the youngest brother will talk, including the youngest brother.

Review — 3.5 bayonets:

In this tight script by Irve Turnick, the moral dilemma is faced by the guest stars, not the regulars. Lamas struggles with decisions about his younger brother. How interesting, though, would it have been, if the same plot could have been adapted to one of the regulars? What would Saunders have done in that situation if it were his brother Chris about to betray them?

Both Mineo and Lamas are excellent as the dissimilar brothers. Ted Knight, in his third *Combat!* appearance, plays a German officer shocked at the Frenchman's fanaticism. With disgust, the German orders the execution of this madman who would murder his own brother

About Filming the Episode:

Dick Peabody said in his column in the Mountain Democrat, "The most entertaining guest we ever had was the late Fernando Lamas. Fernando was both erudite and earthy. From a wealthy family in the Argentine Republic and educated in Europe, he had the manner and the manners of the manor. But not always. Sometimes he was as funky as we were. He enjoyed doing our show so much that he would badger his agent to put him up for any role he could possibly play—mostly Frenchman or Germans. Besides English, Fernando spoke French, German, Italian and Spanish. His stories about his days as an MGM contract player should have been a book (X-rated), but Fernando was a talker not a writer."

Notes, Oddities, and Bloopers:

• When the squad ambushes the Germans, Caje throws himself backwards as he attacks a German.
• Hanley has an extra seven in his serial number.
• Typical fifth-season blood bath at the end: four unarmed Americans slaughter fourteen Germans.

The Furlough (135)

Written by Paul Playdon and Bob Frederick
Directed by Bernard McEveety
First aired 27-Dec-1966 (Episode 15 of Season 5)

CAST:

Regulars: Morrow, Hogan
Guest Star Carol Lawrence as Ann Tinsley
John Williams as Edmund Tinsley
Jon Walmsley as Andrew
Tony Fraser as Phillip
Chris Charney as Paulette (now Christine Baranski)
Cindy Eilbacher as Cynthia
Maria Lennard as Dolly
Jacquelyn Hyde as Maggie
Merri Wood-Taylor as Mrs. Davis
Paul Picerni as Vincent

Synopsis:

When Private Vincent dies before going on furlough, he asks Saunders to deliver a bequest for him. Saunders travels to England to fulfill his promise, bringing Vincent's money to Ann Tinsley, director of an English orphanage. While in London, Saunders views the war through the frightened eyes of children and shares a bittersweet relationship with Ann.

Review — 3.5 bayonets:

Let me get the major flaw with this episode out of the way. The script suffers from hopeless predictability. The soldier who likes orphans might as well have a target on his forehead. When the mistress of the orphanage turns out to be a lovely young woman (Carol Lawrence), who could not predict that Saunders would spend his furlough with her? And when they share their first tender kiss, her fate was sealed.

With that said, what a wonderful episode! I will take predictable scripts any time if they are so gorgeously performed and directed. Vic Morrow excelled in his portrayal of Saunders in a non-military situation. In London, he is not in charge and is deliciously at a loss as how to behave. His usual style of underplaying a scene worked particularly well here as his character tries to remember how to behave in a domestic situation.

The climactic scene of Saunders' return to the orphanage to find his love is so effective — an excellent example of how TV has changed over the decades. The long shot of Saunders turning slightly and seeing the corpse, the camera slowly panning in as he realizes that she is gone, panning in and in . . . and you wait for the cut to the corpse (or an arm out from under a beam or something of the like), but the shot just keeps panning in and in. And suddenly, I found myself afraid that they *would* cut to the corpse; in that excruciatingly long shot, Morrow made me afraid to look at the death that he was seeing. Today, not only would you see the corpse and blood, but probably some dismemberment. But that slow closeup on Saunders, as we watch his hopes die, was more eloquent than anything seen on contemporary television.

Notes, Oddities, and Bloopers:

•Ann was married, but is called Miss Tinsdale by the children.
•Anne's husband died just after D-Day. After that she set up the orphanage. When did the American private spend his weekends at the orphanage? Was she entertaining soldiers so soon after his death?
•The upstairs hallway of the orphanage is the hotel set in "Gunsmoke."
•The POV shot of the sniper sighting the American: he is sighting on a Garand M1, not a Mauser.
•Christine Baranski (listed in episode as Chris Charney) plays Paulette and Jon Walmsley, of "The Waltons," plays Andrew.

Cry for Help (136)
Written by Sheldon Stark
Directed by Richard Benedict
First aired 20-Dec-1966 (Episode 14 of Season 5)

CAST:
Regulars: Jason, Hogan, Peabody, Carter
Guest star Robert Duvall as Peter Halsman
Faith Domergue as Madam Fouchet
Jacques Roux as Anton Fouchet
Gene Kirkwood as Danny
David McFarland as Henri Fouchet
Chris Howard as German Officer
Horst Ebersberg as 1st German
Lou Robb as 2nd German

Synopsis:

On a mission to destroy an observation post, Hanley's patrol encounters a German machine gun nest, losing two men and picking up a German medic, Peter Halsman. Kirby objects to

bringing the medic. But he proves useful when he saves the life of the son of their French contact. Halsman and Doc form a bond until Doc's life is in the German medic's hands.

Review — 1.5 bayonets:

Moral of story: Medics are nice, no matter what uniform they wear. The message is a little thin to hang an entire hour upon, but the cast does a fairly nice job in this middle-of-the-road episode that's just below par.

Robert Duvall has several poignant scenes: one of the best is his farewell to the German soldier he was unable to save. A gentle, quiet "Es tut mir leid." (I'm sorry). Kirby is once again a butthead with the German prisoner, reverting to his first-season character.

The best moment of the episode is the scene in the farmhouse between Conlan Carter and Robert Duvall — a quiet moment between two strangers who share a common bond, delicately punctuated by a silent Kirby reading his newspaper.

About Filming the Episode:

Conlan Carter says of Robert Duvall: "He was so good, he's frightening. He works so easy that you don't see it happening. You see it on film, and you see all the stuff happening, and you think 'Oh my god!' He's just one of the best."

Notes, Oddities, and Bloopers:

•The same farmhouse used in "A Child's Game," with the bullet-holes patched up from last week's filming.
•In his previous Combat! appearance, Duvall was billed in the opening credits. Here his name appears only in the closing credits.
•Doc should tell Kirby to keep his unsterile hand out of his medic's kit.
•In scene with Duvall, Doc says he doesn't think he could manage a tracheotomy. Later in the season, Doc is willing to attempt one in "Decision."
•The squad, again, captures a tri-lingual prisoner.

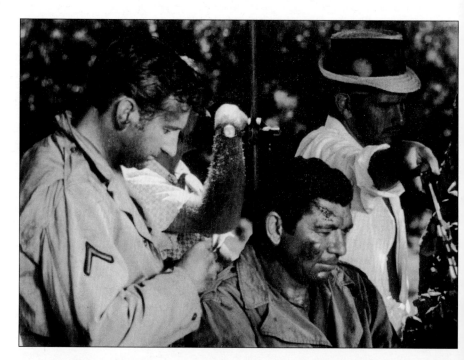

The slateman (right) is ready for the start of a scene with Conlan Carter and guest Claude Akins in "Ollie Joe." Akins also appears in "Ask Me No Questions."

Ollie Joe (137)

Written by Frank Moss
Directed by Bernard McEveety
First aired 27-Sep-1966 (Episode 3 of Season 5)

CAST:
Regulars: Jason, Morrow, Hogan, Carter, Peabody
Guest Star Robert Walker [Jr.] as Ollie Joe
William Bryant as McCall
Warren Vanders as Lt. Earnshaw
Tom Pace as Otto
Special Guest Claude Akins as Pelton

Synopsis:
The squad picks up two survivors from Charlie company: the company's number one goldbrick, Charlie Pelton, and the eagerest of beavers, Ollie Joe Brown, boy army. Ollie is an orphan who has found a home in the Army and thinks of himself as G.I. to the core. But his over-eagerness brings anxious moments and danger to the squad. His demeanor switches from born killer one minute to gentle as a lamb the next, until his friend Pelton is killed and Saunders learns that Ollie killed his lieutenant for fear of being sent back home.

Review — 3 bayonets:
Is he a G.I. perfect soldier? Is he a lost child? Is he dangerous? Yes, to all of the above. Robert Walker, Jr. as Ollie Joe creates a multi-layered mosaic of a character in this 3-bayonet thriller. In less-skilled hands, this character would have been unbelievable and annoying. Walker makes Ollie a real person, haunted by personal demons. Only slowly does he let the audience realize that his demons have taken possession of him.

The clever script by Frank Moss first shows Ollie as a jolly fool who has risen past personal tragedy. Step by step, it marches the audience to the realization that Ollie was not made stronger by these tragedies, but destroyed by them.

About Filming the Episode:
According to Joanne Strobl, Manager of Hop Kiln Winery, "An episode of *Combat!* was filmed at Hop Kiln Winery back in 1967. Most of the filming was done inside the old brick kilns. Scenes using dud grenades were also filmed."

"Ollie Joe" was filmed prior to the restoration of the brick kilns. Originally built for drying hops, the structure was restored as a winery and tasting room. It is located in Healdsburg, California.

Notes, Oddities, and Bloopers:
• No one is wearing backpacks or carrying extra equipment. When they break for chow, ration-boxes and eating utensils appear from nowhere.
• Long and undramatic opening battle sequence.
• Stuntman Earl Parker is the G.I. in foxhole who gets killed in the opening.
• Filmed at Hop Kiln Winery.
• A bloodbath at the river where the squad slaughters 17 Germans without taking a single hit.

Gadjo (138)

Written by Phillip W. Hoffman
Directed by Michael Caffey
First aired 17-Jan-1967 (Episode 17 of Season 5)

CAST:
Regulars: Morrow, Hogan, Carter, Jalbert
Guest Star Ricardo Montalban as Barbu
William Bryant as McCall
David Sheiner as SS Major Krieghoffen
Pat Renella as Razna
Anthony Benson as Andras
Hank Brandt as Sgt. Denfler
Beau Vanden Ecker as Gypsy
Larry Grant as Gypsy
Eugene Iglesias as Kako

Synopsis:
French gypsies vie with Saunders' squad over possession of a German prisoner. The German officer slaughtered their camp of 78 men, women, and children and the gypsies want vengeance. But the pursuers become the pursued when the gypsies are pinned down by a German attack and must depend on aid from Saunders.

Review — 1.5 bayonets:
Watching and listening to Ricardo Montalban is always a pleasure. His mellifluous voice can be mesmerizing, even reciting the banalities of this rather silly script. The odd description of the Gypsy afterlife he delivered with passion and intensity. As in "Mountain Man," this is a character who thinks the war has nothing to do with him.

Those who enjoy battles scenes should find "Gadjo" entertaining. The squad and Gypsies go from one battle to another in this high-action episode. But the firefights seem just an excuse for action, not really progressing the plot. They are disjointed and unreal in their frequency.

The resolution comes out of nowhere. Why the sudden change of heart in the Gypsy? This unmotivated transformation is unbelievable and unsatisfying. Why is he suddenly willing to break his sacred promise to the spirits and take up Saunders' philosophy, suddenly believing that it is his war, too? Especially coming so soon after clutching his young brother's dead body in his arms.

Notes, Oddities, and Bloopers:
• Paul Busch is the Major killed in the staff car at the opening of the show. He's also the German soldier leading the patrol that next attacks the squad.
• In scene where German soldiers are firing at the squad, one of their guns jam. You can see the German mutter "Damn" and bangs on the gun to get it to work.
• Filmed at Franklin Canyon. Opening sequence is filmed at Bronson Canyon. The reservoir scene was shot on the southeast edge of Elysian Park near the 110 (Pasadena) Freeway.
• At the end of the episode, the Gypsies have the high ground but are supposedly pinned down.
• Wardrobe man Beau Vanden Ecker appears as a Gypsy.

Headcount (139)

Written by James Menzies
Directed by Michael Caffey
First aired 01-Nov-1966 (Episode 8 of Season 5)

CAST:
Regulars: Morrow, Hogan, Peabody
Jan Merlin as Lt. Geiben
Ray Stricklyn as Pvt. Earl Konieg
Ron Soble as Cprl. Wiltz
William Schallert as Major Fisher
Tom P. Pace as Kurt Shiller
Richard Kindelow as Driver
Gerd Rein as German Prisoner
Paul Busch as German Prisoner
Mike Masters as German Prisoner
David "Buddy" Pantsari as German Prisoner
Jeff Pomerantz as German Prisoner
Oliver C. Stein, Jr. as German Prisoner
Hank Brandt as Karl Schiller

Synopsis:

Saunders is saddled with 18 German prisoners with only four men to guard them. Transporting them by foot, he encounters unexpected hazards and complications from a mysterious prisoner, Corporal Wiltz, who had allowed himself to be captured. When a land mine explodes, one of the prisoners grabs Saunders' pistol, threatening to kill him unless the prisoners are freed, but help comes unexpectedly from Wiltz. Safely back at battalion, they discover that Wiltz is an American intelligence officer.

Review — 3 bayonets:

"Headcount" is a tightly directed episode. Each act offers a neat twist and a new danger. The use of the mysterious German prisoner (Ron Sobel, who also was featured in the third-season episode "More than a Soldier") was interesting. He was never central to the action in any of the acts, but he was always there, always in the background, creating suspense as to when something was going to break with this character.

The major flaw with the script involves Saunders. As usual, Saunders has all the answers. He anticipates the Germans' escape attempt and out-thinks them at every turn. However, the script dumbs down Kirby and Littlejohn. A more confident script writer could have made Saunders brilliant on his own, not just in contrast to those around him.

Despite these minor detractions, this is an enjoyable episode with a strong performance by Morrow and the collection of Germans. Peabody is especially good in this episode. His scene where he discovers that he has accidentally killed a wounded man is understated and touching. William Schallert is fine in a too-small role. It would have been interesting to learn more about this Major who passes on his obsession to Saunders. Center stage throughout the episode is a gaggle of faces familiar to *Combat!* fans. Not since "Operation FlyTrap" have so many of the supporting German soldiers been featured in an episode.

Notes, Oddities, and Bloopers:

•A long German barrage starts the episode. So many powerful explosions in the forest, yet every tree remains standing.

•During the fight in the stream, Littlejohn is completely submerged, but when he gets ashore he is wet only from the chest down.

Telly Savalas, as a resistance fighter, relives the past with his wife (Anne Wakefield), who was killed by the Germans in "Anniversary.

Anniversary (140)

Written by William R. Yates
Story by Edward J. Lakso
Directed by Michael Caffey
First aired 01-24-67 (Episode 18 of Season 5)

CAST:
Regulars: Jason, Hogan, Jalbert, Peabody, Carter
Guest Star Telly Savalas as Jon
John Van Dreelen as Lt. Kramer
Anne Wakefield as Anne
Emile Genest as Robierre
Richard Jeffries as Pvt. Heller
Michele Montau as Dressmaker
Chris Howard as German Medic
Chris Anders as Karl
Sofia-Marie as Marie

Synopsis:

A French resistance fighter, Jon, who has lost his wife and daughter in the war, becomes a lone avenger, killing Americans and Germans alike. Suffering from shock and delirium, Jon captures a German officer and threatens Hanley's life.

Review — 1/2 bayonet:

This psychological drama is a change of pace for the series. I applaud the producers for trying new styles in the fifth season. Unfortunately, this experiment fell flat. Telly Savalas, as Jon, has all the right moves as an alternately troubled, then dangerous, man trapped in the past. Ultimately, though, he is an unsympathetic madman.

The show has no substance, especially contrasting it with "Cry in the Ruins." The two episodes share a similar premise — a person is driven mad by a tragic loss. Both stories were by Edward J. Lakso (though the teleplay for "Anniversary" was written by William R. Yates). In "Cry in the Ruins," Lakso uses the tragedy of the mother to shed light on the larger issues and to bring two warring factions together. In "Anniversary," no greater message is attempted, no insights offered.

Director Michael Caffey provides some lovely aerial shots and pans of the French village. With creative camera work, Michael Caffey creates beautiful contrasts between Savalas' idyllic memories of a perfect marriage and perfect village, and the reality of a home torn asunder by war. The shots slipping into and out of his memory in the dress shop are well executed. His camerawork surpasses the quality of this episode's script. The show ends symbolically with Savalas' broken body on the ground below and the puppet, now hanging from one string, above in the church.

Notes, Oddities, and Bloopers:

• When Telly Savalas is in the church loading his German rifle, he fumbles with the new magazine for several seconds. In the next cut, from a different angle, the magazine easily snaps in.

• Robierre played the collaborator in "The Tree of Moray" and the innkeeper in "Any Second Now." Telly Savalas starred in the episode "Vendetta."

The Outsider (141)

Written by Shirl Hendryx
Directed by Richard Benedict
First aired 22-Nov-1966 (Episode 10 of Season 5)

CAST:

Regulars: Jason, Hogan, Jalbert, Peabody
Guest star Jason Evers as Pvt. Jim Culley
Steven Marlo as Blake
Biff Elliot as Doctor
Richard Miller as Young Soldier
Stasa Damascus as French Girl
Paul Busch as German Sgt.
David "Buddy" Pantsari as German Patrol Leader
William Bryant as McCall

Synopsis:

Private Cully is a moody misanthrope who joins the squad. The farm boy meets with hostility because of his anti-social

attitudes. At Littlejohn's urgings, Kirby and squad take pains to make sure Cully feels wanted.

Review — 1/2 bayonet:

In "The Outsider," Jason Evers has the thankless task of portraying an unlikable cur who the squad takes to heart. Cully cares about no one but himself, has no manners, looks down on his squad members, will not help Caje when he is pinned down, and will not even say thank you when Caje saves his neck. After all this, Littlejohn wants to give him a tractor.

The direction by Richard Benedict does not help Evers with the role; the camera could have been used to either soften his attitude, reflect on his thought processes, or let viewers see something redeeming about Cully. But the camera work is less than revelatory, just a notch below ordinary.

"The Outsider" features a warm and fuzzy Kirby. The first season Kirby would not have put up with any of Cully's nonsense. A nice job by new *Combat!* regular William Bryant as McCall. He plays McCall like the old Kirby. The poker scene between Kirby and him is delightful.

About Filming the Episode:

Dick Peabody says of Richard Benedict, "He was the only director that I hated his guts. Most directors on established shows know that they are more expendable than the regular cast. Not this dude. He came on like Otto Preminger from the moment he walked on the stage." On the first day of shooting, Peabody and Benedict disagreed over a scene in the church where Peabody had entered and removed his helmet. "Littlejohn always takes his helmet off in a church. He's from a farm in the Bible Belt. That's how he was raised." Peabody would not leave his helmet on and Benedict called the producer to enforce his authority. They did not back him up and the film was shot with Peabody removing his helmet. Vic Morrow then arranged with producer Gene Levitt for Benedict not to return as a director. He was originally signed to do three episodes, but they bought out his contract after two.

Notes, Oddities, and Bloopers:

• At Cully's first entrance, he's standing just outside the door, then in the next cut he's inside the house, without having moved.

• Inside the church, Cully is holding the tractor picture as Hanley enters. Later cut to Cully and the paper is out of his hands. He never laid it down.

• Same scene, Caje is seated behind Kirby and McCall smoking a cigarette. After the commercial break (when no time has passed in the scene), Caje is now standing by the door, not smoking.

• The radio operator, Steve Marlo, was also Hanley's radio operator in "Hills Are for Heroes" and "The Leader" and McCall's second on the bazooka in "The Bankroll."

• McCall slaughters a German, shooting him ten times with an eight-shot M1.

Nightmare on the Red Ball Run (142)

Written by Dan E. Weisburd
Directed by Michael Caffey
First aired 02-28-67, Episode 23 of Season 5

CAST:
Regulars: Morrow, Hogan, Carter, Peabody, Jalbert
Guest star Claude Akins as Rosie
William Campbell as Corporal Sloan
John Carter as Major
Paul Busch as German Tank Commander
Mike Masters as Medic
Beau Vanden Ecker as Markum
(Note: Medic is mis-credited, is actually Walt Davis)

Synopsis:

The drivers of the Red Ball Highway are overworked to the point of danger, pushed by the fanatical Sergeant Rose. The truckers must accept Kirby and Littlejohn as replacements. They volunteered believing that riding would be easier and safer than walking. Transporting explosives over bumpy roads and collapsing bridges, they encounter snipers and a halftrack that blocks their path. Rosie saves the day when he rams the half-track with his truck, at the cost of his own life.

Review — 1/2 bayonet:

Claude Akins, as the sergeant-with-an-attitude, and William Campbell, as right-hand-man Corporal Sloan, have fun in this episode filmed at Franklin Canyon. Campbell appeared in fourth-season's "More Than a Soldier." This is Akins' third appearance on *Combat!*

The pacing in this episode is abominable. Nothing much happens, and what does happen, does so slowly. The characters drive through a series of contrived predicaments with no real dramatic tension. But Hogan and Akins have an easy-to-watch chemistry, as do Peabody and Campbell. Pity this story could not have been accelerated to allow them to interact more.

Watch for the small role of the Major in this episode. It is played by John Carter, who is the real-life brother of Conlan Carter ("Doc").

Notes, Oddities, and Bloopers:
•Opening nighttime barrage includes much historic footage, colorized.
•The snipers have the element of surprise and the high ground, but still are easily picked off.
•The trucks drive all night, yet they arrive at the front and encounter the same medic (Walt Davis) they left behind the night before.
•Disappointing that no black actors were cast for this tribute to the drivers of the Red Ball Express.
•The Germans who ambush the truck wear U.S. camoflauge pattern HBT jackets and one has a camoflauge helmet cover in the U.S. pattern.
•Kirby tells Rosie he has never fought a half-track. Not true.

Gulliver (143)

Teleplay by Paul Playdon and Bob Frederick
Story by Shimon Wincelberg and Richard Shapiro
Directed by Vic Morrow
First aired 06-Dec-1966 (Episode 12 of Season 5)

CAST:
Regulars: Morrow, Peabody
Stefan Arngrim as Henri
Vicki Malkin as Christina
Jeremie Paul Andre as Marcel
Don-Antoine Fabrice as John
William Bramley as Desk Sgt.
Sasha Hardin as German Lt.
Paul Busch as Sgt. Kolcheck
Horst Ebersberg as German Sentry
Joe Stead as Johnson
Angelo De Meo as Jeep Driver
Oliver C. Stine, Jr. as Corporal
Beau Vanden Ecker as G.I.
Larry Grant as U.S. Soldier

Synopsis:

Two miles from Lyon, Saunders sends Littlejohn off for a day of R&R. But his vacation is prevented by a Messerschmitt that strafes him. He is rescued/captured by a band of French urchins. They are scavengers who strip the dead of money, food, and clothing. And now they've scavenged Littlejohn, holding him prisoner in their houseboat hideout. When their attempt to ransom him to the Americans fails, they try to trade him to the Germans.

Review — 0 bayonets:

"Gulliver" has the potential for high tragedy, but misses the mark. The episode was written to feature Hanley, but Vic Morrow, as the director of the episode, convinced the producer to change it, giving an opportunity to Dick Peabody. The switch in central character hurts the story. The plot was not strong to begin with, but the change from an officer to an enlisted man put too many obstacles in the script, making the urchins not very bright. The children's actions make more sense if they had a real officer in their clutches.

Any actor, Peabody or Jason, would have been a waste in this role. The show is carried by the children, and not very well. The children are not up to the calibre of past child actors on the show, such as Andrea Darvi. Vicki Malkin, as Christina, does her best playing a demented Wendy to these gun-toting lost boys.

The story desperately calls for a PPT at the end, but the script and Morrow have Littlejohn simply flat on his back for the conclusion. Littlejohn is the constant victim throughout the show, offering no insight, no action, and no resolution.

About Filming the Episode:

Dick Peabody says, "I didn't like 'Gulliver,' in which I was the lead. I think my agent [Meyer Mishkin] discouraged me from liking it. I asked him to see a screening, to see if I should run an ad. So we screened it for him and he said, 'Save your money.' Great agent I had. He said it was too inactive a part. 'You really didn't do anything, you were just lying around being

Littlejohn (Dick Peabody) is strafed by a P-51 Mustang piloted by Frank Tallman in "Gulliver." Dick Peabody injured himself during this scene and spent the next three months on crutches.

wounded.' . . . I can't be objective about my own work. I've had a lot of good comment from 'Gulliver' from other people, other than my agent. I don't know. How does one judge their own work?"

Notes, Oddities, and Bloopers:
•The plane strafing was filmed at Thousand Oaks, with a P-51 mustang acting as the Messerschmidt.
•Dick Peabody ripped his cartilage filming the scene where he is strafed by the airplane.
•The French children have international tastes in music. They sing "London Bridge is Falling Down," in English, and listen to Wagner.
•Well-educated children: three speak English and French. Henri is tri-lingual.
•Why would the children try to bargain for German money? They are trying to make it to the coast, which is in Allied hands.

Decision (144)

Teleplay by Esther & Bob Mitchell and Paul Playdon
Story by Peter Barry
Directed by Georg Fenady
First aired 15-Nov-66 (Episode 9 of Season 5)

CAST:
Regulars: Jason, Morrow, Hogan, Jalbert, Carter
Guest star James Franciscus as Pfc. Charles Harris
William Bryant as McCall
Maurice Marsac as Elderly Frenchman
Louis Elias as Adams
David "Buddy" Pantsari as G.I.
Wes Bishop as Wounded Soldier

Synopsis:
Saunders is tasked with knocking out a radar and commu-nication setup with help from a demolition expert, Harris. He is a former physician who has turned his back on his profession. Though he has given up saving lives, he cannot bring himself to take a life with his own demolitions. He must re-evaluate his decision when the life of an officer depends on using his med-ical skills.

Review — 1/2 bayonet:
James Franciscus plays Harris, a man so afraid that he cannot live up to his father's legacy that he abandons it. He has a crip-pling fear that he might do something that will kill somebody, both as a doctor and as a demolition man.

Franciscus and Morrow are both good here. Morrow shows that incredible intensity that makes Saunders so memorable. But the Harris character comes off as whining.

The resolution is simplistic. Franciscus comes to the realiza-tion that, "It's not easy when you've been afraid of something as long as I have, but, I'm going to give it a try." The moral of this story is, just try. Ho hum.

Notes, Oddities, and Bloopers:
•Same cave as in "Entombed."
•As the squad marches out just before the title credits roll, one soldier's M1 gets caught in the camoflauge netting and is knocked from his shoulder.
•McCall's flesh wound required a tourniquet.
•Doc runs to help McCall when he's hit, but he ignores Adams.
•An incredibly long and uninteresting firefight, with much repeated action. The sequence contains fifteen instances of Caje jumping around the same tree and firing his rifle.
•Littlejohn is only in the opening sequence. He was on crutches from his "Gulliver" injury and could not film the action shots.

COMBAT!

The Gantlet (145)

Written by Paul Playdon and Bob Frederick
Directed by Michael Caffey
First aired 07-Feb-1967 (Season 5, Episode 20)

CAST:

Regulars: Morrow
Tom Skerritt as Sgt. Decker
Bill Glover as Sgt. Crandall
Tom P. Pace as Pvt. Jackson
Peter Church as British prisoner
Terence Mitchell as British soldier
Kurt Landon as German doctor

Synopsis:

Captured by Germans, Saunders is placed aboard a prison train bound for Germany. He escapes and is saddled with Sgt. Decker, who would have been content to sit out the war in a P.O.W. camp. Switching into German uniform, Saunders becomes shot and finds treatment at a German evac hospital. During a barrage, he is left to wander the countryside in a drug-induced haze.

Review — 0 bayonets:

Except for glimpses of a dashing Saunders motorcycling through a barrage and impressive night-time pyrotechnics, this episode offers little of interest.

The story was told far better in third season's "Odyssey." This version lacks the emotional appeal of the earlier venture. The episode is devoid of human compassion, even from Saunders. One of Saunders' men dies grasping at the Sergeant's hand, and Saunders is unmoved. He announces the death with the emotion of a weather report.

The Decker character was irrelevant; he did nothing to advance the story and could have been cut without affecting events. The script gives no insight into the cowardly soldier. The shallow script is populated with one-dimensional characters, managing even to make Saunders flat and uninspiring.

Saunders' drug-induced hallucinations could have been an opportunity to delve into the psyche of a soldier or provide some background information about Saunders. Instead, they are an excuse for graphic mayhem. Usually, *Combat!* uses violence to a purpose. Perhaps director Michael Caffey was trying to graphically illustrate the horrors of war, but failed. This was another fifth-season effort for change-of-pace that fell flat.

The cinematography during Saunders' hallucination is reminiscent of the hokey style of the "Hawaii Five-O" psychedelic trips. The script is full of happy coincidences. Under morphine, not only does Saunders avoid blurting out something in English, he is capable of driving a motorcycle. He cannot distinguish between a German soldier and a German Shepherd, but can tell clutch from accelerator. The writers copped out on scene transitions. Three separate times, Saunders blacked out in order to move to the next scene.

Notes, Oddities, and Bloopers:

• One-size-fits-all German uniforms.

• Germans lean an unconscious Saunders against the gate of the truck; though passed out, Saunders pops the left leg under him to support his weight.

• During dog attack, second German runs up, stops, wipes his mouth, Saunders moves around the rock; the same sequence repeats from a different angle.

• After five years as a G.I. expendable and German cannon fodder, Tom P. Pace gets a featured role as Jackson.

• Saunders, in his hallucination, fights and kills himself.

Entombed (146)

Teleplay by Paul Playdon and Bob Frederick
Story by William Bast
Directed by Bernard McEveety
First aired 03-Jan-1967 (Episode 16 of Season 5)

CAST:

Regulars: Jason,
Guest star Skip Homeier as Lt. Karl Mauer
Special Guests Michael Constantine as Jacques Patron
and Margaret O'Brien as Marianne Fraisnet
King Moody as Toulon
Mark de Vries as Pvt. Wexler
Michael Hausserman as Johann Schiller
Barry Ford as German Captain
Beau Vanden Ecker as Emile
Tom Fielding as Pfc. Tommy Bishop
(uncredited: Walt Davis as Sentry)

Synopsis:

After rescuing captive French resistance fighters, the squad regroups in an abandoned mine. When the Germans attack, Germans, French, and Americans are all trapped. They form a pact to work together to dig their way out of the cave, and soldiers learn something about the humanity of the enemy.

Review — 3 bayonets:

Strong acting, evocative directing, and tight editing can work wonders on a goofy plot. This script is a half-bayonetter, but director Bernard McEveety's touch saves the day. Like a magician, the director distracts you from the idiocy of the dialogue and action with striking mood pieces.

McEveety draws fine performances from Rick Jason, Skip Homeier, and especially from Michael Constantine as French Resistance fighter Jacques. Margaret O'Brien, an angelic child actress from the forties, is cast as the hated French collaborator. Though well performed, the emotion and sentiment of Lt. Mauer's (Homeier) speech seem out-of-place in the *Combat!* mileau. A professional soldier admiring a deserter who chooses his lover over his country? *Combat!* usually deals with the big sacrifice, putting others before yourself. These two lovers put their own interests above all others.

I would have liked a regular squad member in this instead of the new character of Bishop. Can you imagine the emotions if Littlejohn would have had to kill the German he befriended? Alas, Dick Peabody was still on crutches and was unavailable for this episode.

The Bankroll (147)

Written by Shirl Hendryx
Directed by Georg Fenady
First aired 13-Dec-1966 (Episode 13 of Season 5)

CAST:

Regulars: Jason, Hogan, Jalbert, Carter, Peabody
Guest Star James Stacy as Farley
William Bryant as McCall
Norbert Meisel as German Sergeant
Mike Farrell as Doctor
Steven Marlo as Carson
Mike Masters as Poker Player
Louis Elias as Lou
Oliver C. Stone, Jr. as Whitey
Dave Armstrong as Poker Player
Larry Grant as German Soldier
Buck Taylor as Jeetleman

Synopsis:

After an exhausting 24-hour pass that left him broke, hungover, and happy, Kirby gets a new guy to back him in a poker game. They win a $1,600 bankroll, half in markers from Pvt. Farley. After a firefight, Farley makes sure Kirby knows that the markers are worthless if Farley dies. Kirby learns that Farley has welched on every bet in his former units. Kirby collects half the money from Farley and gives it all to the kid, who was wounded while Kirby tried to protect his markers.

Review — 1/2 bayonet:

"The Bankroll" offers Kirby at his cuddliest. He is just a harmless little fuzzball in this episode about an obnoxious welcher who owes Kirby and a fellow G.I. a pot of money. Kirby is so nice and noble at the end — what went wrong?

The bankroll gets Kirby thinking he has enough money to buy himself a stake in his Uncle's bowling alley, giving him something to go home to, "something that means something." Buck Taylor as Jeetleman gives another fine performance in *Combat!* He was last featured in the episode "The First Day" as the soldier who didn't make the mark his first time under fire.

Notes, Oddities, and Bloopers:

- Hanley's helmet is so bright and shiny that it reflects lights during the firefight. It looks almost polished.
- In the first scene, Kirby uncorks the wine bottle with his teeth, but in the next frame the bottle is again corked and then in next shot is uncorked again.
- Shot in Franklin Canyon and the MGM backlot.
- Kirby gives Jeetleman $400 more than he's owed.
- Dick Peabody is still on crutches, so is not in action sequences.

For five seasons, Combat! *used the Franklin Canyon reservoir outside Los Angeles as a stand-in for the countryside of France. This photo of the lower reservoir of Franklin Canyon shows the area had changed little by 1997. Today, many of the* Combat! *locations are disappearing under the restoration work being done in the park. Fans Marty Black and Dion Osika have spent hundreds of hours and many trips to Franklin to document the filming sites, and have verified over 30 episode locations at Franklin Canyon.*

COMBAT!

The Masquers (148)

Written by William R. Yates
Directed by Georg Fenady
First aired 14-Feb-1967 (Episode 5 of Season 5)

CAST:

Regulars: Hogan
Guest Star Nick Adams as Corporal Marty Roberts
Co-starring Jack Hogan as Kirby
Roger Perry as Carl Driskoll
Gavin MacLeod as British Corporal Tommy Behan
Maurice Marsac as Paul
Earl Parker as Squad Leader
Paul Busch as German Sergeant
John Nealson as 1st G.I.
Don Knight as British Soldier
Skip Battyn as G.I. Soldier

Synopsis:

No one can tell friend from foe as Germans infiltrate dressed as Allied soldiers. Kirby, separated from the squad, interrogates Driskoll, an American G.I. who thinks Kirby is a German. Both are captured by British corporal Tommy Behan, who thinks one or both of them are Germans. Confusion mounts when Behan captures American Cpl. Marty Roberts, who speaks fluent German and has just escaped from American M.P.s.

Review — 2.5 bayonets:

"Who's out there?" is the central theme of this story of suspicion. But beware any episode that starts with the dialogue, "It's quiet. Too quiet."

Jack Hogan does a credible job in this solo outing that was originally written for Vic Morrow. That explains why the cute, cuddliness of the fifth-season Kirby is missing in this episode. Kirby is as hard-as-nails as Saunders.

In his second guest appearance, Nick Adams stars as a conniving sneak who may be a German infiltrator, but claims to be an American deserter. The story by William R. Yates is fairly clever, but occasionally predictable. Many of the characters are written to be expendable. Gavin McLeod gets in a few nice scenes before his time is up. But the pacing is flawed and no believable tension is drawn.

About Filming the Episode:

Director Georg Fenady says, when asked about favorite episodes of his, "It's hard to not have a little place in my heart for that first one. But I did one with Nick Adams, it was the last year in color, where it was the enemy was infiltrating in American uniforms. With Nick Adams, Jack Hogan, Roger Perry who is a fine actor, and Gavin MacLeod, the 'Love Boat' guy. And the thing was, 'Who was the German?' And it really came off very well. I was very pleased. Nick Adams was unbelievable, he'd do Jimmy Cagney impressions for us."

Notes, Oddities, and Bloopers:

• Filmed at Franklin Canyon.
• Infiltrator claims to be from A Company, weapons platoon. Serial number 36327448. From Cleveland (maybe he knows

Saunders!)
• Kirby abandons his B.A.R. when captured. Bet he has it again for next week's episode.
• I wish Kirby would realize after five seasons that he's a member of King Company, not Baker Company.
• Kirby says his serial number is 14327230, from B Company.
• Paul Busch dies again.
• At end Kirby says good-bye to Marty. When did they get on a first-name basis?
• That head wound of Kirby's moves around his forehead.
• British character is listed in credits as a Corporal but is wearing Sergeants' stripes.

Encounter (149)

Written by Frank Moss
Directed by Bernard McEveety
First aired 31-Jan-1967 (Episode 19 of Season 5)

CAST:

Regulars: Jason, Morrow, Hogan, Peabody, Jalbert, Carter
Guest star James Daly as Capt. Cole
Special Guest Star James MacArthur as Jack Cole
Karl Sadler as German Soldier
Buddy Pantsari as Squad G.I.
Paul Busch as German Officer
Richard Ever as Pvt. Kean

Synopsis:

Jack Cole, a war correspondent, encounters his estranged father while covering the war. His father, Captain Dewey Cole, is an Engineer Corps veteran whom the platoon has been assigned to assist. The captain resents his son's civilian status and refuses to allow him to accompany them in the field. But when facing death together, father and son reconcile.

Review — 2 bayonets:

Take one domineering, no-nonsense military father, mix with one sensitive, Mamma-raised intellectual son, stir in long-held resentments and what do you get? A heart-tugging reconciliation before the final credits. Nothing original here. But director McEveety tries his best to put a little spit and polish on the old theme. The acting is solid, direction professional, the plot predictable. When all is said and done, in "Encounter" you spend a pleasant hour with the squad without overly taxing your brain or your emotions.

The show ends with Saunders coming over the hill like the U.S. Cavalry. He and the squad mow down the entire German patrol without taking a single casualty in a pristine bloodbath.

"Encounter" is the closest to a "squad" episode that viewers get in fifth season. Only four fifth-season episodes feature the entire cast. This is the only one that has good squad interaction.

Notes, Oddities, and Bloopers:

• Filmed at Franklin Canyon.
• A German leaves behind his rifle to advance and toss a grenade into the house. He then shoots Private Kean with his rifle (which he did not bring with him).

A Little Jazz (150)

Written by James Menzies
Directed by Michael Caffey
First aired 21-Feb-1967 (Episode 22 of Season 5)

CAST:

Regulars: Morrow, Hogan, Jalbert, Peabody, Carter
Guest Star Dan Duryea as Bernie
Special Guests Noah Beery as Hank
and Dennis Hopper as Zack
Joe Maross as Will
Robert Easton as Woody
Hank Brandt as German Lt. Knubel
Mike Masters as German Sgt.
Paul Busch as German Cpl. #2
Walt Goodrich as German Cpl. #1

Synopsis:

A USO jazz troupe, led by arrogant Bernie Wallace, causes Saunders trouble. Saunders rescues them from a German attack and their gratitude is underwhelming. When a German patrol traps them in a mill, Wallace panics and, without Saunders' knowledge, puts out a flag of truce. The jazzmen heroically opt to stay and support Saunders. In the nick of time, an American patrol arrives to save the day.

Review — 1½ bayonets:

Dan Duryea makes his second *Combat!* guest appearance as jazz band leader Bernie Wallace, a character as self-centered and cowardly as the correspondent that Duryea played in "Dateline."

A pity the central character is so unsympathetic and unbelievable, because two of the supporting characters were not only interestingly written, but strongly portrayed. Dennis Hopper as the 4-F drummer who wants to be a hero is heartbreakingly convincing and Noah Berry as the over-aged conscience of the jazz group was touching. All the jazzmen are well-drawn and well acted — from Woody, the happy soul who insists on carrying his bullet-ridden bass across the countryside, to Will, who makes a failed plea to Saunders to understand Bernie's behavior. But the on-screen time of these characters is limited and overshadowed by the Duryea character.

This is one of director Michael Caffey's best episodes. The battle sequence where the bass and drums are destroyed musically with orchestrated bullet shots is inventive. After the 4-F drummer becomes a hero, the shows ends on a plaintive note with the death of the bass player. The scene fades out as the clarinetist plays a lonely dirge.

About Filming the Episode:

Dick Peabody particularly enjoyed Dan Duryea as a guest. In an article in the *Mountain Democrat*, Peabody said, "He joined us in our stupid games, laughed at our dumb jokes, and was an enthusiastic spectator at our unauthorized jeep races through the western streets of MGM's back lot No. 3. Dan was older by 20 years but he fit in as not many guest stars did. He said working with us reminded him of his college days at Cornell. He had belonged to a fraternity whose members were as wild and irreverent as we were."

Dick Peabody says that Dennis Hopper was crazy, so he fit in perfectly with the gang of Morrow, Jalbert, and Peabody. Peabody and Hopper had gone to the same junior high school, but not at the same time. "We wondered if that experience could have negatively impacted on our brain cells."

Notes, Oddities, and Bloopers:

- Paul Busch is killed twice in this episode.
- Both Germans and Americans have radio contact. Why does neither call in a barrage?
- In the scene after the fiddle player and Caje are shot, Caje's helmet is alternately on his head and on the floor next to him.

Relaxing in their "civvies" are Pierre Jalbert, Dick Peabody (still on crutches from his "Gulliver" injury) and Vic Morrow.

The Partisan (151)

Written by Ed Waters
Directed by Michael Caffey
First aired 03-14-67 (Episode 25 of Season 5)

CAST:

Regulars: Morrow, Jason, Hogan, Jalbert, Peabody, Doc
Guest Star Robert Duvall as Michel (not in opening credits)
Special Guest Star Claudine Longet as Babette
Paul Busch as German Officer
Hank Brandt as German Soldier

Synopsis:

Saunders goes on patrol to locate German artillery. Ambushed, Saunders is wounded and left behind while Caje is wounded and captured. Saunders finds help in the home of a blind girl who is hiding an American deserter in her cellar.

Saunders rescues Caje from the Germans and returns to the French girl's house. The deserter reluctantly helps Saunders bring Caje to the American lines, taking the girl with them. He comes through in the end, helping Saunders capture a German jeep to drive Caje to safety.

Review — 1 bayonet:

"The Partisan" was the last original episode of *Combat!* to air. Robert Duvall returns for his third *Combat!* guest role as a downed American navigator hiding from the war in the arms of a blind-but-beautiful French farmgirl — until Saunders spoils it with a patented pep talk.

The beginning of the episode was filler to save expenses, since the season was running over budget. The footage is the same used in the opening of "The Losers." Those shots are intercut with footage shot in Franklin Canyon and new footage of Saunders driving the truck.

The script by Ed Waters is disjointed — giving us the strange first act that served little purpose and ending with a long journey forced on the French girl and deserter for little reason. The situation is similar to "Missing in Action," except instead of a downed Colonel falling in love with his French rescuer, it's now a downed navigator.

Notes, Oddities, and Bloopers:

• Some remarkable nighttime pyrotechnics as Saunders blows up the ammo dump.

• Saunders has no canteen or ammo belt while rolling down the hill, though he had them earlier.

• Saunders loses his helmet at the top of the hill; it comes crashing down through the brush next to him, nearly hitting the camera.

• When Michelle is nursing Sarge in the basement, she wrings out a dry cloth in an empty pan.

• The beginning of the episode was filler to save expenses, since the season was running over budget. The footage is the same used in the opening of "The Losers." Those shots are intercut with footage shot in Franklin Canyon and new footage of Saunders driving the truck.

Jonah (152)

Written by Richard Wendly and William Fay
Directed by Georg Fenady
First aired 07-Mar-1967 (Episode 24 of Season 5)

CAST:

Regulars: Jason, Morrow, Hogan, Carter, Jalbert
Guest Star Tom Simcox as Dolan
Peter Haskell as Richards
Peter Duryea as Simmons
James Dobson as Greely

Synopsis:

Private Dolan is a replacement convinced that he sponges good luck from his squad mates. Hanley is in charge of this outing plagued by bad luck from the beginning. Two expendables die at the Jonah's side, falling to unusually unlucky whims of war. Faced with a string of calamities, the squad starts to believe that they really have a Jonah in their midst.

Review — 2.5 bayonets:

In the last episode filmed, Tom Simcox plays a man burdened with the curse of seeing friends die around him while he remains unscathed. Doc and Hanley resist falling prey to the fears of having a jinx among them, but Caje and eventually even pragmatist Kirby begin to wonder if their luck has finally run out.

William Fay and Richard Wendly wrote this story that examines the fears and superstitions among frontline soldiers, and how they adversely affect combat readiness. "Jonah" is the flip side of first season's "High Named Today." That episode showed a soldier convinced that he would die; "Jonah" has a soldier convinced that he will live, but only at the expense of those around him. The screenplay looks inside both the Jonah and the squad. The Jonah is tormented by his fate; the soldier in "High Named Today" was unmoved and unemotional, not caring how he affected those around him.

I missed having Littlejohn in this episode, who was still hampered by his "Gulliver" injury. Of all the regular characters, he is the most superstitious.

Peter Haskell puts in a good performance as the friend of Simcox that comes to fear his buddy may be the jinx that he claims. (Haskell appeared earlier this season as the less-than-sympathetic G.I. in "A Child's Game." He also appeared as the German prisoner in "Hear No Evil.")

Notes, Oddities, and Bloopers::

• Rank has no privileges in this episode. Hanley is leading the troops through the rain and the mud while Saunders remains safely in a dry house giving instructions on the radio.

• The show opens with one of *Combat!'s* better staged hand-to-hand fights.

• Caje, though wounded in his shooting arm, still fires his M1 with deadly accuracy. Hanley must have great confidence in Caje: when Hanley scouts ahead, he takes with him the wounded Caje.

• Kirby has adopted the inner tube around his helmet, emulating Lee Marvin.

CHAPTER 7

After Combat!

Selmur Productions replaced *Combat!* with the series "Garrison's Gorillas," using the same crew, the same sets, and similar characters who, as Pierre Jalbert said, worked cheaper. Jack Hogan guested on the show, experiencing *deja vu*. "The same people were there, they were wearing our uniforms!"

Pierre theorizes about why *Combat!* went off the air. "Selmur Productions was a subsidiary of ABC. And all the millions of dollars that they put into pilots was down the drain. They were broke. They were hoping to merge with ITT and the federal government cut them off because of anti-trust. So they wanted to syndicate so they could get money from those 152 episodes in the can."

Jack Hogan says, "About that time, it was getting so there was no 'good war' because of Viet Nam. There was no justifiable war in those days, right then, with all that was going on. Also, it was time to renew all of our contracts."

Since 1967, when Selmur Productions rushed it off the air, *Combat!* has been in continuous syndication. It is one of the most popular syndicated shows in Japan. "Garrison's Gorillas," the show that replaced *Combat!*, lasted one season.

The MGM backlot town that was used for the filming of the *Combat!* village scenes no longer exists. It was bulldozed over and is now a housing development, though part of the famous "Euccy Road" remains. *The Stuntman* was the last film to shoot in the French village. The movie deliberately destroyed parts of the lot, knowing that it was slated to be demolished. Thousand Oaks is now Westlake Village condominiums.

Combat! continues to have a legacy. Fans remember the show and its lasting effect on their lives. "I served three years in Viet Nam. We watched the show all the time and really enjoyed it. We used to say we watched it to see what we were doing wrong."— Red Wilson

It went on to influence future television series. The producers and writers of the series "Tour of Duty" were admirers of *Combat!* Some of the writers would take their videos of *Combat!* into the conference room late at night to watch them. At least one episode was inspired by a *Combat!* plot.

Whenever *Combat!* is aired, it gains new fans. When running on the History Channel (Canada) and Encore Action channel, it was among their most popular shows.

Like the greatest generation they helped to dramatize, the creators of this show are slowly leaving us. Since this book was first issued in 1997, we have lost five of the contributors: Dick Peabody, Rick Jason, A.D. Flowers, Burt Kennedy, and Earl Parker. They have "taken the point" but will always be with us in the legacy of film they left behind.

Publicity shot of Vic Morrow as Sergeant Saunders.

The quiet, soft-spoken A.D. Flowers was the first special effects man for *Combat!* He attended the 1998 and 2000 cast reunions, where his lifetime joy in blowing things up was evident to all. He took great pride in creating havoc and chaos with impeccable safety — everything from brief firefights to full-scale invasions.

Whether the script called for a simple effect, such as a bullet biting into wood, or complex effects such as a village-leveling bombardment, A.D. Flowers and the special effects wizards who followed him, made sure no real casualties were taken.

A.D. Flowers, had been detonating things as a special effects man since 1941. In his later career, he won two Academy Awards for special effects.

The tools of a special effects team include explosive compounds such as rifle powder, flash powder, and black powder, as well as detonators, peat moss, cork, balsa wood, electric wires, batteries, switches, iron pots, butane gas, gas tanks, valves, burners, and special weaponry.

In an article for Showtime newspaper in 1964, Flowers said, "We rent the practical (working) firearms for the show. I did build the rifles used for firing pellets. Special effects men are particular about equipment like this and we are constantly rebuilding and changing the original model."

The Showtime article said that "lightweight balsa wood, cork and plastics serve as debris flung about by the blasts. Butane, flaming from a series of burners concealed around and within a building, creates the illusion of a flaming structure without really damaging it.

At the 1998 reunion, A.D. Flowers answered the most frequently asked question from *Combat!* fans, that is, how to make it appear as if bullets are striking around the actors.

He said that in the series they used two different effects for that. To simulate gunfire, *Combat!* effects men used two tricks. One was to plant squibs (small charges) inside posts or other soft material which could then be detonated remotely. To simulate bullets striking stone or masonry, they would fire dust pellets from an air rifle.

CHAPTER 8

Special Effects and Technical Credits

ABOVE: Pierre Jalbert, Conlan Carter, and A.D. Flowers at Recon 2000 in Las Vegas.
LEFT: Sgt. Saunders (Vic Morrow) and a German infiltrator (James Coburn) engage in a deadly game in "Masquerade." **157**

COMBAT!

Also in the 1965 article, Flowers said, "Some special effects men use a slingshot. I prefer the rifle. It's much more accurate, and its force makes the pellet-burst more effective. To simulate bleeding, we fill a thin, synthetic casing with 'blood.' When the actor is 'shot,' pressure applied by the actor on this casing forces the 'blood' through a small copper tube and out through a torn piece of covering cloth. For mortar shots and other large-scale explosions, we put the iron pots to use. These mortars are wide at the top, narrowing toward the base. This forces the power generated by the explosion up, and not out. It's something like a balloon bursting. If you hold the balloon by the stem and burst it, the force release is equal on all sides. Put the balloon in a bowl, pop it, and the force is all upward. By applying this principle, the actors can work in close to the explosion without danger.

"These pots are usually buried with only a small part above ground. Covered with peat moss, they are invisible to the camera. The charges vary according to script demands, and are used to simulate shell bursts from big guns, mortars and grenade explosions.

"When detonated by pushing a button on the special effects panel, they blow in a planned direction. The peat moss, which to the camera looks like dirt, scatters, leaving the actor safe. In three months last season, we used 1,500 bags of peat moss.

"During the same period we used 15,000 bullet hits. These charges cost $1.30 each. In one episode we had 20 special effects men working on the bombardment and destruction of a French village. It took us two days, cost more than $25,000 for labor and required 300,000 feet of electrical wire ... There are dozens of ways to do each of the effects we use on the show. Every special effects man experiments to decide what works best for his show. The goal is authenticity. ... Creating and executing these effects is a combined effort. Fifty per cent of the credit has to go to the camera and dolly operators. Without them even the most spectacular explosions would be duds. No one knows better than a special effects man just how important camera angles are.

"Of course, the most important part of the action centers on the actors, and the guys in *Combat!* are the best. They never hesitate to do what is necessary to achieve the desired effect. And I am with them every minute, looking out for their safety. They are as anxious to keep our accident record clean as I am."

Asked what he considers the most difficult effect to control, Flowers answered, "Firing a mortar when an actor is running toward it. This demands split-second timing on the part of the actor and myself. The slightest error could be extremely dangerous."

A.D. Flowers passed away in 2001.

Season One Technical Credits

Produced by: Robert Altman, Robert Blees, Burt Kennedy, Gene Levitt, Richard Maibaum, Paul Stanley
Music by: Leonard Rosenman (for "Survival" music composed and conducted by George Bassman, music supervision by John Fresco)
Director of Photography: Robert B. Hauser (Emmett Bergholz for "No Hallelujahs for Glory")
Art Direction: George W. Davis and Phil Barber (Addison Hehr for "Next In Command" and "No Time For Pity")
Assistant Directors: Michael Caffey, Morris Harmell, Lou Morheim
Set Decoration: Henry Grace and H. Web Arrowsmith
Sound Recording: Franklin Milton and Bill Edmondson
Casting: Stalmaster-Lister Co.
Supervising Music Editor: Richard Lapham
Sound Effects Editor: Finn Ulback
Associate Producers: Richard Caffey, Lou Morheim
Film Editors: Richard L. Van Enger, Jack W. Holmes, William Mace
Production Executive: Richard Caffey, James Moore (none listed for "The Chateau")
Post-production Executive: James Moore
Executive Producer: SELIG J. SELIGMAN
SELMUR PRODUCTIONS In Association with ABC TELEVISION NETWORK
Filmed at METRO-GOLDWYN-MAYER STUDIOS

One of the important tools of the trade of Virgil Beck (one of several special effects men who worked on Combat!) *is the air rifle. Looks are deceptive. This mean-looking weapon shoots only dust pellets to simulate bullets striking pavement and masonry.*

Season Two Technical Credits

Produced by: Gene Levitt
Music by: Leonard Rosenman
Director of Photography: Emmett Bergholz
Story Consultant: Richard P. McDonagh
Art Direction: George W. Davis and Carl Anderson / Phil Barber / Eddie Imazu
Assistant Directors: Michael Caffey, Georg Fenady, Morris Harmell
Set Decoration: Henry Grace and H. Web Arrowsmith / Budd S. Friend
Sound Recording: Franklin Milton and Bill Edmondson
Casting: Stalmaster-Lister Co.
Film Editors: Richard L. Van Enger, Robert L. Wolfe, Basil Wrangell
Supervising Music Editor: Richard Lapham
Sound Effects Editor: Finn Ulback
Associate Producer: Richard Caffey
Post-production Executive: James Moore
COMBAT! Series Developed by: ROBERT PIROSH
Executive Producer: SELIG J. SELIGMAN
PRODUCED BY: SELMUR PRODUCTIONS INC.

Season Three Technical Credits

Produced by: Gene Levitt
Music by: Leonard Rosenman
Director of Photography: Emmett Bergholz
Art Direction: George W. Davis and Phil Barber/Marvin Summerfield
Assistant Directors: Michael Caffey, Georg Fenady, Morris Harmell
Set Decoration: Henry Grace and H. Web Arrowsmith / Francisco Lombardo / Bud S. Friend
Special Effects: A. D. Flowers, Bill Ferrier, Virgil Beck
Music Coordinator: John Fresco
Sound Recording: Franklin Milton and Bill Edmondson
Casting: Stalmaster-Lister Co.
Film Editors: Jim Faris, Richard L. Van Enger, Robert L. Wolfe
Music Supervisor: Richard Lapham
Sound Effects Editor: Finn Ulback
Associate Producer: Michael Caffey
Post-Production Executive: James Moore
COMBAT! Series Developed by: Robert Pirosh
Story Consultant: Richard P. McDonagh
Executive Producer: SELIG J. SELIGMAN
PRODUCED BY: SELMUR PRODUCTIONS INC.

Season Four Technical Credits

Produced by: Gene Levitt, Richard Caffey
Music by: Leonard Rosenman
Director of Photography: Emmett Bergholz, Neal Beckner
Art Direction: George W. Davis and Phil Barber/ Preston Ames
Assistant Directors: Michael Caffey, Georg Fenady, Harker Wade, Eric von Stroheim, Jr.
Set Decoration: Henry Grace and Don Greenwood, Jr.
Specials Effects: A. D. Flowers, Bill Ferrier, Bill Pearson
Music Coordinator: John Fresco
Sound Recording: Franklin Milton and Bill Edmondson
Casting: Marvin Paige
Film Editors: Jim Benson, Richard L. van Enger, Tom McCarthy, Robert L. Wolfe
Music Supervisor: Richard Lapham
Sound Effects Editor: Finn Ulack
Associate Producer: Richard Caffey (part of season)

Production Executive: Georg Fenady (part of season), Tom Walker, Jr. ('Ask Me No Questions')
Post-Production Executive: James Moore
COMBAT! Series Developed by: Robert Pirosh
Story Consultant: Richard P. McDonagh
Executive Producer: SELIG J. SELIGMAN
PRODUCED BY: SELMUR PRODUCTIONS INC.
In Association with ABC Television Network

Season Five Technical Credits

Produced by: Richard Caffey
Music by: Leonard Rosenman
Director of Photography: Emmett Bergholz
Associate Producer: Georg Fenady,
Art Direction: Phil Barber
Assistant Directors: Ralph Ferrin, Harker Wade
Set Decoration: Donald E. Webb
Specials Effects: A. D. Flowers, Bill Ferrier
Music Coordinator: John Fresco
Sound Recording: Woodruff H. Clarke
Casting: Marvin Paige
Production Supervisor: Tom Walker, Jr., Dennis L. Judd II
Film Editors: Richard L. Van Enger, Tom McCarthy, Robert L. Wolfe
Music Supervisor: Richard Lapham
Supervising Sound Effects Editor: Jack Finlay
Production Executive: Lloyd E. Anderson
Post-production Executive: James Moore
COMBAT! Series Developed by: Robert Pirosh
Story Consultant: William R. Yates
Executive Producer: SELIG J. SELIGMAN
PRODUCED BY: SELMUR PRODUCTIONS INC.
In Association with ABC Television Network

Rick Jason and Vic Morrow in "Bridgehead."

159

Much *Combat!* merchandise was sold during the show, some licensed and some not. The show sparked an interest in WWII weapons as toys for children; many of the Tommy guns sold were positioned to attract *Combat!* fans but did not bear the *Combat!* logo. The "official playset" by Superior Toys consists of tanks, trucks, artillery, and toy soldiers. The "*Combat!* Battle Gear Playset" includes a machine gun, pistol, grenade, helmet, and plastic knife.

For kids, two board games were produced: "The Fighting Infantry Game," which is a typical boxed board game, and "At Anzio Beach," which came in a large envelope and is the more difficult of the two to find. Milton Bradley produced a *Combat!* card game and two 125-piece jigsaw puzzles. At least three different coloring books were issued, and perhaps a fourth that had a black-and-white photo on its cover. These coloring books came in two different sizes. Hasbro released several paint-by-number sets.

In addition to the mass-market collectibles, fans also collect original memorabilia from the show. These include props such

CHAPTER 9

Collectibles

as the German bayonets, costumes, and original scripts. Such items occasionally come up in Hollywood auctions and at online auction houses, such as eBay. One of Saunders' original helmets was auctioned in 1996 and sold for over $5,000. Another of the original helmets sold for over$10,000. Autographed items are also of interest, especially original *Combat!* photos signed by Vic Morrow, which can go for upwards of $500.

Above: "Command," original artwork by Susan Moar, based on the episode "Hills Are for Heroes." Oil on canvas.
Left: Vic Morrow as Sgt. Saunders.

COMBAT!
Magazines and Newspaper Supplements

Combat! and its stars regularly appeared on the covers of TV magazines and TV listings. Shown here are issues of TV News and TV Showtime and supplements in the Detroit Free Press and the Chicago Tribune.

Combat! TV Guides

TV Guide had eleven issues that mention *Combat!*

Sept 6, 1962: Fall preview

Sept 15, 1962: "This Means War" *Combat!* vs. The Gallant Men

June 1, 1963: "A River Flows in Hollywood"

June 15, 1963: "The Private War on Lot 2" (cover story)

August 3, 1963: "Stop the War, it's Chow Time"

February 1, 1964: "How to Wage War Safely"

May 9, 1964: "The Not So Secret Life of Rick Jason" (cover story)

April 18, 1964: Review by Cleveland Amory

October 10, 1964: "That's Snow Business"

October 2, 1965: "The Sergeant's Private War"

April 15, 1967: "With Time on Their Hands"

Photo Credits: Nostalgia magazine is from the collection of Jo Davidsmeyer. All other items on this page are from the collection of Dennis Hasty.

Books

Lancer Books published three *Combat!* paperbacks during the show's run. The first book had a red cover, the second a white, the third a blue, giving the colors of the US flag.

Whitman Publishing also published a hardcover children's book "Combat! The Counterattack."

Lancer paperback

Lancer paperback

Lancer paperback

Above: Coloring book
Below: Puzzle

Combat!
continues to remain tremendously popular in Japan. The Japanese-language magazine, Combat, features information not just about the television series, but about all things military. From top to bottom: the January 1997 issue featured a 12-page spread about Comboat! '96. The June 1993 issue continues their "Combatlogy"—a detailed look at the show. Vic Morrow, with his trademark Thompson, graced the cover of the August 1980, issue, and the December 1992 issue includes more "Combatlogy"—a detailed look at the show, the characters, the weapons, and the uniforms.

Japanese magazines from the Jo Davidsmeyer collection. Coloring book and puzzle from the Dennis Hasty collection.

Toy Guns and Military Equipment

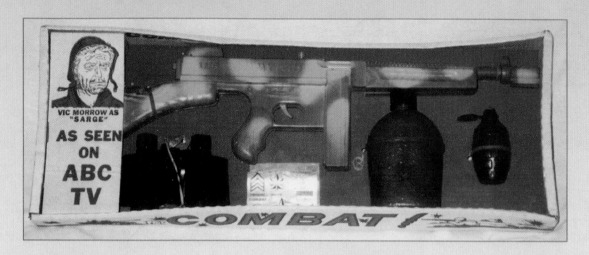

Games

All items shown here are from the Dennis Hasty collection.

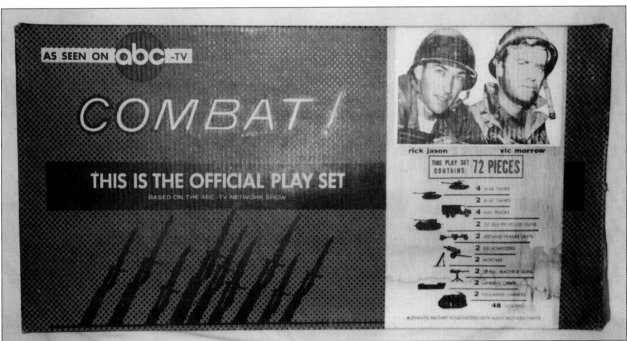

COMBAT!

The wrapper for Don Russ Co Series 1 cards., Memphis, Tennessee.

Bubble Gum Cards

The Donruss company, known primarily for their baseball cards, produced two sets of black-and-white *Combat!* trading cards. Each set contains 66 cards depicting characters and scenes from the television show. Cards were originally available in wax packs of 5 cards containing a stick of gum. The captions on the backs of the cards often have little to do with the picture on the front, but if you read the cards in order, then each set of captions tells a complete (if not very well-written) story.

Donruss only had a license to use the images of the regular cast members. If an extra was also in the photo, instead of using a different photo, they hand-drew new faces on the extras. This make some of the cards very cartoonish.

Series 1: Issued 1963

The story on this set of cards is about the squad being captured and then escaping from a POW camp. Throughout the story, the characters are identified by the actors' names, instead of the character names (for example, Sgt. Morrow, Lt. Jason, Pvt. Rogers). Besides scenes from the show, the cards also depict formal studio portraits of Morrow and Jason and posed shots of the squad in uniform. (Photo of series 1 wrapper provided by Dave Sanders). Don Russ had licensing problems while creating these series.

Series 2: Issued 1964

This set features scenes from episodes shown during the latter half of the 1963/64 season. The cards also document military equipment and hardware used in the series. The captions for these cards show none of the naming errors so prevalent with the first series. This second set had a much shorter print run and is the more valuable of the two sets.

Prices

Price guides list the value of each card (in near mint/mint condition) to be $2 to $5. Star cards (those with Vic Morrow or Rick Jason) are the most expensive with commons often going for as little as $1 each. A complete set of series 1 and 2 in mint condition can cost upwards of $500 (U.S.). By 2002, it's much more difficult to find mint condition original sets.I've seen combined series 1 and 2 sets in mint condition sell for over $500. Good to fair condition individual cards comes up frequently on eBay.

Arcade Cards

Two arcade cards were issued in the 1960s: one with Vic Morrow as Saunders and another with Rick Jason as Hanley. These can often be found in Fine or better codition for $10 to $25 each.

Items pictured are from the Dennis Hasty collection.

Paint Sets

Hasbro released at least three *Combat!* Paint By Number sets in 1963. One features a landing craft on the cover, and another a tank, both of which came in a cardboard carrying case measuring 15 x 17 inches. A third set came in a 14 x 20 inch box.

Each set has three 12 x 16 inch pre-numbered sketched canvases, 28 vials of paint, and 3 brushes.

At the end of the 1990s, already painted paint-by-number art became quite collectible — so if you painted yours and you still have it, it's got value. Military paint-by-numbers already painted became especially popular post September 11, 2002.

Current values for the carry case versions: in good condition $100, in excellent condition $115, in mint condition $125.
Current values for the boxed edition: in good condition $75, in excellent condition $90, in mint condition $100.

Original Props and Costumes

Saunders' helmet was made from fiberglass and covered with camo parachute silk. At first, only Morrow and Jason had the light-weight helmets, but eventually the costume department made molds tailored for each of the regular actors, from which their fiberglass helmets were made. This let them avoid the weight of authentic metal helmets. The helmet pictured is an original from the show (photo by Tim Kiser, helmet courtesy Chris Andersen). The costumes for the regular actors were made of cotton and fashioned to look like authentic wool costumes.

The German canteen and ammunition pouches shown here were made from wood in the prop shop and painted. The metal belt buckle and German bayonet are metal made from molds.

G e r m a n uniform props from the collection of Jo Davidsmeyer

167

Songs of the COMBAT Years

I'll walk alone / Sentimental journey / Blues in the night / I'll never smile again
Lili Marlene / Mam'selle / American patrol
Coming in on a wing and a prayer / This is the army, Mr. Jones / Black magic
Praise the Lord and pass the ammunition / COMBAT Show Theme

Record Albums

The *Combat!* theme was released as sheet music in 1965 and in the collection "The Hollywood Book of Motion Picture and TV Themes," published by Hansen. "Songs of Combat Years" from Columbia Records, was released in 1963. It features the *Combat!* theme and a variety of WWII songs. *Combat!* is also featured in the album "Anita Bryant invites you to See America with AC." In the nineties, the music from the series was included in a CD called "TV Themes of the 60s."

During the series run, Dick Peabody released a 45 rpm record called "My Sarge."

Anita Bryant
invites you to
"See America with AC"

on "COMBAT" Tuesday nights starting September 14 on ABC-TV.

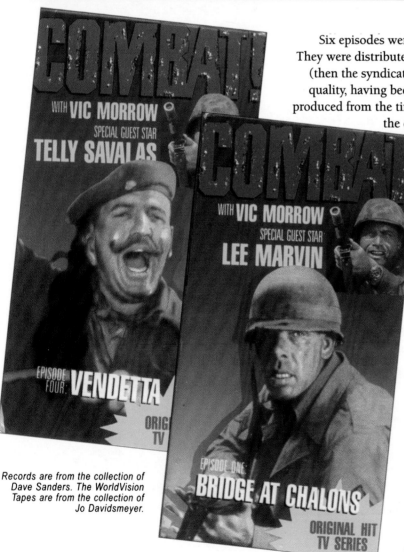

Records are from the collection of Dave Sanders. The WorldVision Tapes are from the collection of Jo Davidsmeyer.

Six episodes were commercially released in the USA on videotape. They were distributed in the late eighties by WorldVision Home Video (then the syndicator of the series). These tapes were not the highest quality, having been recorded in LP mode. They are uncut, but were produced from the time compressed versions in syndication, so are not the original air length, Still, these are highly prized by collectors, going for upwards of $20 each in the original boxes on eBay's auction site. Episodes in this series are: "Bridge at Chalons," "Heritage," "Masquerade," "Vendetta," "Doughboy" and "S.I.W."

In Japan, several laserdisc sets were released in the 1990s. In 2002, Beam Entertainment in Japan released a 10-DVD set of episodes with two *Combat!* episodes per DVD. These DVDs are also sold separately. All are in English with Japanese sub-titles. The boxed set costs 34,200 yen, with separate DVDs selling for 3,800 yen each. The set is from Region 2, so American fans will need a DVD player that bypasses region encoding to play them. The episodes included in this set are:

#1 - A Day in June / Any Second Now
#2 - Cat and Mouse / Escape to Nowhere
#3 - Off Limits / Forgotten Front
#4 - The Steeple / The Hostages
#5 - The Ringer / The Cassock
#6 - Beneath the Ashes / Gideon's Army
#7 - The First Day / The Flying Machine
#8 - More Than a Soldier / Odyssey
#9 - The Casket / Nothing to Lose
#10 - Ask Me No Questions / Run, Sheep, Run

In 1962, *Star Cine Vaillance*, a French-language cinema magazine, featured *Combat!* stories in three of their issues. Each has the complete story of a *Combat!* episode told in black-and-white pictures with balloon-bubbles for dialogue. Issue 49 features the episode "Any Second Now." The cover incorrectly lists the stars as Rick Jason and Dick Morrow. Issue 52 of *Star Cine Vaillance* features a photonovel version of the episode "Just for the Record."

Items photographed are courtesy of Jo Davidsmeyer.

The boys of Combat! *in an October 1996 photo during the Comboat cruise. Back row: Rick Jason, Dick Peabody. Front: Conlan Carter, Tom Lowell, Pierre Jalbert, Jack Hogan. Photo by Jim Duffy.*

Starting in 2004, Image Entertainment began releasing COMBAT! *on DVD. Available both as sets and the complete season, these DVDs boast DVD extras produced by Steve Mitchell.*

Buttons and dog tags associated with Comboat '96. Items courtesy of Jo Davidsmeyer.

Comboat '96 Reunion

Though always in syndication, only since the emergence of the Internet have the show's devotees been able to easily band together. The *Combat!* Internet group (the first group organized by Nancy Durgin) who first came up with the idea of a reunion of the cast of *Combat!* This idea was implemented and organized by the author of this book, Jo Davidsmeyer.

It was not easy to re-assemble the cast. One of the actors was MIA since leaving the acting profession and some were leery of the thought of looking back so far. But with the enthusiastic support and assistance of Dick Peabody, such problems were overcome. Neither Dick nor any other of the Los Angeles actors knew where to find Conlan Carter and the search went out far and wide to find him. After finally getting a letter to him via a friend of a friend of his daughter, it turned out theat Conlan lived within driving distance of Jo. It's definitely a small world!

COMBOAT! '96, the *Combat!* Reunion Cruise, took place October 21, 1996. Six of the members of the cast joined fans on a Mexican cruise. This was the first time they had all been together since the show. The closest they had come beofr that to a reunion had been at Vic Morrow's funeral, when all but Conlan Carter, who was working in Europe at the time, met under less pleasant circumstances. As it turned out, this was to be both the first and last time the remaining cast would be together.

The cruise was a wonderful time for renewing old friendships and making new acquaintances. The reunion was a success, with actors mingling warmly with all, being as silly and excited as their fans. Jack Hogan did his impression of Paul Busch dying and imitated Pierre Jalbert padding his French dialogue. The question-and-answer sessions were exciting, along with an impromptu one Tuesday morning, where five of the actors just got on the stage and made themselves available to one and all. That was characteristic of the whole week. At the autograph session, the actors and their wives were collecting autographs alongside the fans.

Actors and fans mingled freely on the cruise, sharing meals, watching videos, going on shore excursions together, and just having fun. Also on board was Steve Rubin, co-producer of a project *Combat!* film from Paramount.

Rick Jason said on board, "You all do us an honor by coming here to help us pay tribute to something that we enjoyed so much for five years. It's sort of like being awarded a prize for something *you* should be given a prize to, and everyone of us who were in the show feel that way."

Pierre Jalbert said, "I want to thank you all for being here. It's really a pleasure. It's really for us, our Academy Award. I'm pleased to recognize your incredible interest in our work. For us it was a pleasure. It was a moment in our lives that we will never forget."

CHAPTER 10

Cast Reunions

Dick Peabody said, "I never took the show that seriously. All I knew was that it was so much fun and games for five years and forming lasting friendships. And we just had a ball. It was the best working experience any of us have ever had. It was a pleasure to go to work and we even got together in the evenings and on weekends. We just couldn't get enough."

Recon '98 Reunion

In 1998, Jo Davidsmeyer organized a second *Combat!* reunion, dubbed Recon '98. At that reunion, actors Rick Jason, Dick Peabody, Pierre Jalbert, and Tom Lowell re-united in Simi Valley, California. Also in attendance were A. D. Flowers , Burt Kennedy (director and writer, who helped form the character of the show, also author of the book *Hollywood Trail Boss*), and Steve Rubin, co-producer of the planned *Combat!* film. The highlight of the weekend was a guided tour through Franklin Canyon, where so many *Combat!* episodes were filmed. Fans not only got to walk where the squad walked, but could photograph themselves in the famous culverts. Fan Craig Covner brought his restored WWII-era jeep to the Canyon and fans got to ride the trails in style. Encore television sent a film crew to the reunion to do interviews with the stars. These interviews have aired often during Encore's marathons. You can see Dick Peabody in his interview seated in Craig's jeep at Franklin Canyon. This was the last film footage taken of Dick Peabody before his death.

Recon 2000 Reunion

Recon 2000, organized by fan Jeanette Healey, was held in Las Vegas, Nevada. Attending the millennium reunion were Conlan Carter, Jack Hogan, Pierre Jalbert, Rick Jason, and Tom Lowell, and special guests Tina Peabody, Muriel Seligman, Emile Genest, A. D. Flowers, Dick Kindelon, and Col. William Byrns, the show's military advisor for several years.

Combat! is enjoying a renaissance among television viewers. Much of the fan activity centers around the Internet. On the *CombatFan* mailing list, fans from around the world share old memories and make new discoveries about a show that was canceled thirty years ago.

This interest amazes the cast. Pierre Jalbert says, "It's like a renewal of our marvelous moments. We're appreciative of your concern and interest and your love for us."

To find out more about *Combat!* and *Combat!* fandom, visit the Web page at www.CombatFan.com. There you will find a discussion forum, news, photos, and much information about the show and cast.

New Stories from the Pros

Early in the eighties, Tom Lowell and his writing partner developed a treatment for a *Combat!* story. The story was set in 1968 in San Francisco (23 years after WWII). It involved Kirby in his search for a wayward child lost in the hippie generation in San Francisco. But the project never went forward.

Robert Pirosh was also anxious to launch another *Combat!* story. According to actor James Beaver, "A young writer-producer named Steve Mitchell and his partner, whose name I've forgotten, had joined forces with Robert Pirosh to put together a *Combat!* feature film in the time period of around 1987 or '88, if I remember correctly. I had done a rewrite on a film that Steve had been involved with, called *Sweet Revenge*. We had hit it off, and when he started putting this *Combat!* film together, he called me about writing it, not knowing that I was a huge fan of the series. The plan was that the film would feature Sgt. Saunders and the squad as their unit participated in the Battle of the Bulge. I began researching the Battle of the Bulge and was very excited about the project, as you can well imagine. However, the film did not ever get funding, and then, after a number of delays in getting anything underway, Robert Pirosh died and that was the last I heard of the project."

Writer Steve Rubin started going after rights to *Combat!* in 1988. He was working at that time with Robert Pirosh. He had interviewed him for one of his books *Combat Films*. Pirosh wrote a treatment in '89, Pirosh wanted to do a Battle of the Bulge story, so they went off to get the rights. WWII at that time was out of fashion, after "War and Remembrance" was a ratings disaster on TV. "WWII DEAD AS GENRE" the article came out in Variety the week after Rubin acquired rights to *Combat!* Rubin had a sixth-month option and couldn't get anyone interested in the project. In the fifth month Robert Pirosh died. The project sunk into oblivion. In 1993 Rubin reacquired the rights. Bill Wisher connected with Bruce Willis. Steve Pirosh's son heard Bruce Willis on a talk show saying

CHAPTER 11

Combat! Lives

what a fan he was of *Combat!* Once Willis was signed on, a bidding war went on. Savoy Pictures purchased it, but subsequently went out of business. The project was sold to Paramount.

Wisher's first draft had Saunders and squad fighting an Alamo-style defense of Mortain against two Panzer units. The second script has Saunders involved in a raid to liberate German scientists and save New York City from Hitler's wonder weapons.

The project is still under development at Paramount. "Passion fuels Hollywood," says Steve Rubin. "When you love something so much, it gets made. And I know these nine years have not been for naught." Paramount not only owns the rights to new projects, but also purchased the rights to the old series. Fans are hopeful that this finally means the series will be commercially available on tape or DVD.

New Stories from the Fans

Impatient for a *Combat!* from Hollywood, fans have forged ahead and created their own stories. From around the world, the USA, Canada, Japan, and elsewhere, fans are writing continuing adventures of the squad to share with friends and their fellow Combat-ants. In addition to this fan fiction, followers of *Combat!* have created original artwork (see page 161 for a beautiful example), photo collages, and original songs and parodies.

Hollywood may never send Hanley and Saunders on new missions, but the original squad lives on. The series is now 40 years old, and we are living in a new century. The show's newest fans are several generations removed from the men and women who served in WWII and paid such a high cost for the freedoms we enjoy today.

Still, the human drama of men in combat speaks to new generations with a voice and message that is ageless. And with a reminder that freedom is never free.

Left: Ready for action—Hollywood style. The cast poses in front of a photo landscape. Top row: Vic Morrow, Rick Jason. Bottom row: Pierre Jalbert, Dick Peabody.

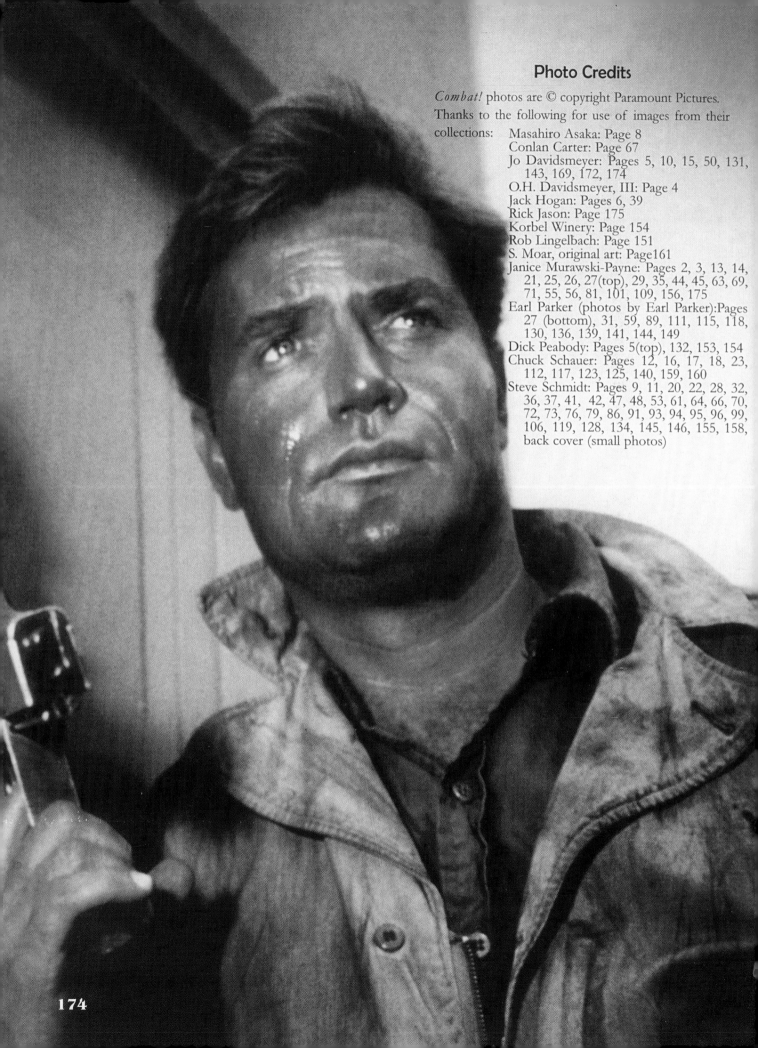

Photo Credits

Combat! photos are © copyright Paramount Pictures.
Thanks to the following for use of images from their collections:

Masahiro Asaka: Page 8
Conlan Carter: Page 67
Jo Davidsmeyer: Pages 5, 10, 15, 50, 131, 143, 169, 172, 174
O.H. Davidsmeyer, III: Page 4
Jack Hogan: Pages 6, 39
Rick Jason: Page 175
Korbel Winery: Page 154
Rob Lingelbach: Page 151
S. Moar, original art: Page 161
Janice Murawski-Payne: Pages 2, 3, 13, 14, 21, 25, 26, 27(top), 29, 35, 44, 45, 63, 69, 71, 55, 56, 81, 101, 109, 156, 175
Earl Parker (photos by Earl Parker):Pages 27 (bottom), 31, 59, 89, 111, 115, 118, 130, 136, 139, 141, 144, 149
Dick Peabody: Pages 5(top), 132, 153, 154
Chuck Schauer: Pages 12, 16, 17, 18, 23, 112, 117, 123, 125, 140, 159, 160
Steve Schmidt: Pages 9, 11, 20, 22, 28, 32, 36, 37, 41, 42, 47, 48, 53, 61, 64, 66, 70, 72, 73, 76, 79, 86, 91, 93, 94, 95, 96, 99, 106, 119, 128, 134, 145, 146, 155, 158, back cover (small photos)

Index of Episodes and Guest Stars